SCREENWRITING
UPDATED

SCREENWRITING UPDATED

New (and Conventional) Ways of Writing for the Screen

LINDA ARONSON

SILMAN-JAMES PRESS   LOS ANGELES

First Silman-James edition 2001

10 9 8 7 6 5 4 3 2 1

Library of Congress Cataloging-in-Publication Data

Aronson, Linda, 1950-
Screenwriting updated : new (and conventional) ways of writing for the screen /
Linda Aronson.-- 1st Silman-James ed.
        p. cm.
Originally published: St. Leonards, Australia : Allen & Unwin, 2000.
Includes bibliographical references and index.
ISBN 1-879505-59-2 (alk. paper)
1. Motion picture authorship. I. Title.

PN1996 .A76 2001
808.2'3--dc21

                                            2001031143

Acknowledgment is made to the following for their kind permission
to reproduce the material indicated:

Beyond Simpson Le Mesurier Pty Ltd for the extract from "Getting to Know You" Episode 5,
Something in the Air written by Cliff Green, Edited by Jo Martino
(©1999 Beyond Simpson Le Mesurier Pty Ltd.)
Something in the Air is a Beyond Simpson Le Mesurier
ABC Co-production;

Michael Wiese Productions for extract from Christopher Vogler,
The Writer's Journey: Mythic Structure for Storytellers and Screenwriters
(© 1992, Michael Wiese Productions, California).

Silman-James Press
3624 Shannon Road
Los Angeles, CA 90027

Contents

Part III: Getting it onto paper

Foreword

The rules of the game

Screenwriters today are a pretty savvy bunch. In most cases they've been to film school, they've taken short courses or they've attended industry seminars. They've read every authority on dramatic writing from Aristotle to Robert McKee. They know the principles and the processes from concept to final draft. They can identify a protagonist, an inciting incident, an obstacle, a turning point, a substory, a climax and a resolution in their sleep. They know the rules of the game.

However, in recent years the writers with whom I have been working in England, Australia, France and the United States seem to be stepping back from the dramatic conventions that are promoted in the classroom. They have started to question the classical models described in the textbooks. The films that most excite this new wave of screenwriters include *Pulp Fiction, Mystery Train, Short Cuts, Decalogue, The Ice Storm, Sliding Doors, Happiness, Festen (The Celebration), Magnolia, Run Lola Run, Beautiful People* and *American Beauty*. These films are unconventional in so far as they might employ multiple protagonists, parallel stories, voiceover, flashbacks, or non-linear narratives. Each in its own way is an exception to the rule.

It is difficult to say why so many recent movies are unconventionally structured. It would be nice to think it is an attempt by contemporary writers to reflect an increasingly complex world with accuracy. We live in confusing times. It is an enormous challenge for the storyteller to impose artistic order on current chaos and to extract some kind of significance from the avalanche of meaningless events that bombard our lives. In the opening days of the twenty-first century, people are celebrating an economic boom that they do not understand while denying the economic misery before their eyes. The globalization of the marketplace allows capital to flow unpatriotically across borders while labor is not permitted to do the same. Peacekeeping forces provoke the very conflicts they claim to prevent. Sanctions hurt the people they are supposed to protect and in the age of the Internet, millions are dying of starvation. Even in the richest country in the world, one in six children goes to bed hungry, one in ten has a parent in prison, a quarter of the population is illiterate and children carry guns to school. It may be that the contradictions of our times can no longer be convincingly represented by a single protagonist overcoming overwhelming odds in two hours of screen time. It may be that the modern screenwriter has to choose between perpetuating old myths or telling new truths ... and this choice might require the rewriting of some of the rules.

Curiously, the public raised on the multiple storytelling techniques of episodic television is perfectly capable of following the interwoven narratives of modern cinema. Someone, somewhere, someday, will undoubtedly write a learned piece on how much Kieslowski's *Decalogue* owes to *The Young and the Restless*, but in the meantime we have Linda Aronson's book to help us bridge the gap between high art and popular culture.

Screenwriting Updated: New (and Conventional) Ways of Writing for the Screen also covers the great divide between the exception and the rule.

Linda Aronson's book is an invaluable work of reference for the aspiring and established professional. It provides an intelligent and thoughtful investigation of new and conventional narrative, pinpointing and analyzing four separate types of parallel narrative. It explains how each of these is related to traditional narrative and gives practical guidelines for getting each onto the page. For writers who want to use the conventional three-act model, the book provides a range of "Development Strategies," together with useful tips and techniques for developing ideas and overcoming the fear of writer's block. It offers analyses of screenplays as diverse as *Pulp Fiction* and *The Piano*. *Screenwriting Updated* functions as a personal script editor and gets as near as any book can to overcoming the loneliness of the long-distance screenwriter.

Linda Aronson is a multi-talented, award-winning writer of plays, screenplays, television drama and novels. She has written widely for the screen in the U.K., Australia, New Zealand and for U.S. television. Her credits include *Kostas*, directed by Paul Cox, the stage play *Dinkum Assorted*, which premiered at the Sydney Opera House, the best-selling novels *Kelp: A Comedy of Love, Seaweed and Rupert Murdoch* and *Rude Health*, and an extensive range of TV drama including award-winning episodes of *GP, Singles* and *Learned Friends* for Australian television. Linda is also a highly regarded teacher of screenwriting, conducting courses for the Australian Writers' Guild, the Australian Film, Television and Radio School as well as the University of Technology, Sydney. Her remarkable body of work covers the mainstream as well as the margins of her profession and this experience gives authority to her voice. Linda's respect for the traditions of her art and her love of the conventions of her trade are balanced by her enthusiasm for the most innovative and experimental works of contemporary cinema. She is clearly thrilled by the exception as well as the rule.

In our quest to write the elusive great original screenplay we will undoubtedly need the wisdom to respect the rules and courage to break them. In this task we would do well to remember Brecht's view that "there is only one great inflexible rule that the proof of the pudding is in the eating." Enjoy this book.

Paul Thompson
Associate Professor (Film/Television)
New York University
1 May 2000

Preface

Screenwriting is getting harder. It is no longer enough to study the traditional three-act rising structure. As well as a whole variety of flashback narrative forms (in films like *The End of the Affair* (1999) or *The English Patient* (1996)), writers have to take on "ensemble" structures (*The Big Chill* (1983), *American Beauty* (1999)) and a bewildering range of complex multiple-story and non-linear forms as seen in movies like *Pulp Fiction* (1994), *Magnolia* (1999), *Short Cuts* (1993), *Go* (1999), *Crimes and Misdemeanors* (1989) and *City of Hope* (1991).

The job is made tougher because these new structures are bewildering to the point of paradox. Why do flashbacks in *The Remains of the Day* (1993) make the audience understand and identify with the main character, while flashbacks in *The Usual Suspects* (1995) leave the audience finding the character unknowable and sinister? Why does a reunion film like *The Big Chill* succeed and a reunion film like *Parallel Lives* (1994) fail? How does *Pulp Fiction* – a film which breaks all the rules and should, theoretically, be a mess – maintain pace and achieve such satisfactory closure that at the end its audiences regularly applaud?

In the face of such complexity, where does the writer start? How does someone actually go about constructing a film with nine time-frames or eleven stories or forty actors? What are the rules?

So far there is little in the way of theory for writers who want to write film using parallel narrative structures. Consequently, in *Screenwriting Updated* I have tried to establish some basic laws and principles. The book isolates four major categories of parallel narrative (flashback, tandem, sequential and multiple protagonist/antagonist), providing detailed explanations of how each works and of the problems each has with unity, pace and closure.

It explains the practical mechanics of the new structures, charting why and where plots intersect. It identifies structural components like the macro plot, the portmanteau plot and the triggering crisis. It describes and analyzes a range of frequently appearing characters, including the enigmatic outsider, the investigator, the traitor within and the dominant character. It looks at unsuccessful films built on the new structures and tries to discover their faults. Crucially, it provides highly practical diagrams, cross-references, summaries and structural breakdown charts so writers can explore and analyze the new forms for themselves.

As I studied these new structures, I was surprised to find how much they used the nuts and bolts of traditional three-act narrative to create unity and rising jeopardy in individual plots and across the film as a whole. It became increasingly clear that writers who wanted to master the new forms needed a very firm grounding in the old. They also needed a reference system so that as they studied how the new structures used the nuts and bolts of the old, they could remind themselves of what that nut or bolt actually did in the old structure and, most importantly, how it might fail.

I have provided help in three ways. Firstly, I have summarized a number of different approaches to traditional narrative to give writers a variety of ways to understand its nature and problems. Secondly, I have created a combined learning and reference system called the Script Development Strategies. Each Strategy addresses a new structural component by describing it and providing questions for the writer to ask and answer. Studied one after the other, the Strategies build a three-act film in logical steps. The questioning process provides focus and distance. It forces new writers to consider complex craft issues and it stops experienced writers from dropping into automatic pilot, a perennial problem.

There are other Development Strategies to deal with specific plotting problems in forms such as short films, journey films, adaptation and comedy/satire. The Strategies are also useful at the rewriting stage because they provide objectivity at a time when the writer is highly subjective.

Like many writers, I have found that it is often easier to understand why something works by looking at what happens when it doesn't. As a result, my third aid to understanding traditional narrative is a chapter entitled "Lost in the telling." This analyzes a range of films which, despite fine performances, premise and direction, fail because of specific structural faults. Where possible, "Lost in the telling" is cross-referenced with the Development Strategies, so that when writers encounter a new structural element, they can check to see what happens when it goes wrong.

I come to the first section of the book last of all. This part is devoted to creativity, specifically, to what is happening when writers write well and what is happening when they write badly. I particularly wanted to isolate practical techniques for getting a range of good ideas under pressure (in a script meeting, for example), because much of a scriptwriter's life involves writing to order for people who want the script yesterday. Now that writers have to master twice as much narrative theory as they used to, any practical aid to creativity under pressure should, I think, be very welcome.

We take the writing-to-order aspect of our craft for granted, but in fact it makes our job vastly different from the job of novelists or poets, who have all the time in the world. It is one thing to be full of ideas and write well. It is another thing to be full of ideas and write well at a specific time and place and with a looming deadline.

Really we are more like musicians or dancers, performing to order. And like musicians and dancers, we need highly developed skills of concentration and focus. For our specific branch of performance, the devising and writing of scripts on command, we need a range of imagination triggers we can call up at will.

I found that if I applied Edward de Bono's theories on creativity to my own writing experiences and what other writers said about writing, I could produce some simple concentration techniques that produced ideas on command and counteracted the relentless pull towards cliché that happens when writers are under stress. The basic principle is that imagination is not proactive but reactive, so if we consciously throw stimuli at it, it will trigger ideas.

The method gives writers simple rules so that they can consciously manipulate imagination and logic in the way that happens naturally when they are writing well.

While this may sound cold-blooded and formulaic, it actually derives from Wordsworth's practical writing methods as described by him in the Preface to the *Lyrical Ballads*. I show how to trigger ideas from a variety of sources, including screen genre, myth, fairytale, fable, theme, historical material, photographs and words chosen at random.

My hope is that this book can be a practical desktop guide for new and experienced writers who want to consolidate their understanding of conventional screenwriting and be more imaginative in ideas and narrative structures. To help less experienced writers, I have included information on getting the work onto the page (dialogue and treatment writing) and on writing under pressure generally.

As far as parallel storytelling is concerned, I am conscious that *Screenwriting Updated* has barely scratched the surface. Much is left to be done. The new narrative structures have entered mainstream cinema and they are becoming more complex all the time. As writers we must be versatile and accept the challenge. We need to master the new structures, indeed, we need to take them even further, always recognizing that while they seem to blow apart the old rules of storytelling, in fact it is in traditional narrative that they have their core.

Many people have helped me with this book. I am greatly indebted to Paul Thompson, not only for writing such a complimentary foreword but because I first became interested in theories of writing after attending one of his excellent workshops. I am also indebted to other writers whose workshops and master classes I have attended over the years, most particularly Carl Sautter and John Vorhaus. For his invaluable comments and his kindness in taking on board yet another manuscript, I thank Ken Methold. I thank Jan Sardi for letting me read and study the manuscript of his screenplay, *Shine*, and Cliff Green, Jo Martino, Beyond Simpson Le Mesurier Productions and ABC TV for permission to reproduce material from *Something in the Air*. I thank my students at AFTRS and UTS for test-driving the theories and providing such useful feedback. For their patience in waiting for a manuscript that took so long to complete, I thank AFTRS, most particularly Meredith Quinn, and for their great help in the final stages, I thank my editor Jo Jarrah, designer Maggie Cooper., and Grahame Ramsay for bringing the project to completion. For the U.S. edition, special thanks to Jim Fox at Silman-James.

To my family, as ever, I owe the deepest thanks of all.

Linda Aronson
April 2001

Part I
Getting ideas

1. Creativity and general problem-solving

The two perennial writing problems in the screen industry are getting good ideas and structuring them properly. The enemy is pressure, particularly pressure of time, because it triggers a panic reflex which tempts filmmakers either to clichés or to story material that strains credibility.

That so many clichéd and incredible films are made every year is testament to the power of this panic reflex. It would be reassuring if all of these weak films were made by inferior talents, but the sobering reality is that the people creating and funding such films – the people seduced and dazzled by what will present to the rest of the world and, eventually, to themselves as a second-rate movie – are usually highly talented, sophisticated and commercially savvy people with a history of successful credits, otherwise they would not be in the position of making films in the first place. The lesson is that pressure has the power to warp the judgment of the best of us. Unfortunately, since we can't slow the industry down, the pressure is not going to go away. Time pressures have been part of the dramatist's job description since at least Shakespeare's day and the reality for screenwriters is that the job is not just about talent but about a capacity to be talented on command and to a deadline.

So what can we do? The first choice is to ignore the problem and hope that it will never happen to us. The second choice is to attempt to define and pinpoint what is happening intellectually when we make stress-related writing mistakes, and what is happening when we are writing well. That way, not only should we be able to short-circuit the stress-related impulse towards cliché and the incredible, but hopefully – if we can just work out what is happening mentally when we are writing well – we may be able to reproduce the process to order, finding techniques through which we can be creative at speed, under pressure and for long periods of time.

Understanding the writing process

Many accounts of the actual writing process exist, all remarkably similar. They describe an interaction between imagination and technique, a dual process whereby a logical, craft-skilled part of the writer's mind works to filter and make sense of streams of ideas, images and words coming from another part of the mind, usually loosely termed the "imagination," "subconscious," "right brain" or, in earlier times, "fancy."

Interestingly, this division between imagination and technique, instantly recognizable to all kinds of writers, it is also recognizable in terms of Edward de Bono's ground-breaking theories about the workings of creativity in *Lateral Thinking* (1970). In fact, de Bono's theories provide such a useful breakdown of the process that writers have been describing for centuries, that they can be used in a very practical way to pinpoint how good writing happens, and how poor writing can be improved.

De Bono's creativity theories and screenwriting

De Bono describes two sorts of creativity. Writers will immediately recognize these from their own work patterns. The first, **vertical thinking**, is a step-by-step logic that results in "right" and "wrong" answers. It's the sort of thought process that we apply in arithmetic, and writers use it for such tasks as judging whether a plot point is credible, or whether a piece of dialogue sounds lifelike. The poet Coleridge called it 'the organizing spirit of imagination'. We call it craft or technique. Its negative side is that it can push us to produce technically correct clichés. Vertical thinking makes up the 'ninety per cent perspiration' side of the writing process. It could be depicted as shown in Figure 1.1.

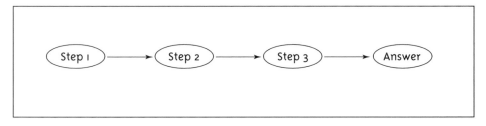

Figure 1.1 Vertical thinking

The second sort of imaginative thought process, **lateral thinking**, makes up the "ten per cent inspiration." It is a generative and very personal, associational, stream-of-consciousness thought process that is interested in providing as many answers as possible regardless of quality. The **lateral mind** is what is unique about each writer. In the old days it was called the writer's "fancy" or "muse." It is what is at work when we write about emotions or intuit clever links between disparate things and, because it lacks any judgment, it is also what is at work when our work becomes "over the top" or unfocused. Visually it could be depicted as shown in Figure 1.2.

Good writing happens when craft (provided by vertical thinking) and the writer's unique view of the world (provided by lateral thinking) are inextricably mixed to produce a work of striking originality. For screenwriters who regularly work under pressure of time, in the rush to finish the script it is easy either to underuse the two sorts of thought process, or else to use each for the wrong jobs. The result is writing that is less original and less technically skilled than it needs to be.

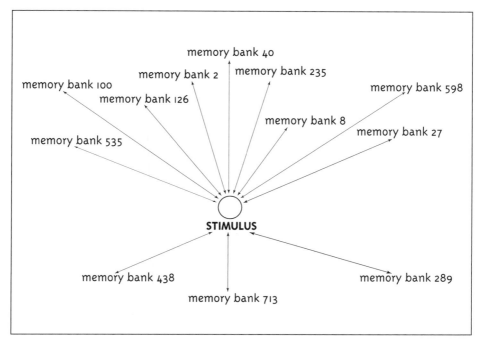

memory bank 40

memory bank 2   memory bank 235

memory bank 100

memory bank 126

memory bank 598

memory bank 8

memory bank 535   memory bank 27

STIMULUS

memory bank 438   memory bank 289

memory bank 713

Figure 1.2 Lateral thinking

What causes weak writing

Few writers have escaped the depressing experience of finding that something they thought to be a fine piece of writing turns out, in the cold light of day, to be clichéd or unbelievable or just simply over the top. How precisely does this happen? How can a fine, experienced writer produce technically correct but clichéd material? How can an exciting new writer let a good idea fizzle out into cliché, or become incredible or silly? How is it that we do not recognize poor work at the time of writing?

Weak writing seems to happen when there is an imbalance between vertical and lateral thinking.

Dangers of being too vertical

Being too vertical can make writers produce clichés without being aware of it. Because vertical thinking is based in experience, learnt skills and logic, it can only repeat and classify information that it has encountered before – in the case of screenwriting, what it has encountered before on screen. Functioning as it does on facts, accuracy, and the idea of "right" and "wrong" information, vertical thinking tends to seize upon the first possible solution to any problem and stop there, quite uncritically, convinced that this is the right answer. In screenwriting, the effect is to make the writer produce a cliché and be happy with it (this is how fine writers can turn out cliché). In all areas of screenwriting requiring originality (premise, characters, backstory, dialogue etc.), vertical thinking can only give back what has been done before on screen. Hence, an over-reliance on vertical thinking will always pull towards cliché.

For example, given the problem of creating the screenplay for a film centered on police and a police station, vertical thinking will conclude that the right way to do it is to have a range of stereotype characters with stereotypical backstories, speech and plotlines (the rebel cop with the bad marriage paired with the conservative cop with the good marriage; the disapproving chief detective who constantly threatens the rebel with dismissal; the cynical, uniformed female cop, and so on).

In addition to this, the emotional authenticity of stories and characters created by vertical thinking is always shaky because the writer is not getting into the characters' heads and trying to feel the emotion. Instead, the emotions and dialogue are being written up from memory of other films and television shows, which this way of thinking is convinced will show what people say and feel in the given situation.

Overdependence on vertical thinking often happens through exhaustion (particularly for storyliners/consultants on television series), and is a perennial problem for established writers, making them write "on automatic pilot" without being aware of it.

In *Selling Your Screenplay* (1988), Carl Sautter gives an interesting example of vertical thinking at work when he was story editor on the U.S. TV drama series *Moonlighting*. Part of his job was to listen to writers pitching story ideas.

> I was astonished that almost every writer pitched variations of exactly the same plots. The most popular: Maddie and David are trapped together…. Each writer pitched this isolation idea with fervour, confident that it was the most original and compelling notion of all time.

Dangers of being too lateral

An over-reliance on lateral thinking makes the writing pull towards the incredible, silly, repetitive, unfocused and overly emotional. Lateral thinking is prone to all kinds of problems connected with poor technique and the "real," because lateral thinking has no interest in such things; indeed, it lacks any kind of critical faculty at all. Lateral thinking pushes the writer to write for the sake of writing, unconcerned about structure, focus, repetition, intelligibility, and redundancy. It falls in love with its own cleverness in devising dialogue or ideas or jokes, and doesn't know when to stop. In plot and characterization, this means it is unable to discriminate between what is real and what is over the top. It is at work in all of those thriller films where the audience finds itself thinking: "Why don't these people just call the police?" or "Why are they walking into what is so obviously a trap?" In characterization, it will pull towards the maudlin and the overly personal. It will frequently make the writer too visible, and often pulls towards the preachy and the overt.

Because its whole approach is that more is better (quantity rather than quality), it can unwittingly produce the same scene (in essence) over and over again. Actor–writers are highly prone to this fault because lateral thinking is the major imaginative skill they have to use in improvisation, and when they come to write they automatically resort to it. This means that they tend to create a unique character and keep showing it doing the same thing over and over again. *Mr. Saturday Night* (1992), produced, written, and directed by Billy Crystal, is a good example.

Lateral thinking can also pull the writer to write in "real time," meaning they create scenes as they would actually happen in real life, not for how they cleverly push forward the plot and characterization under the guise of naturalism. Lateral thinking cannot monitor how much exposition or backstory to include or when. It doesn't know when enough is enough. It typically produces screenplays with several apparent endings before the real one.

Why is it so easy to get vertical and lateral thinking out of balance?

In their separate ways, vertical and lateral thinking are immensely seductive. Each creates an enormous and false sense of self-confidence. What makes things worse is that, in the pressured world of the film industry, the process of stopping to check that vertical and lateral thinking are in balance is counter-intuitive. Every instinct is to jump at the first half-decent idea, whether it is a cliché resulting from vertical thinking or a half-baked idea resulting from lateral thinking. At every turn there is pressure to get something on paper. And of course, once scenes and dialogue are on the page, it is almost impossible for a writer to throw them away. The result is that writers can easily become deeply committed to ideas – just because they were the first ideas that occurred to them – that do not do them justice.

While both new and experienced writers are capable of imbalances in either direction, stress will typically make the more experienced writer rely on vertical thinking's craft skills, forgetting originality and jumping with relief at the first half-decent idea so as to get at least something on paper; meanwhile, the less experienced writer will typically get carried away on the imaginative roller coaster that is lateral thinking, throwing credibility and all critical faculties to the wind.

Vertical thinking is seductive because its quick answers make the writer feel totally in control. Lateral thinking is seductive because its lack of self-criticism not only results in fluent, fast writing, but convinces the writer that everything written is wonderful. In both cases, the combination of fluency and self-confidence is hard for any writer to resist.

And writers are not the only ones to succumb to imbalance of this kind: the fact that there are so many scripts that are incredible or clichéd means that directors, producers, and network executives are also susceptible. The hard economic truth is that imbalances between vertical and lateral thinking cost the film industry many millions of dollars a year.

How to use vertical and lateral thinking

Successful pieces of screenwriting – perhaps of all sorts of writing – are always credible, but highly original, which means in the words of Carl Sautter (1988), they are always "real but unusual." They might take a traditional genre or situation, just as *Strictly Ballroom* (1992) takes the Cinderella story, but the old story is always given a strikingly new twist. Even if the work produced is avant-garde and non-naturalistic, the "real but unusual" factor applies because what is "real" in such cases is an emotional or intellectual reality, or sometimes both.

This balance between real and unusual seems to be a key to success in everything from the initial idea through to things like structure, characterization and dialogue. In fact, it's useful to follow Carl Sautter's advice to think of the phrase "real but unusual" as a motto for writing generally.

We can use lateral and vertical thinking to give us these real but unusual components. "Real" seems to be linked with vertical thinking, and "unusual" with lateral thinking. To achieve a balance between the real and the unusual during writing, we can consciously switch between lateral thinking, which can generate new and original ideas, and vertical thinking which, with its logic and analytical skills, can monitor the credibility and appropriateness of suggestions created by lateral thinking. The trick is to know which jobs are best done with vertical thinking and which are best done with lateral thinking.

The analogy here is with driving a car. You can't drive a car without alternating between the brake and the accelerator. To "drive" a script, alternate the accelerator pedal (lateral thinking, which drives the script forward by originality and emotion) with the brake pedal (logical vertical thinking, which keeps the script in control – that is, structured and real). It is easy to be either too clichéd (using only the vertical imagination) in which case the "car" will grind to a halt, or too emotional, unstructured and "over the top" (using only lateral), in which case the car will go off the road.

In practical terms, we can trigger the vertical imagination by thinking *real* and the lateral imagination by thinking *unusual*. Another way to come at it is to remind ourselves that vertical thinking does anything *real*, while lateral thinking does anything *unusual*.

The idea is to consciously apply the right sort of thinking to the tasks for which it is suited. But what tasks are these?

Tasks for vertical thinking

1. Identifying the requirements of any pattern

Vertical thinking helps identify the normal characteristics of patterns (like genres) or character types. So, if the job is to create a coming-of-age movie or a war movie, vertical imagination will run through all its memories of such material in books, films, and life, and define what they have in common. If the job is to write a movie about, say, a schoolteacher, vertical thinking will call up everything of that type read, seen, or experienced in fact or fiction. This information provides a strong sense of "what film we are in," something vital to know. The information can then be handed over to the lateral imagination to brainstorm uncritically in the hope of generating new approaches.

2. Monitoring the originality of lateral ideas

Vertical thinking is very good at picking what is original because it works on what is not. So, once you have brainstormed all the lateral ideas generated by the vertical definition of, say, "the personality of a schoolteacher," vertical thinking can be called upon again to choose a range of elements which are simultaneously new but consistent with reality.

3. Keeping ideas real

Vertical thinking is very good at identifying credibility gaps in ideas and characterization.

4. Checking for schmaltz and anything "over the top"

Vertical thinking is very good at identifying anything overly subjective or emotional.

5. Writing to formula

Vertical thinking is very useful for analyzing elements for purposes of mimicry. This is a skill much needed in television series and serial writing, where a writer must be able to reproduce an established style.

6. Defining the task at hand

Vertical thinking is excellent at pinpointing problems, ready to hand over to lateral thinking for brainstorming.

Tasks for lateral thinking

1. Generating unique ideas

Lateral thinking is uninfluenced by pattern. If faced with a pattern-like genre or character type, it will provide unique, personal ideas. Not being constrained to think logically, it will often provide "left-field" ideas. In all ways, lateral thinking pulls against cliché.

2. Generating lots of ideas

Being uncritical and interested in quantity not quality, the lateral imagination is very good at producing large numbers of unusual ideas and approaches to any given pattern such as genre or character type. These will range widely in quality but, as we will see later, often a poor idea will trigger a novel idea.

3. Finding an emotional core

Lateral thinking, seeing everything as unique and outside of pattern, is very good at perceiving the emotional uniqueness of a situation and keeping us fresh in the way we think about and present emotional interaction. It will send writers back into their own emotions to recreate how characters feel an experience. This process is very close to what Wordsworth was describing in the Preface to *Lyrical Ballads* (1800) when he famously spoke about how, to get the emotions of the poem right, he would consciously psyche himself back into the situation he wanted to write about. This he called "emotion recollected in tranquility." Screenwriters call it "getting into the character's skin."

Figures 1.3 and 1.4 show what each sort of thinking seems to be good and bad at, and how those skills translate into writing tasks to do with keeping the script real but unusual.

The Development Strategies method

Is there any way to control the balance between vertical and lateral thinking so that we can write to our best? While of course no method is absolutely foolproof, it is possible to duplicate the process that happens when vertical and lateral are working well together. This process breaks down into three steps which are repeated over and over again:

1 Vertical thinking defines the task at hand (for example, inventing a speech for a specific character that will get across specific plot and theme details while remaining credibly in character).

2 Lateral thinking brainstorms the task, running through a number of possibilities and making as many original connections as possible.

3 Vertical thinking chooses the best "real but unusual" answer.

This natural three-step problem-solving and imagination-boosting process can be applied to all kinds of writing problems by using a set of questions and reminders which I have devised and given the name *Development Strategies*. The Development Strategies guarantee that the imagination is fired by a variety of good triggers while ensuring that the resultant ideas are based in human truths and presented with sound technique. The aim is to keep lateral and vertical thinking functioning properly in tandem to make the

What vertical is good at (Keeping it real)	What lateral is good at (Keeping it unusual)
1. Logic, structural instinct, learned knowledge, technique.	Intuition, inspiration, originality, energy, receptiveness to new ideas.
2. Socially conditioned world view.	Idiosyncratic world view.
3. Poor at writing emotion, but good at judging how real it is.	Good at writing emotion. Pulls towards over-emotionalism, melodrama.
4. Selective, logical.	Generative, illogical.
5. Objective.	Subjective.
6. Linear processing tasks.	Associational tasks.
7. Pulls toward cliché. Chooses what it has seen before.	Hates cliché. Seeks links between disparate bodies of information.
8. Looks for one right answer.	Seeks many answers. Non-judgmental.
9. Has sound judgment.	Poor judgment.
10. Concentration.	Lack of concentration.
11. Sense of continuity.	Moves from moment to moment.
12. Pleasure in unity.	Not interested in unity.
13. Interested in the normal, usual.	Interested in the abnormal, unusual.
14. Pleasure in set-up/pay-off.	Not interested in set-up/pay-off.
15. Cynicism, reluctance to suspend disbelief.	Untroubled by the incredible.
16. Circular, derivative.	Asymmetrical, original.
17. Taste, self-control.	No taste or self-control.
18. Sense of everyday life.	Instinct for myth, archetype.
19. Critical, cautious, lacking confidence.	Uncritical, optimistic, confident.

Figure 1.3 Vertical and lateral creativity in scriptwriting

screenplay work to its best. There are 29 Development Strategies. Development Strategies 1 and 2, described in the following pages, are designed to help with general writing problems. Later Development Strategies form a step-by-step method to create and revise a classic three-act narrative.

Development Strategies 1 and 2: diagnosis and general problem solving

As we have seen, in the haste to finish a screenplay it is very easy to rush through general problem solving and end up, quite unconsciously, either with a piece of writing that is clichéd or unbelievable or, in the case of a rewrite, one that does not really address the problems raised. In situations where there is enough development money and a large enough pool of available writers, the solution is easy. Simply employ a new writer to bring new skills and insights. In situations where money and writers are scarce, the project may flounder or even die – all for the want of time spent consciously and carefully defining the script's problems and devising a range of answers.

Vertical		Lateral	
Advantages	**Dangers**	**Advantages**	**Dangers**
1. Provides credible plotting.	Can become clichéd.	Can give original ideas at every stage of plotting.	Can become unfocused.
2. Has good structural sense.	Can become overstructured.	Pushes to transcend limits and clichés of structure.	Can become unstructured.
3. Has good sense of the everyday.	Can become mundane.	Will pick up the archetypal, mythical.	Can become incredible, silly.
4. Has good sense of naturalism.	Can become predictable, boring.	Will provide unusual ideas.	Can become incredible.
5. Sense of unity, perfectionism.	Can cause rigidity, lack of originality.	Provides a personal voice.	Can become overly subjective.
6. Good critical sense.	Can become overcritical.	Open to all ideas.	Lacks capacity for criticism.
7. Strong intellectual content.	Can be overly theoretical.	Provides powerful emotions.	Can result in melodrama.
8. Commercial instinct.	Can be overcautious.	Provides original voice.	No commercial instinct.

Figure 1.4 Advantages and dangers of vertical and lateral thinking in writing tasks

This section introduces *Development Strategy 1* (which is about diagnosis, defining the task) and *Development Strategy 2* (which is about brainstorming a range of real but unusual solutions; in other words, remedy). Development Strategies 1 and 2 provide the starting point for all problem-solving in screenplays, from the finding of good, original ideas to the final editing process. They are also an all-purpose troubleshooting device particularly useful in panic situations. In a crisis they should be the first recourse. This section demonstrates how Development Strategies 1 and 2 can be used as general troubleshooting tools. Later parts of the book will show how they can be used in conjunction with a range of story triggers to kick-start lateral thinking and generate large numbers of good story ideas at speed.

Development Strategy 1: Defining the task at hand

Define the task at hand before considering remedies.

Questions to ask:

Do I know the task (for example what film we're in, the point of this scene)?

What am I supposed to be doing here?

Do I understand the definitions?

1

It is frighteningly easy to jump in and start writing before you really know what writing task you have on your hands. Be conscious that your instinct for survival will push you to rush. Resist that instinct. Think: "What am I supposed to be doing here? What is the problem here?" For example, if you are asked to submit ideas for a low-budget thriller film, have you defined to yourself precisely what the demands and potential pitfalls of a low-budget thriller are? Or, if you have to plan the second act of your film, have you defined to yourself precisely what the second act is supposed to do? Again, if you feel there is something wrong with your first act, before you start pulling it apart, have you tried to define as precisely as possible where the problem might be? Or, if you are writing a scene, have you defined to yourself precisely what you need to do in this scene before you start putting in the dialogue?

Use Development Strategy 1 to help define to yourself whatever task you have at hand. Once you are clear about what the task involves, you can use Development Strategy 2 to brainstorm a range of ideas from which to choose.

Once Development Strategy 1 has provided a range of questions that need to be asked, Development Strategy 2 can brainstorm a range of real but unusual answers for filtering later. It is important to realize that brainstorming, being lateral, is counter-intuitive, particularly in the situation when it is most needed, that is, a crisis. In a crisis,

Development Strategy 2: Brainstorming the best "real but unusual" remedy

Allow lateral thinking to generate original or unusual ideas to be filtered by vertical thinking.

Questions to ask:

Is what I am creating credible enough?

Is what I am creating unusual enough?

Have I let lateral thinking generate enough ideas?

Once I've got all the lateral ideas, am I using vertical thinking to filter out poor ones?

2

every vertical thinking instinct will (a) be pushing us to jump at the first possible answer, which is likely to be a cliché, and (b) be trying to filter out the more extreme or silly ideas coming from the lateral imagination.

The crucial thing to remember about this ideas-generating stage of the process is that any idea, however weak or crazy, is acceptable because it can lead by association to something useful. As writers, we are so used to rejecting substandard ideas immediately that at first this is a difficult process. It can feel like a rejection of our hard-earned skills of discernment. But in fact the process is liberating and empowering. Instead of finding ideas by default ("this one isn't good enough;" "that one isn't good enough;" "this one is good, let's go with it …") we end up with a range of good ideas from which to choose.

It takes real discipline to brainstorm in a crisis, because brainstorming requires you to daydream about a problem rather than taking action. It is rather like being faced with a charging tiger and asking yourself not to run, but to consider the patterns on the tiger's coat.

To use Development Strategy 2 to maximum effect, writers need to stay calm and give themselves permission to think of silly or outrageous answers on the way towards exciting and original ideas. It takes practice and a conscious effort to be calm in this situation. One simple way to control the panic instinct that says brainstorming is a waste of time is to use a stopwatch to set a time for brainstorming – even ten minutes can produce a fund of ideas.

How Development Strategies 1 and 2 assist the writing process

Boosting confidence

Development Strategies 1 and 2 genuinely boost a writer's confidence, because they can be relied upon to give a range of ideas for whatever problem they are addressing. This is particularly important in the film industry where factors like budget or the practical exigencies of shooting may rule out the first idea, or mean a new solution has to be found immediately.

Helping the collaborative process

Development Strategies 1 and 2 help collaborators better understand each other because they force them to analyze the problems they are sharing. This helps keep everyone 'in the same film'.

Maintaining a high standard of writing generally

Development Strategies 1 and 2 are not merely useful in an emergency. They can help writing generally. It is very easy for writers to drop into automatic pilot, writing without really checking that the decisions they are making are the best ones. Development Strategies 1 and 2 can help with this by forcing the writer to maximize options.

Helping the writer understand the script better

Development Strategies 1 and 2 give writers a much better understanding of the themes and structure of the screenplay than they would have if they were writing intuitively. This is an enormous help in the script development stage, helping writers to defend damaging revisions of the script and assist positive ones.

Development Strategies 1 and 2 seem so obvious that it is easy to assume that we use them automatically, but it's not as simple as that. Imagine a screenplay coming back from readers with the general criticism that it is uninteresting because the female characters are too passive. This seems like an easy problem to solve. The problem has been defined ("female characters are too passive") and the answer seems to be just a matter of plotting and writing extra "proactive" scenes into the existing plot.

In fact, Development Strategies 1 and 2 have not been used because the diagnosis of the readers has been accepted at face value. What if the readers' diagnosis is wrong? Even if it is right, the chances are that the scenes written in response will have been devised so quickly and with such little thought that they are likely either to be a cliché (coming straight out of a vertical imagination desperate for an answer) or incredible (coming straight out of a lateral imagination lacking totally in judgment). (For more information on using Development Strategies 1 and 2 in rewrites, see "Using criticism to best advantage" in Chapter 6.

2. Getting good ideas fast from screen models

Good ideas are essential, and the ability to get a wealth of ideas under pressure is a vital screenwriter's skill. The clue to getting good ideas at speed is to realize that imagination is *reactive*. We are used to thinking of the imagination as something overwhelmingly proactive, a powerful force that takes us over and dominates our lives. And so it is, once it has got an idea to run with. But if, as writers, we look back at how we got ideas for original work, almost invariably the answer is that something in the world around us – an event, a story read in the newspaper or told by a friend, an anecdote, a thought – provoked in us a response that demanded a story.

In other words, the business of getting an idea for a story was *a reaction in response to a stimulus from the outside world*. It did not come from inside us. This process is reflected accurately when we say of writers that something fired or caught their imagination. It's also what the ancients were thinking about when they thought of the idea of a muse, which was a separate, and petulant, supernatural entity in charge of ideas.

To experience how outside stimuli fire the imagination, try this simple task. First of all, give yourself ten seconds to think of as many one-sentence film ideas as possible. The chances are you will be lucky if you have one or two. Now give yourself ten seconds to think of film ideas on the topic "earthquake." This external stimulus will make it much easier to make connections and produce ideas. Finally, give yourself ten seconds to think of film ideas that combine earthquake with another stimulus – say, a theme like 'self-esteem', or a simple plot model like a Cinderella story. You will find that the extra connections make it surprisingly easy to think of ideas (although the quality of many will be poor).

This associational activity is what happens naturally in the creative process. Since we screen professionals rarely have time to wait for the great idea to come to us, we can artificially create the natural stimulus/reaction process ourselves, by using vertical thinking to pick a stimulus which we then run past our lateral imagination so as to trigger associations and unusual connections. We can catch our own imagination and be our own muse.

This chapter and the next deal with using Development Strategies 1 and 2 in combination with a variety of story triggers to kick-start lateral thinking and get a wealth of story ideas at speed for three-act films. They also introduce *Development Strategy 3*, which is about pinpointing the components of a specific genre, and *Development Strategy 4*, which shows how to get more ideas by consciously making links between very different things. This chapter looks at using screen models (genre) to trigger plot ideas. The next chapter looks at other triggers, including fairytale, myth and fable; real life events; characters; themes; events; and random combinations of ideas.

Isn't a model a fast track to cliché?

Before we look at models we need to ask the obvious question: why use models? Isn't a model (particularly something like genre) a fast track to cliché? Why, in a search for the new and unusual, are we returning to formats that some would say have been done to death?

Unfortunately, it is a sad fact of writing life that any model, after a while, can produce or mask clichés. But this is not the fault of the model. It is because the writer has unconsciously let vertical thinking take over and preempt lateral imagination. Models are not necessarily a fast track to cliché. Models are successful patterns that audiences enjoy and, in some cases, have been enjoying for thousands of years. The chances are that audiences will like them again, as long as lateral thinking is brought into play to push the boundaries and give the format a new and original slant. It's interesting to remember that *Hamlet* was a commercially commissioned piece of formula writing, written within the very rigid format of *revenge tragedy*, a genre akin to the modern-day Mafia or gangster movie, full of murder and betrayal. Hamlet himself was a typical revenge tragedy protagonist, a melancholy malcontent who had to avenge a murder and found it difficult to do so. As usual, Shakespeare transcended formula and stereotypical characterization. Of course, Shakespeare's plays themselves have now become models: some very obviously – for example, Baz Luhrmann's *Romeo + Juliet* (1996) – and some less obviously – for example Disney's *The Lion King* (1994) which, with its self-critical crown prince deposed by a wicked uncle, is really a version of *Hamlet*. A good pattern can give us endless good stories. The trick for writers is to avoid being kidnapped by vertical thinking and pushed into a weak rehash of the pattern.

Writing to a screen model

Screenwriters are so often asked to write to models that it makes sense to deal with that approach first. Television series and serials are the most obvious example of writing to models, but writing feature films often requires writing to a model or genre. Typical writing-to-model tasks would be the following:

- ideas for a low-budget romance (feature)
- the premise for a 50-minute TV drama series
- ideas for a package of three science fiction telemovies for the teen market
- ideas for episodes in a TV anthology on the theme of motherhood.

The trick of getting lots of ideas for models is, as we might expect, knowing how and when to use lateral and vertical thinking. For experienced writers the hardest part will be to switch vertical thinking off after it has defined the requirements of the model, so that it is not allowed to get ideas but only to choose them after lateral brainstorming. For newer writers, the temptation will be to sidestep the vertical task of defining the model's requirements and jump straight into lateral brainstorming.

The approach can be summed up quite simply. Define the model, then give yourself permission to brainstorm it freely through a *variety* of triggers, keeping all the ideas so that later, when you are completely sure you have brainstormed enough, you can select the best. The importance of varying the story trigger cannot be sufficiently stressed. The same trigger, used over and over again, is likely to result in the creative process being hijacked by vertical thinking, so that you think you are brainstorming but in fact you are only producing clichés and ideas that you had the last time you used the trigger (this is typically what is happening when TV storyliners go into burn out).

Give yourself as much time as possible to work on this vital ideas part of the project. Remember, a good idea virtually writes itself. If you choose a poor idea, you will be spending a huge amount of time trying to make it sparkle.

Rejecting the first idea

Remember that this stage of the process is not about getting complete plots. It is about getting a wealth of one-sentence story ideas – fragments from which a choice can later be made. Moving into plotting too early can preempt the creative process. It is frighteningly easy to commit to a poor idea just because it was the first one that came to mind. In fact the first idea is usually a derivative one springing from the vertical imagination. Instant, second-rate ideas are one of the great traps of vertical thinking and one of the great dangers facing experienced writers, whose craft skills are so extensively developed and who, as a consequence, can so easily drop into automatic pilot. Matters of detailed plotting come later.

Getting ideas for a film (for example, low-budget romance)

As an example of how this works, let's look at the low-budget romance feature film. As we've seen, getting good ideas is all about finding useful triggers for lateral thinking. A model of the simplest kind, like the words "low-budget feature romance," can sometimes act as a good trigger in itself. So this is where to start. Remember, all you are looking for at this stage are one-sentence ideas. Keep to one sentence because if you start to plot a whole story you will commit to it, thereby shutting out a whole range of other potential stories.

Step 1

Reminding yourself that finding the right idea is going to take some time, apply Development Strategy 1: defining the task at hand (see page 10) so that you can brainstorm ideas. Make sure you know what the task is, for example, what film you're in, what the point of the scene is and what you are supposed to be doing. While the task might seem obvious, consciously define it for yourself, because that precision helps vertical thinking to keep you unpanicked.

Here the task is to think of ideas for a low-budget feature romance. You will imme-diately notice that business issues are present, but don't allow them to inhibit the next stage of the process, which is brainstorming. Put them aside for later, even better, jot down a memo on a separate piece of paper.

Step 2

Having pinpointed the task, utilize Development Strategy 2: brainstorming the best real but unusual remedy (see page 11) to come up with as many one-sentence ideas for a feature romance as possible. Ask yourself whether what you are plotting is unusual enough. Have you let lateral thinking generate enough ideas? Are you letting vertical considerations – like business issues or quality – limit you?

Before brainstorming, consciously shed preconceptions about what a romance should be. Give yourself permission to be flippant, grim, ironic – anything, so long as you keep yourself open to all ideas. Also, shed anxieties about quality. Quality issues come later. Try for 20 one-sentence ideas. Here are a few random, even ridiculous, ideas on the topic of a real but unusual romance. Let yourself bounce out from the first idea.

Ideas for a real but unusual romance feature

1. A postal worker falls in love with a letter, which could be developed to a postal worker falling for the addressee, for a computer, or for the sender, in the latter case because they have beautiful handwriting, or the letter smells engaging.
2. An elephant falls for an ant, which takes up the idea of opposites or unlikely people attracting each other, such as the power-broker falling for a powerless person; an old person falling for a younger person; people of different races become attracted; the Romeo and Juliet idea.
3. A divorced couple falls in love again.
4. Two murderers fall in love.
5. A person falls in love with their disease, which could be developed to a person who functions by thinking of themselves as weak or victimized finding strength through falling in love with someone who challenges that approach.

Step 3

Write all these ideas down.

Step 4

Get other triggers from the model. This is because, while a limited model like "romance feature" can sometimes trigger excellent ideas, usually stress will cut in and make us switch into vertical thinking before our lateral imagination has had a chance to work properly. The result is limited, clichéd ideas.

To help yourself, you can use Development Strategy 1 to give yourself a range of other triggers. For example, having defined the task by determining that you are getting ideas for a feature romance, you can define the task more precisely by asking "What is a feature romance?" In other words, what are the *story components* of a feature romance? Logical vertical thinking will give us answers like these:

Story components of feature romance

1. Setting (place and era).
2. Personal details of lovers (age, class, occupation, etc.).
3. Way lovers meet.
4. Non-human barriers to lovers (social, health, misunderstandings, distance, etc.).
5. Rivals to lovers.
6. Ending – happy or sad?
7. Point of view (one or other of the lovers, a friend, a parent, a rival, etc.).

Each of these character and plot components can be run past the lateral imagination as a trigger for brainstorming. Let's look at an example. We will take the idea of a real but unusual setting for a feature romance. Switching to lateral thinking, we might get the following examples:

Unusual settings for a feature romance

1. Mars, outer space, spaceship, flying saucer.
2. Zoo – lovers as animals, actually or symbolically?
3. Place of work – office, factory, bakery, garage, car yard, ferry depot, houses in the same street, chemistry lab, cancer ward, Alcoholics Anonymous meeting, deathbed, radioactive dump, school, university, gardens, parks, racing stables, building site, studio, garbage dump, recycling facility, symphony orchestra, theatre, cinema, roller-skating rink, sports field, restaurant, hotel, bank.
4. Desert island, emotional island of some sort, railway station (when both parties are stranded, emotionally isolated).
5. Across the Internet – two people in different towns.
6. Medieval era or some other period in history, or a museum where both are enthusiasts for one era. Love in a cult setting of some kind, perhaps a religious cult setting (but period might be too expensive).
7. Fantasy land, fairy land, psychiatric hospital, beauty parlor.
8. Big house – one lover rich, the other a servant.
9. Small country town, big country town, big city, small rural pocket in big city.
10. Cemetery, funeral parlor, shoe store, clothes store, shopping centre (he's the butcher and she's the newsagent, etc.).
11. Old people's home, children's playgroup, children's sports club.
12. Love at a health farm, love at a resort, people out of context (will love last?).
13. Love on an archeological dig or in the jungle (city as jungle). Beware budget.
14. Love in a swamp, in the desert, after a plane crash at the North Pole.
15. Penguins in love – anything polar in love.

Already, the range of ideas has opened up enormously. The ideas show everything from the mundane (lovers meeting at a resort) to the apparently bizarre (penguins in love). But it is important to realize that without the mass of other ideas surrounding it, "lovers meeting at a resort" might not have seemed so weak. As for "penguins in love," while it looks out of place here, it could look quite respectable as an idea for an animated children's film.

Also, while of itself it seems unpromising, it could be the feeder idea for another concept. This could be comedy romance about two scientists fighting to become the first to document the mating habits of a rare penguin, or it could be a thriller with a romantic subplot about industrial espionage in the Antarctic. Note that staying open to tragic ideas permits ideas like love in a cancer ward, which lifts the topic into a whole new range of emotions.

You can now go on to brainstorm each of the components. This will give you a huge range of ideas.

Step 5

When you feel you have enough ideas from all of your idea triggers, take your favorite six or so ideas and hand them back to your vertical imagination for a "business issues" check. This is another way of defining the task. It requires you to define the business components your idea needs to have to be genuinely a low-budget feature romance.

Business issues of low-budget romance
1. Low budget, so must not require expensive locations, special effects, etc.
2. Must not be period because of the expense.
3. Must not be written with expensive actors in mind.
4. Is it my producer's kind of product (if a producer is attached at this stage)?
5. Is it to be aimed at a certain demographic? Should I choose?
6. Are there any co-production issues here that might affect ingredients of the story (location, actors, etc) ?

If a producer is already involved in the project, that person will probably appreciate receiving and perhaps contributing to this list. Lists like these are very helpful in helping the collaboration process run smoothly because they ensure that everybody knows what the writer is supposed to be doing.

Step 6

When you have defined the story components and business issues, take a moment to define the potential pitfalls of your story or stories, using as a reference point poor examples of your model. So, if you are writing a science fiction movie, take a few moments to note down what was wrong with the bad science-fiction movies you have seen. As the writing proceeds, check from time to time that you haven't fallen into the pitfalls.

Genre and audience expectations

Now that you have six or so story ideas, you need to double check that you know "what film we're in," so that you can give the audience the best possible version of the model it expects. In this instance, the model is a *genre*. Identifying the genre of the film you intend to write provides even greater insights on the matter of the Development Strategy 1 question: 'What film are we in?' This is firstly because it provides further details about plot and characterization requirements, and secondly, because understanding what genre we are in helps remind you of the exact ways in which the film needs to grab the emotions and intellect of the audience. It reminds you that a thriller must be extremely thrilling, or that a spy story must be extremely full of suspense. It reminds you that a whodunit must keep us guessing. In the case of the love story, it will remind you that the screenplay must make the audience feel romantic, exhilarated and touched by the story. It will remind you that the audience needs to empathize strongly with the main characters. It reminds you of the need to convince your audience until the very last moment that the lovers will break up – and so on.

This might all seem very obvious. In fact pressure makes it very easy to rush into creating specifics of storyline while forgetting the core requirements of the genre or, more precisely, what experience the audience is looking for when they come to this sort of film. The sort of questions that have to be asked, quite cold-bloodedly, are things like: "Before I go any further, is my film actually exciting enough for a thriller?" or "Before I commit to this whodunit, does it really have enough twists and turns?" Such things can never be assumed.

But what if the writer wants to play games with the audience's genre expectations? This certainly can be done but, just as we need to understand the form before we copy it, so we must understand the form before we play tricks with it. Before you try to write in a particular genre, take a moment to pinpoint the audience's expectations of that genre. That is the essence of Development Strategy 3.

Development Strategy 3: Pinpointing genre to check audience expectations

Identifying the pattern or genre you are writing in, remembering that genre = pattern + relevant emotion + real + unusual.

Questions to ask:

Am I including events and characters that will provoke high levels of the right emotion (for example, fear, amusement, suspense)?

Have I identified all the components of the pattern?

What plot and character points must I have for the audience to identify this as the chosen pattern?

Have I pinpointed the danger areas of the genre (for example, cliché, credibility gaps)?

Have I run Development Strategy 2 to make sure I have got a highly unusual but credible version of the pattern?

3

Development Strategy 3 is actually a development of the "real but unusual" rule that we've seen is a useful screenwriter's motto. It is the first Development Strategy to have a highly specific function, and its function is to make sure that the writer knows enough about the demands, clichés and nuances of any chosen genre to recreate it in a powerfully original way that will fulfil – hopefully exceed – the audience's expectations. Because it focuses on the scenario that could develop from the idea, it shifts the idea closer towards creation of a complete story with a proper structure. While it is still too early at this stage to start close-plotting any of the ideas, it is useful to begin considering the general demands of a genre. Doing so helps filter out inappropriate ideas and shift more promising ideas to the top of the pile. It is much better to pinpoint the demands of genre *before* close-plotting any one story because choosing a story means you have emotionally committed to it. This could blind you to its inadequacy as a vehicle for the genre you have to write in.

How can we pinpoint the components of a genre? There is an old comedy writer's rule that runs "silly plus real is funny, but silly plus silly is stupid." For example, in a successful comedy like *Muriel's Wedding* (1994) a plain girl agrees to a loveless arranged marriage (credibly real, vertical thinking) for the comically ridiculous reason that she is desperate to have a white wedding (unusually silly, lateral thinking). The result is a premise that is engagingly funny. But if *Muriel's Wedding* had been about a girl who thinks, in a comically ridiculous way, that she's from Mars and, also in a comically ridiculous way, is desperate for a white wedding, the result would have been stupid. This sound advice is another way of saying that if you remove vertical thinking from the equation, your comedy gets too over the top. There is also the obvious point that if you remove lateral thinking, the unusual component of the comedy, all you will have is a completely vertical equation of real plus real, which is not funny at all.

Just as we can describe comedy films as being "silly plus real," so we can define thrillers as 'exciting plus real', and tragedies as "deeply sad plus real." *That gives us the emotion we want to arouse in our audience.* We can also use the "silly but real" motto to remind ourselves that an overdose of the relevant emotion will wreck any film. So that "deeply sad plus deeply sad" will be over the top. The "real" must always be there.

If we add to this equation the basic pattern of the specific genre (by which I mean that the pattern of a spy film, for example, is "what spies do," and the pattern of a love story is that "people fall in love"), we have a quick way to prove that our film is getting the audience via the emotions and story patterns that its genre should. Or alternatively, that it is playing games with story patterns and emotions (as in *Pulp Fiction*, which adds comedy and the mundane to the normal gangster movie pattern of fear, excitement and underworld atmosphere). Playing games with genre is of course entirely permissible; in fact it is the premise behind all film spoofs and many cult films.

We can even create a table to remind us how the basic genres break down into tasks, as shown in Figure 2.1. Pattern components and credibility are handled by vertical thinking and emotion and originality are handled by lateral thinking.

Genre	=	Pattern	+	Emotion	+	Credibility	+	Originality
Comedy	=	pattern components	+	silly	+	real	+	unusual
Thriller	=	pattern components	+	fear	+	real	+	unusual
Action story	=	pattern components	+	excitement	+	real	+	unusual
Love story	=	pattern components	+	romance	+	real	+	unusual
Tragedy	=	pattern components	+	pain	+	real	+	unusual

Figure 2.1 Breaking down genres into tasks

A similar chart could be used as a brainstorming tool for the film you are writing, with each element as a heading, as shown in Figure 2.2.

War story	=	Pattern (normal components of war story)	+	Frightening	+	Real	+	Unusual
Historical war or invented war? Internal, mental war? War with invaders from outer space?		Setting up both sides. Explaining cause of conflict. Battle scenes, tender scenes, thoughtful scenes.		Many different frightening events, plus suspense.		Research (into historical wars of the same type and/or the sort of conditions that would apply).		Use unlikely protagonists. See it from viewpoint of the enemy — for example, from the view of an invader from outer space? From the view of a non-combatant? From the view of a machine? Use flashback narrative structure?

Figure 2.2 Genre table for a war movie

Pitfalls of genre

Every genre contains its clichés and pitfalls. Rather than ignore the possibility of clichés and other pitfalls, define what they are so you can avoid them. For example, a cliché of war films is that the coward will behave in a cowardly way and endanger others. Consider varying this in some way, or dispensing with it altogether.

Combining genres

An interesting way to avoid cliché and find new and interesting patterns is to combine genres. This approach can produce a wealth of interesting ideas. It is dealt with at length in Ken Dancyger and Jeff Rush's absorbing book, *Alternative Scriptwriting* (1995), but the theory in essence is to brainstorm the plot possibilities of combining different genres (for example, combining a gangster film with a war film, or combining a love story with a war story) and see what interesting plot combinations suggest themselves. Interesting structural combinations might also suggest themselves as a result of the process, as for example in the case of *The English Patient,* which uses flashbacks to tell its combination of love and war stories.

Inventing genres

Brainstorming of the kind demonstrated with a low-budget feature can be used equally well with other genres. In fact an interesting brainstorming exercise is to think up new genres, then use them as triggers. For example, you might brainstorm literal and figurative treatments of the "buried treasure" movie, the "other woman" movie, the "pride before a fall" movie; the Samson movie (hero destroyed by passion gets revenge), and so on. Be careful not to be drawn in to close-plotting of one or two ideas. The purpose is still to generate as many ideas as possible.

3. Getting good ideas fast from fairytale, myth and fable

Stories that have engaged audiences for hundreds or thousands of years are clearly stories that work and therefore stories that make good models. Myths, fairytales and fables are actually easier to use as models than genre types because they specify protagonist, supporting characters and details of scenario. Since they also typically possess a very sound traditional three-act narrative structure, they are ready-made templates. While, to modern minds, using an existing story might seem like a form of plagiarism, in fact inventing stories from scratch is a relatively recent idea, and for writers before, after and including Shakespeare, using an existing story was the norm, the issue being how the story was made relevant to modern times.

The screen industry continues this tradition to its great profit, constantly recycling myths, fairytales and fables. One very dominant fairytale, particularly in mainstream cinema, is Cinderella, the story of the triumph of the underdog. It is such a prevalent and consistently successful model (particularly in Hollywood) that it deserves close attention. Clearly, Cinderella is evident in a movie like *Pretty Woman* (1990) but it crops up in many other less obvious forms, in everything from *Strictly Ballroom* (1992) (Cinderella for ballroom dancers) to *Babe* (1995) (Cinderella for pigs), to *Shine* (1996) (Cinderella for concert pianists) to the *Rocky* movies (Cinderella for boxers), and not forgetting that entire genre of movies like *The Mighty Ducks* (1992) (almost exclusively North American) that feature a losing sports team winning against the odds. Even extremely serious films can be Cinderella stories. Both *The Killing Fields* (1984) and *Awakenings* (1990) are Cinderella stories. Since *Cinderella* is such a versatile and successful model, it is a useful starting place for looking at story-triggering strategies for fairytale, myth and fable.

Getting story ideas from *Cinderella*

The task in getting ideas from *Cinderella* – as with getting ideas from a genre – is not to think of complete stories, but rather to devise a long list of one-sentence fragments from which a final choice can later be made. Seizing on the first idea can, as ever, be a fast track to cliché.

All ways of getting story ideas from *Cinderella,* or indeed any other fairytale, myth or fable, start by defining the task (Development Strategy 1). In this case, the task is "get as many one-sentence ideas as possible for new versions of *Cinderella.*" The next step is to use Development Strategy 2 to brainstorm as many 'real but unusual' answers – at least twenty. What follow are four different methods of stimulating lateral thinking to trigger ideas from *Cinderella.* Really, each is just a different vertical definition of *Cinderella.* They work by providing an external stimulus that sets the lateral imagination to work creating links. However, it is very important to remember that all imagination triggers can be hijacked by vertical thinking and pulled towards cliché. Assume that each method will cease to produce exciting ideas after a while, and have no reservations about abandoning it for another. In fact, as a matter of routine, try as many methods as you can before you commit to one story idea.

Method 1: "*Cinderella* for ..."

Think "*Cinderella* for…" then insert a social role or type, a thing, or even a place, for example: *Cinderella* for librarians, *Cinderella* for street-sweepers, *Cinderella* for stamp collectors, *Cinderella* for multimillionaires, *Cinderella* on the stock market, *Cinderella* in a UN peacekeeping situation, *Cinderella* in a lab, *Cinderella* in a traffic jam, *Cinderella* at the zoo, *Cinderella* in a retirement home, *Cinderella* for musicians, *Cinderella* for endangered species, and so on.

Note that examples like "*Cinderella* for street-sweepers" could be further brainstormed to produce ideas based on metaphorical interpretations of "street-sweepers" – such as bouncers, or police, or social workers, who also "keep the streets clean."

Method 2: One-sentence template

Use Development Strategy 1 (define the task) to create and write down a one-sentence template of the plot, in other words, "what film we're in," then highlight all changeable components. An obvious one-sentence template for *Cinderella* is the following:*Likeable, oppressed person* encounters *fairy godmother* whose *actions* help them achieve *their greatest wish.*

Devising a template like this might seem time-consuming and unnecessary, but it is actually a very useful way, firstly, of summing up the film that is to be written (always a good idea early in the process); secondly, of getting distance on the plot; and finally, of forcing oneself to consider all the options. The latter is the reason for highlighting changeable components. Without highlighting the components, it is easy to drop into the assumption, for example, that planning a Cinderella story has to start with devising new versions of Cinderella herself. In fact a good Cinderella story could equally well start from brainstorming versions of a fairy godmother figure or a wish.

Having devised the template, brainstorm plot ideas from the highlighted elements. For example, for likeable oppressed protagonist, possibilities might include likeable oppressed vet, airline attendant, parent, IT expert, Vietnam veteran, manicurist, nurse, psychiatric patient, dog, etc. From this list of possible protagonists, you could then brainstorm real but unusual versions of a *fairy godmother* figure, fairy godmother figure's *actions* and a *greatest wish*.

Alternatively, you could start by brainstorming the notion of *greatest wish* (for example, to make the best model train set in the world, to achieve recognition as a cheese maker, to save a rainforest, to bring together warring family members), then work backwards to create a protagonist and a fairy godmother figure.

Alternatively, you could start from fairy godmother figures (criminal, builder, animal, disease, etc.), then work backwards to find original protagonists.

Yet another possible starting point is to think of original *actions/transformations* a fairy godmother figure might employ (for example, people hostile to the protagonist could be forced to be helpful or subservient, superior equipment might be acquired for the protagonist etc.).

Of course, the entire nature of *Cinderella* can be changed by changing the one-sentence template. Cinderella could become: "Irresponsible person in authority risks national security by liaison with unskilled laborer." Or "Animals exploited by agent of social climber."

Creating different templates for well-known stories is a method of getting a fresh approach and a variety of ideas. It is another way of working out what film we're in. The trick to devising other templates is to see the story from the point of view of players other than the normal protagonist.

Method 3: Summarizing part of the action

Create a template that summarizes a striking part of the action, then brainstorm the changeable components of that template. This is another use of Development Strategy 1 skills of defining on the page what film we're in' For example, Cinderella's transformation by the fairy godmother could be described as: "*Magic* turned *a poor servant* into *a glamorous wealthy person* for *a short time*, after which things returned to normal."

This could inspire Dr. Jekyll and Mr. Hyde stories along the lines of: "*Technology* turned a *socially unglamorous person* into a *glamorous person* for *a short time*, after which things returned to normal."

This last example is actually the premise of Eddie Murphy's *The Nutty Professor* (1996). But if it was rendered in a different way, it could be the premise of many war or natural disaster films. The following is almost a description of the Tom Hanks character in *Saving Private Ryan* (1998): "*Cataclysmic events* turned *a normal person* into *a hero* for *a short time* after which things returned to normal."

Method 4: The twist ending

Reverse or significantly change the fairytale's ending. For example, using the Cinderella template, look at an ending in which marriage to the prince becomes another form of slavery.

To find a good twist ending, define the underlying assumptions of the fairytale (or other story model) and question them. In Cinderella, one of the basic assumptions is that a marriage that gets a woman out of domestic slavery is good. If that is questioned, other stories start to suggest themselves, along with interesting ideas for more subtle characterization. Brainstorming from a twist-ending version of the model can produce a whole range of interesting story ideas, probably because twist endings provide the normally simplistic characters of fairytale with the opportunity for psychological complexity and development.

Fairytales as templates for thrillers

While *Cinderella* is probably the most common fairytale used in the film industry, others are evident, most often as templates for different sorts of thrillers. For example, "Little Red Riding Hood" is the model for many thrillers featuring the villain in disguise. *Psycho* (1960) is a surprisingly close rendering of Little Red Riding Hood, even down to the wolf dressing up as an old woman (although the twist is that the audience as well as the protagonist are equally ignorant of the old woman's real identity).

Similarly, "The Three Little Pigs" is the basic model for the serial killer film (although *Home Alone* (1990) is a comic inversion of the idea) and, in "Jack and the Beanstalk," where the intrepid hero hides out in the house of the ferocious giant, we have a model for spy and heist films (complete with dramatic final chase). If fairytale models for thrillers seem too simplistic, it is worth remembering that *Being John Malkovich* (1999) is actually a Jack and the Beanstalk story. A young man sent out to raise money finds not a magic beanstalk leading to the home of a giant but a portal which takes him into the giant's head, in this case a "giant" of the screen. Of course, *Being John Malkovich* goes on to tell a much more complex story than "Jack and the Beanstalk" because modern film requires much more plot than the normal fairytale, which usually has very simple second and third acts. But suspenseful fairytales are very useful because they provide very simple and very accessible maps of the dramatic high points of the genre, particularly in the way that suspense is built towards a final climax. For this reason, fairytales like "Little Red Riding Hood," "The Three Little Pigs," and "Jack and the Beanstalk" are not only very useful templates from which to start devising modern-day thrillers, but they also provide a quick way of checking that the thriller you are writing has the right components to provide proper drama and suspense.

It is easy to identify the dramatic high points of these thriller fairytales because they are the parts that everyone remembers: "Fee, fie, fo, fum;" "Oh, Grandma, what big …;" "I'll huff and I'll puff …" If everyone remembers these bits of thriller fairytales, they must be dramatically powerful, and it makes sense to write modern equivalents of them. Hence, in a "villain in disguise" movie, one of the questions to ask is whether the audience is being given enough opportunities to see the innocent protagonist face to face with the villain and realize that something is wrong but not be able to define precisely what. For example, the scene in "Little Red Riding Hood" that has the most impact is the one in which the protagonist questions the disguised wolf about his odd appearance, but doesn't make the connection that he is a murderous impostor.

Similarly, in a spy or robbery film (Jack and the Beanstalk model), one of the points to check for is that there is sufficient treatment of moments when the highly dangerous antagonist can sense that the Jack figure is nearby and almost finds him. Notice that *Being John Malkovich* contains a large section in which Malkovich comes hunting the Jack figure, Craig. These are very simple checks; indeed, they might seem childishly simple, but their very simplicity and directness can help when we are so immersed in the details of writing that we can't see the wood for the trees.

To get ideas for a thriller, brainstorm real but unusual modern versions of the three fairytales using the same four methods we used with the Cinderella template.

Method 1: "'Jack and the Beanstalk' in the world of ..."

Start by inventing as many versions as possible of "'Jack and the Beanstalk' in the world of ...," for example, Silicon Valley, the United Nations, educational organizations; or, Little Red Riding Hood as a dancer, a nurse, a cable TV installer; or, "The Three Little Pigs" for accountants, prostitutes, plumbers.

Method 2: One-sentence template

Create a one-sentence template of the plot, highlighting the changeable components. For example: "*Likeable young man* is forced by poverty and *magic* to enter *a new world*, commit theft and get away with it,"

The changeable components (protagonist, nature of the magic and the new world) can then be brainstormed to produce a variety of scenarios. When the template is exhausted, create others by looking at the story from the point of view of characters other than the protagonist. Note how "Jack and the Beanstalk," seen from the giant's point of view, becomes a tragedy of betrayal. One result might be: "*Elderly rich man* is betrayed by *his wife* then robbed and murdered by *a ruthless interloper*." Do not worry that this template does not accurately reflect "Jack and the Beanstalk" as we know it. The point is merely to create another trigger for lateral connection-making.

Method 3: Summarize part of the action

Create a template by summarizing a compelling part of the action, for example: "*An apparent con trick* offers *an entry* into *a new, dangerous but potentially profitable world*." Or, more simply: "*Magic* creates *a promise* and *a threat*." The latter could result in everything from a vampire story to *Field of Dreams* (1989).

Method 4: The twist ending

Reverse or significantly change the fairytale's ending. The twist ending can work just as well for a thriller model as it can for *Cinderella*. Questioning the basic assumptions behind "Jack and the Beanstalk" (that killing of the giant is good) could result in a model where, say, Jack is irredeemably brutalized by the murder of the giant. Brainstorming the idea of a hero brutalized by a deed that initially seemed positive provides a whole new variety of thriller story. This is because, as we saw with *Cinderella,* the twist ending permits the normally simplistic and unselfconscious characters of fairytales the potential for psychological complexity, which is highly useful for enriching the story.

Myth, fable and literature
The hero's journey

It is impossible to talk about the use of myth in film without mentioning Christopher Vogler's brilliant and seminal book *The Writer's Journey*. Vogler (1992) takes the ancient and very pervasive myth of the "hero of a thousand faces" (in which a hero has to go into another dangerous world to save the tribe and achieve personal salvation) and demonstrates how its scenario, its protagonist and its range of compelling archetypes can be identified in modern screenplays of all kinds, from action movies to subtle psychological drama, as well as being used as a template for new screenplays. The book is compulsory reading, but to summarize:

- The hero's journey is a circular one, starting and ending at home with a trip to a special world in the middle.
- On the way, the hero meets a range of people, good and bad, who are archetypes, that is, they stand for typical human types or roles. The most frequently appearing archetypes are:
    - mentor (a wise old man or woman)
    - threshold guardian (a fierce person guarding the entrance to the special world)
    - herald (a person who introduces the hero to the quest)
    - shape shifter (a person who keeps changing their role)
    - shadow (the hero's main enemy – a reverse image of the hero)
    - trickster (sometimes a helper, sometimes a hindrance).

Summary of the hero's journey plot

The hero receives a summons to adventure, but is reluctant to go into the special world. Events force the hero to go, taking a magic talisman given by a mentor or teacher. The hero defeats the threshold guardian at the first door into the special world, and goes through. The hero encounters new challenges, new friends and new enemies, eventually passing through the second door, which leads to the innermost cave and the great ordeal, in which the hero is face to face with death. The hero gets the treasure and starts back for the normal world, passing through a third door and experiencing a resurrection. There is a final great battle and the hero experiences victory, returning with the treasure to the normal world.

The huge advantage of this model is that it provides not only a traditional structure and specific scenario, but a range of strongly defined characters with strong needs and specific roles to play in the progress of the protagonist. This not only ensures that the characters have the makings of interesting psychology, but also that each character acts to impel the protagonist forward in the plot. This really is character-driven drama!

Specific scenarios from myth, fable and literature

Vogler argues that mythical heroes like Ulysses and Oedipus are actually all versions of the hero of a thousand faces, with each of their stories being a figurative journey into hell and back. There is a lot to this theory, but for purposes of stimulating the lateral imagination, there is still a lot of mileage to be had in using the specific scenarios of individual myths and fables as triggers. These scenarios can be turned into story templates or templates devised from a story detail, using the same methods we applied to fairytales. Thus, Icarus could be rendered along the following lines: "*A person warned against flying too close to the sun did not heed warnings and was drowned.*" Or perhaps: "*Something strong disintegrated under adverse conditions.*"

Fables – the ultimate character-driven story

Fables are useful models because as well as having compelling plots they possess strongly defined characters. Indeed, because the story of any fable is devised to illustrate the foibles of its main players, fable is always very powerfully character-driven. For screenwriting purposes, this means that fables provide excellent models of how plot must serve character and not exist for its own sake. Since many films, particularly comedies, are about self-inflicted disasters or disasters growing out of character flaws, fable can actively help in keeping a script on track. The way to use fable for this purpose is to try to identify the fable that your film is acting out. Think of your characters as being their counterparts in the relevant fable and check that the action of your film is, like the fable, permitting them to illustrate their failings.

Gangster movies

Many ancient myths figure violent conflict between rival kingdoms and can thus translate easily into models for gangster stories, war stories, or even treatments of corporate warfare. The same four methods can be used as were applied to fairytales, that is, start with the simple name trigger (for example, "Antigone as … the daughter of a CEO"). Next, use a variety of templates, including a summary; and, finally, create a twist ending by questioning the assumptions behind the myth.

Lawyer/detective/adventure/western movies

Lawyers, detectives, and the heroes of adventure and western stories (including space westerns) are all modern-day equivalents of Arthurian knights (hence Indiana Jones in search of the Holy Grail), therefore the Arthurian stories are useful triggers. Robin Hood and Trojan War stories can also be useful. The same four triggering methods can be used as were used for fairytales.

Love stories

Most myths are action adventure stories. A useful classical model for love stories is the myth of Orpheus and Eurydice (perhaps the original blueprint for "boy gets girl, boy loses girl, boy gets girl back," although of course in many versions, Orpheus loses Eurydice forever) and, in the Arthurian legends, the love triangle between Arthur, Guinevere and Lancelot is useful. In literature, *Romeo and Juliet* is of course a perennially successful model – in fact *Titanic* (1997) owed its success not to its historical content but to its Romeo and Juliet story. All of these love story models can be brainstormed using the four methods that we applied to fairytales.

Shakespeare's plays

While *Romeo and Juliet* is probably the Shakespeare play most commonly used as a model, several others frequently appear. *Hamlet* is a common model (even as we have seen in *The Lion King*, 1994), but others often used are *King Lear* and *A Midsummer Night's Dream*. It would be worth considering, if you are given a script to rewrite or a story to write up into a script, whether there is a precedent in Shakespeare that might add any useful dimensions. For example, a story about a dropout finding a place in society might be enriched by adding themes and characters found in *Henry IV Part I* – perhaps, say, a Falstaff figure who is later betrayed. (If this seems like plagiarism, Shakespeare and his colleagues are also guilty of it – indeed, they did it all the time. Shakespeare's *Merchant of*

Venice is his answer to a very similar play by Christopher Marlowe (1633) called *The Jew of Malta*. *The Jew of Malta* was doing such good business at a rival theatre that Shakespeare was told to write something similar.) To brainstorm from a Shakespeare play, use the four methods applied to fairytales.

Comedies

The classic comedies of Molière and Ben Johnson provide excellent triggers for comedy ideas because their protagonists and plots are all about human failings and particular human types. Brainstorming the idea of a misanthrope or a miser or a hypochondriac can provide a whole range of modern comic protagonists. The next step is to think of situations in which the protagonist is confronted with their character flaws – a miser being forced to spend, a coward being forced into battle, and so on. Again, the brainstorming methods used are like those we used earlier for fairytales.

The Pilgrim's Progress

A very persistent model in North American films is John Bunyan's *The Pilgrim's Progress*, in which the protagonist Christian, who stands for all humanity (at least, all non-conformist Protestant humanity), is changed for the better by experience, successfully achieving his goal (heaven) through ordeal. This notion of success through perfectibility – of the protagonist growing and improving and thereby achieving spiritual redemption – is very deeply embedded in the American filmmaking psyche; it is even present in a film like *Pulp Fiction*. So prevalent is it that many American screenwriting theories present growth and redemption in the protagonist as an essential and universal requirement of any story. In fact, not all cultures adhere to this idea. It is essentially a Christian Protestant approach clearly related to America's cultural origins. Many non-American film cultures (for example, Chinese) frequently and actively pursue more depressing protagonist's journeys, in which little is learned and little is – or can be – changed; indeed, determinism rather than personal will runs human affairs. Even in Australian cinema, which is culturally very close to its North American counterpart, the norm (in non-comedy) is to present heroes who are noble failures. This cultural difference is interestingly pinpointed in the different national responses to *Shine*. While Americans saw the film as a story about winning, Australians saw it as a profoundly moving film about noble failure and deeply compromised success.

But regardless of the universality or otherwise of the perfectible protagonist, to understand and write in the US tradition, *The Pilgrim's Progress* is essential reading – and an excellent model if a flawed but growing protagonist is required. Just like the fairytales, it can be used for brainstorming by applying the four methods outlined in this chapter.

4. Getting good ideas fast from non-narrative triggers

S o far, all the story triggers have been fictitious narratives of one kind or another, but a story trigger does not need to be a narrative, fictitious or otherwise. Almost anything can act to trigger lateral thinking. Even a road sign reading "Wrong Way" could be used as a starting point for brainstorming story ideas. What follow are a variety of triggers not based on fictitious narrative. It is extremely important to have a wide range of story triggers because vertical thinking can so easily hijack any one trigger and make us start unwittingly churning out clichés. Never remain exclusively with one story trigger; indeed, anticipate your tendency towards cliché by making a point of switching between different triggers. Even the act of changing triggers is a stimulus to the imagination.

The outside world

Anecdotes, heard or read, can be excellent triggers, as can articles or fragments in the media. Particularly useful are newspaper snippets just a few sentences long ("Two elderly people found guilty of faking their own kidnapping were released on a good behavior bond"). Cryptic headlines ("Tourists return to reality." "Gridlock causes chaos.") are also excellent triggers, as are job ads and personal ads. The names of streets in street maps can be triggers, as can names in a telephone directory. Proverbs or common phrases ("The check is in the mail.") are also useful, and even walking down the street can provide triggers, such as phrases on billboards or, as we have seen, street signs. Always useful is the process of asking yourself "What if …?" and brainstorming possible answers.

To find triggers, simply use Development Strategy 1 to pick a useful trigger from the world around you, then use Development Strategy 2 to brainstorm different "real but unusual" interpretations of the trigger. In cases where the trigger is a phrase or sentence, ideas can be maximized by writing the words down, highlighting changeable components and methodically brainstorming each one.

All story ideas found in this way can be combined with narrative models in genre, fairytale, myth, fable or literature to enrich the basic idea, provide more material for brainstorming, and add structural components. For example, a vague idea for a film about a marriage breakup inspired by a "Wrong Way" street sign could be put beside the myth of, say, Icarus to give a story about a person who aspires too high at work and thereby loses a spouse. Alternatively, the combination could suggest a story about someone who plays with fire and finds their marriage under threat – this is, of course, the basis of *Fatal Attraction* (1987). Linking the idea of a marriage breakup to a genre like "bank heist" could suggest a story in which a marital quarrel affects an attempted bank robbery with terrifying results.

Social roles or behaviors

Some of the methods described above involve using characters from the world around us as story triggers. Another way of using character as a story trigger is to brainstorm real but unusual versions of social roles. The trick to getting interesting story ideas from character-based triggers of all kinds is to pull against the character's stereotype. Metaphorical versions of character types are also a rich source of ideas – so, for example, a "prisoner" doesn't have to be someone behind bars. Some role-based story triggers are:

- character defined by occupation (for example, landlord, lawyer)
- character defined by family role (for example, mother, son)
- character defined by emotional state (for example, avenger)
- character defined by predicament (for example, prisoner)
- character defined by flaws (for example, compulsive gambler)
- character defined by ambition (for example, would-be dancer)
- character defined by one of the seven deadly sins (for example, adulterer, murderer)
- character defined by astrological sign.

With these examples, trigger lateral thinking in the usual way by asking "What are real but unusual versions of [insert role]?" Again, try combining the characters and story ideas found through this method with models from fairytale, myth, fable and literature. This provides more brainstorming material and can actually provide a ready-made structure.

Events

Events are good starting points for stories because they depict characters in a dynamic and emotionally charged situation. Some examples of useful event-based triggers are set out below. As you read through them, trigger lateral thinking by asking what real but unusual versions of, or happenings at, each one would be.

- a social ceremony such as a wedding or a funeral
- a journey
- a crisis such as
    - death
    - war

– an accident in a context, such as a family, school, or business
– a divorce
– a departure
– an unexpected arrival
– new demands, socially or personally
– a mission
– having to make a choice.

Again, try combining the characters and story ideas found through this method with models from fairytale, myth, fable and to provide more brainstorming material and possibly a ready-made structure.

Photographs, music, art works and other sensory stimuli

Non-verbal experiences can also stimulate story ideas. Photographs and paintings, music – even a smell that conjures up memories – can trigger ideas for stories. Although using non-verbal story triggers might at first seem bizarre, it can be very refreshing to use from time to time. Ideas produced in this way can, again, be enriched and expanded by combining them with models in genre, fairytale, myth, fable and literature.

Concepts and themes

Concepts and themes – say, poverty, parenthood, loss, ambition, or the insanity of war – are often behind the most passionate writing. Unfortunately, films based on strongly felt themes can be clumsily structured, clichéd, peopled with stereotypes, and prone to preachiness. The reason for this is that themes and concepts are intellectual entities and as such are governed by vertical thinking, which can very easily take over without the writer realizing. To counteract this tendency and free up the lateral imagination, try creating mind maps or flow charts. Forcing yourself to record your brainstorming on paper is a good way of making sure you are not jumping at ideas and characters too soon. The best way to use a mind map or flow chart in this context is as follows:

1. Choose a theme, such as poverty.
2. Brainstorm different interpretations of the theme in action – for example, homeless people, single parents, starving elderly, child abuse, poverty-related crimes, people caught in a cycle of poverty, the role of the government in poverty, the role of charity organizations, political parties etc.
3. Brainstorm different notions of the theme, even though these may not be what you originally meant by it – for example, poverty of ideas, or poverty of spirit. These can often give you a parallel, metaphorical story to run against your core theme story.
4. Brainstorm real but unusual human connections, that is, characters and their behavior which illustrate the theme – for example, child caught in a cycle of poverty, or a social worker caught between "deserving" and "undeserving" poor.
5. Brainstorm connections with myth, fairytale, fable, literary model, or genre to

find a structure and more story ideas – for example, a poor person as Hamlet, Oedipus, Icarus, or Jack from Jack and the Beanstalk.

Figure 4.1 shows the start of a mind map on the theme of poverty, following these five steps, while figure 4.2 depicts how the same ideas could be organized as a flow chart.

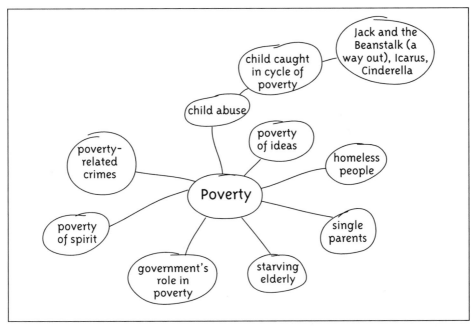

Figure 4.1 Mind map on the theme of poverty

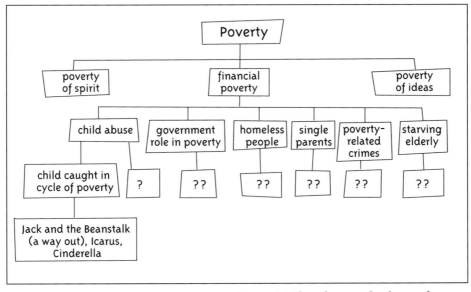

Figure 4.2 Flow chart on the theme of poverty

Finding other triggers

Use Development Strategy 4 to generate a range of other triggers.

Development Strategy 4: Finding other triggers

Throw disparate ideas together and wait for a pattern to form.

Questions to ask:

Could I find a better idea by trying for more combinations or via another method?

Are the new ideas I get this way "real plus unusual"?

4

Sometimes, particularly with time, the triggers described in the last three chapters will not throw up sufficiently original ideas. In cases like these, we can go to a different sort of trigger. So far, the method of finding triggers has always involved using Development Strategy 1 to define the task and give us a model (or pattern) which is then handed over to the lateral imagination, which finds real but unusual links and connections. Now we can use an entirely different method. Instead of starting from a model or pattern and working outwards to real but unusual versions of it, we can throw disparate, unconnected ideas at the lateral imagination and wait for the human brain's innate capacity to find patterns to discover order and connection. For example, we could take a genre (say, love story), then throw it together with a word picked at random from a dictionary, for example, love story/gravity, love story/intrusion, love story/expatriate.

So strong is our ability to find patterns that the results of this process of combining random words together to find stories can seem eerily predestined. Make sure you brainstorm as many possible versions of the combination as possible before choosing. You can then, if you wish, consider combining your story ideas with a model from genre, fairytale, myth, fable or literature.

Part II
Narrative structure

5. Overview of traditional narrative structure

Structure is the business of creating the best vehicle to carry and display the idea. The standard method of approaching narrative structure for the screen is to take a structural model that has worked (usually a three- or four-act model, described in detail in a book or by a teacher) and try to fit story fragments into that shape or progression, adding more until the structure is complete. The advantage of this method is that the structure, being proven, is likely to transmit the story well, and the process of construction itself is a problem-solving device because it reveals the gaps and weaknesses in the story. The disadvantage of the method is that, however good the structural model – however good the book – if we persistently use only one methodology, vertical thinking will take over the process and short-circuit original thinking without our ever realizing it. It will use the method to recycle not only industry clichés but also our own old ideas, generated on the previous occasions when we used the same method. And this is not the fault of the method. It is caused by our own innate panic reflex towards shortcuts and clichéd vertical thinking.

For today's working writer, the reality is that no one method of creating a three-act structure is usable for a lifetime to the exclusion of all others. We can never allow ourselves to feel that we have "the method" to handle structure, and we must make a conscious effort to search out new approaches that will challenge our vertical imagination and permit, rather than suppress, lateral thinking.

This chapter introduces a number of different approaches to a traditional three- or four-act structure – including visual depictions – and provides some practical methods for starting to put such a structure in place. The idea is to provide a number of different ways of looking at structure in order to shake up the lateral imagination generally and, most importantly, to assist with writer's block at all stages of the planning. If one method does not help, then another can be used to give a different perspective on the problem. Later chapters provide the Development Strategies method of creating a traditional three-act structure. Because it works on asking and answering questions, this demands brainstorming and frequently cross-refers to other structural approaches. But, like all methods, it can become mechanical, and special effort must be taken to maintain concentration.

Traditional does not mean boring

These days there is a lot of interest in alternative structures like flashback narrative and other multiple story forms. While these structural forms and the films that use them are fascinating and open up enormous possibilities for the writer, the traditional three-act structure is a remarkable and infinitely variable form completely capable of transmitting modern perspectives on the world. It is worth remembering, as we have seen, that *Being John Malkovich*, one of the most interesting of recent mainstream American films, is constructed in traditional three-act form.

Parallel storytelling is driven by the three-act structure

Parallel storytelling is dealt with in depth in chapters 7–12, but at this stage it is worth mentioning that all of the parallel story structures use elements of the three-act structure within individual stories, and to bind the work as a whole. To understand parallel storytelling, you need to master the three-act structure.

Structure = good timing

The classic narrative structure consists of three acts, punctuated by frequent twists and turns, and leading to a climax and a resolution. All the complex theories of structure and its components boil down to the same basic storytelling problem, namely, how to keep a live audience engaged.

Film is a performing art constructed and executed in the absence of its audience. Screenwriting is the art of second-guessing that absent audience. Poor structure can alienate an audience in the same way that a good joke can be wrecked by poor telling. Thus, structure is largely to do with good timing, that is, knowing how and when to build up suspense; knowing how long to delay before delivering the crucial line; understanding the impact of energy and pause – and so on. Time also impinges in another and more basic way, which is that, because audiences experience screenwriting within a time-imposed framework, sitting down at 8:30 P.M. and getting up at 10 P.M., the film will always present itself to them with a beginning, middle and end. No matter how unconventional the structure or content, time itself imposes this rigid structure and writers have to cope with it as best they can.

In fact everything about film – about *moving pictures* – is connected with time and movement in time, that is to say, action in every sense. Film consists of movement in all ways, physical, emotional and spiritual. In screenwriting, story is movement and our characters move through their own mental landscape.

Traditional theories of structure exploit this inbuilt time component by making the beginning the first act (which introduces the characters and their problem), the middle the second act (which complicates the problem) and the end the third act (where the problem is resolved). Some theories split the middle into two acts, making the end act four. Within this large structure are many other components – essentially twists and turns – which experience shows to have worked with audiences in the past. Some books on screenwriting actually specify the page number in the script where structural high points should happen. Many writers find this worryingly rigid. But if you think of it not as a matter of pages but of screen time, it makes sense, because what is actually being said is that a script needs a twist or turn every ten to fifteen minutes, otherwise the audience will get bored – which is really just common sense.

Essentially, dramatic high points come at the end of the first act, the end of the second act (or, if a four-act model is being used, at the end of the third act) and at the climax, which occurs just before the end of the film and resolves the central dilemma of the story. Early on in the film there will be an event which changes the normal scheme of things and forces the protagonist in a new direction, effectively starting the story. This is called a *catalyst* or *disturbance*. Sometimes the catalyst or disturbance is an apparently harmless event which leads to serious trouble. This is the case in *Thelma and Louise* (1991), where the catalyst/disturbance is the innocent decision to stop at a bar and have a drink. In other films, the catalyst/disturbance is a violent event in itself. This is so in *The African Queen* (1951), where Sunday morning prayers are interrupted by a murderous attack.

Once the catalyst/disturbance has occurred, the suspense builds towards the end of the film to create what is sometimes described as a rising three-act structure, with the *climax* being the most suspenseful moment of the film. This makes sense, of course, because putting the moment of highest tension any earlier would make the action fizzle. These high points are often called *turning points*, because they turn the story in a new direction. Hence we have *the first-act turning point* (the dramatic high point occurring at the end of the first act), and *the second-act turning point*, which occurs at the end of the second act (or third act, if a four-act model is being used). In *Thelma and Louise*, the first-act turning point occurs when Louise kills the man who is attempting to rape Thelma; the second-act turning point occurs when the women are told by the detective that they are being charged with murder (the second-act turning point often involves the protagonist facing death), and the climax is when they drive over the cliff.

The two turning points and the climax form the spine of the story, so writers often try to pick them early. This is not as hard as it might sound because moments of high drama are often among the earliest fragments to present themselves. Really, once you know the two turning points and the climax, you have your film.

Visualizing the three-act structure

To visualize this three/four-act division with all its subdivisions, writers have developed a range of different diagrams (see Figures 5.1–5.3). In its way each presents a different kind of "circuit breaker" for subjectivity, and can be enormously useful. But it should be remembered that while depicting a film diagrammatically in its entirety is an excellent tool for the writer, the piece of screen drama which we produce is not experienced by the audience statically and in its entirety, that is, like a painting. It is experienced as a sequence of events – *moving pictures* – that have to keep the audience's attention. The practical ramifications of this are that however wonderful the third act might be, the audience cannot see it until it has sat through the first and second acts. And if the first and second acts are poor, the audience will not stay for the third act. While this might seem glaringly obvious, it is actually very easy to be so taken up with what comes later in the film that you write a very poor beginning, thinking of it merely as a way of setting up the excellence that is to come. This happens all the time with television series, where the writers get so taken up with later episodes that they perceive the first episode merely as the setup. The result is a weak first episode that loses its audience forever.

Actually, the importance of movement and the fact that a film is absorbed as a sequence is reflected in all of the diagrams commonly used to depict traditional structure. The diagrams are all related to movement, travel and a journey – travelling a road, completing a circular journey, climbing a mountain range. They all depict the protagonist moving through a mental landscape.

To use the diagrams to help you structure your film, simply insert the turning points and climax you propose to use. Check that your versions of each give you a proper movement, and that they will occur at roughly the point in the film's running time that they should. If they are insufficiently dramatic or do not build properly, you will have to pump them up or find others. If they occur too close together, you will have to insert more action between them (always keeping the suspenseful build) or invent others. Sometimes a story will present without one of these turning points, and you will have to invent it.

The mountain

Frequently, to reinforce the need for a build to a third-act climax, the rising action of the traditional three-act structure is depicted as a mountain range with the second act (as is common) being about the same length as the other two combined. Linda Seger, best known for a fine book on screenwriting called *Making a Good Script Great* (1994), is one of the theorists who used models like this one.

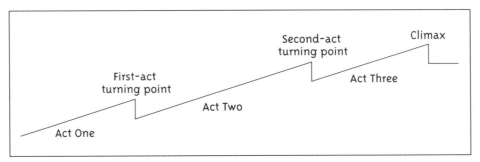

Figure 5.1 The mountain

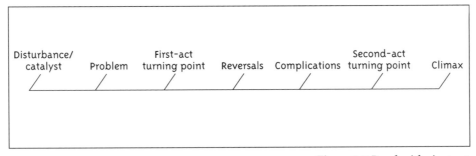

Figure 5.2 Road with signposts

The circle

Yet another way of depicting the three-act structure is to show it as a circle along which are notched the stages on the circular journey of the protagonist. This is the case with Christopher Vogler's (1992) hero's journey model, the steps of which are outlined on page 27.

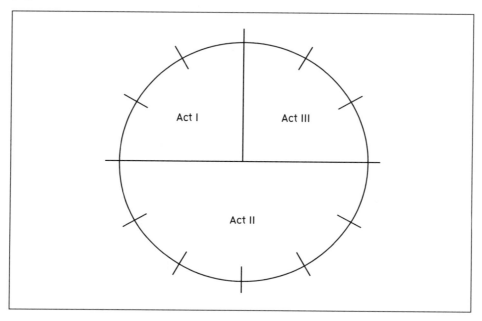

Figure 5.3 The circle

The importance of the protagonist

The movement implied in all these diagrams is that of the protagonist because the main task of traditional structure is to create the journey of the protagonist. The audience needs to walk each step with the protagonist and each step has to lead them (as well as the protagonist) in a specific direction. It's quite useful to imagine the writing task as the job of creating a journey for the audience – like a ride at a theme park. At every point during the journey, the writer has to keep asking what reaction the audience is supposed to be having, therefore what information it needs and what scenario would best transmit such information and create the requisite emotions. This means the process of choosing scenes is not random ("Wouldn't it be good to have a scene about …?") but absolutely focused ("What is the audience supposed to be thinking and feeling here, and what scenario will best achieve that?"). Curiously, it is said that Disneyland designers use Christopher Vogler's hero's journey model as the basis for designing rides, presumably because they believe the model will build in rising suspense and excitement towards a final dramatic climax.

Assembling the fragments

It would be useful if the story behind a film or any piece of literature presented itself in a logical way, starting at the beginning and proceeding through to the end. Unfortunately, stories present in fragments – a character, a scene, a climax – and the writer's job is to find or impose some kind of order on them without preempting the creative process.

The first step is to find a way of collecting and storing all the disconnected fragments until they start to assume some kind of shape. Some writers have a special notebook. Some have a blackboard or noticeboard. Still others write the fragments on pieces of paper which they then crumple into balls and toss into a basket until it is full. A lot of this is about psyching yourself into the right frame of mind, but in all cases there is a commitment to letting the lateral imagination do its spadework over as much time as possible without interference from logic. Screenwriters do not have the luxury of time permitted to novelists, but time given over to accumulating ideas is time well spent. The more fragments, the better.

Making a structure chart

At this point it is very tempting to start writing the screenplay, assuming that problems can be solved along the way. This is not a good idea. It is very hard to throw away a scene once it has been written. An emotional commitment has been made. Subjectivity and protectiveness creep in and writers can end up spending months, even years, on a screenplay that does not do them justice.

Resist the urge to jump into writing and instead, when there are a reasonable number of fragments, construct the beginnings of a three-act structure by means of a chart. All this requires is a page divided into three columns, labelled "Act One," "Act Two," "Act Three" – or, even more simply, "Beginning," "Middle," and "End." As the ideas come, they can be placed, provisionally, where they should happen in the action. The point of a chart is to keep options open while feeling towards the story. It is vital at this stage not to jump into writing scenes with dialogue, not only because once a scene is written it is very hard to throw it out, but because a strong scene can send the story in a direction that will later reveal itself to be quite wrong. By all means think about possible scenes and note down every idea. But do not start putting in dialogue.

A simple structure chart looks like the one in Figure 5.4, which depicts what a chart devised in the early stages of writing *Being John Malkovich* might have looked like had the writer used this method. Of course, the chart is entirely fictitious and the writer might well have used a completely different approach. Note that a lot of options are wide open and much will be thrown out. Notice also how the content is put in the form of questions, so as to resist committing too early.

A number of structure charts can be used. Their advantage is that they permit the writer to devise and compare a whole variety of options without feeling pressed to choose.

When the ideas seem to be shaping up, it is time to add another, more detailed approach to "trapping the story" in the form of a basic narrative structure. This does not mean leaving the charts or ceasing to accumulate fragments. Charts can be made at all stages of the planning process – in fact they are a usefully objective mind-clearer during the actual course of writing. Assume that more out-of-sequence fragments will keep coming, and construct charts to store and define their possible place in the structure.

Nine steps to a three-act structure

This theory breaks the three/four-act form into nine main components (see Figure 5.5). I first came across it in a class on stage writing run by Paul Thompson of NYU, who says that he developed it from Sam Smiley's book on playwriting. I have taken it further because it is such a useful way of putting down a basic narrative structure. It is protagonist-based in that each of the nine steps refers to a crucial event, action or series of actions

Feature film: weird, thought-provoking comedy about being able to get into someone's head. Possible title—'The Portal'?		
Act One	**Act Two**	**Act Three**
Opening? Protag? A man.	Once inside person's head what can he do? Rob a bank? Seduce women? Or do women seduce him? What is his wife or girlfriend doing at the time?	?
Peter? John? Craig?		John Malkovich realises something is happening? Or should this be earlier?
Setting? What is protagonist doing before disturbance?		John Malkovich dies with Craig, Maxine and Lotte in his head? They are trapped in a dead body?
Craig finds portal into someone's mind.	Personal story. Parents? Wife? Love story? Infidelity story? Any way of linking the two stories?	
Where is it? How does he find it? On a walk in the country? In a coat? In a suitcase? Under the bed?		Wife dies? Maxine shoots Craig?
What is Craig's job?	Maxine and Lotte attracted?	Happy ending? Or Craig loses everything? Craig killed by person whose mind he gets into? Craig going crazy, ending up a derelict?
Is he married? Yes, has wife, Lotte, a meek woman.	NB There must be some explanation of the portal somewhere.	
NB What is Craig's job? How can it fit in with the story?		Craig and his wife living happily ever after?
In Act One he meets another woman? Maxine?		
Is there any philosophical content in this, or is it just science fiction? If philosophical content, what?		
What is the ending of Act One? Finding the portal?		

Figure 5.4 Hypothetical structure chart for writing Being John Malkovich

involving the protagonist. This makes it particularly useful because it locks the evolving structure into specific actions driven by the main player – in other words, it ensures that the film is character-driven.

The basic Smiley/Thompson plan (see Figure 5.6) becomes even more useful if we take it a step further and turn it into a narrative sentence along the lines of the beginning of a fairytale.

The beginning of a fairy story or folk tale

Once upon a time there was a [*protagonist*] who lived in [*normality*]. One day when [*protagonist*] was [*doing something normal*], there was [*a departure from normality or strange event – the disturbance*] which made [*protagonist*] decide to [*a plan to cope with the disturbance-induced crisis*]. But suddenly, without warning, [*surprise*] happened, which created [*an obstacle hindering the protagonist for the rest of the story*]. [*Protagonist*] tried many ways to overcome [*the obstacle*] and encountered [*hindrances, complications, substories, more surprises and obstacles*] until finally [*protagonist*] [*climax*], resolving the problem triggered initially by [*disturbance*].

The next chapter will show you how to use a sentence like this as a "fill in the gaps" method of establishing a basic structure, but for now it is only necessary to get a general sense of how the nine-point plan works. Note that what Smiley and Thompson call the disturbance, other writers will frequently call the catalyst. The term disturbance is useful because it clarifies the link between the *protagonist* and what is about to happen, therefore makes identifying a potential *disturbance* easier.

The nine-point plan	
1. Normality	First act
2. Disturbance	"
3. Protagonist	"
4. Plan	"
5. Surprise	"
6. Obstacle	"
	End of first act
7. Complication, substories, more surprises, and obstacles	Second and third acts
8. Climax	
9. Resolution	End of third act
	End of film

Figure 5.5 The nine-point plan

This is how the nine-point plan compares with the three-act model.

Act One		
1. Normality		
2. Protagonist	=	The set-up
3. Catalyst or disturbance		
4. Plan	=	Actions in response to the disturbance
5. Surprise	=	First-act turning point
6. Obstacle		
Acts Two and Three		
7. Complications, substories, more surprises, and obstacles	=	Act two, act three up to climax
8. Climax	=	Climax
9. Resolution	=	How the world goes on

Figure 5.6 Smiley/Thompson nine-point plan and standard three-act model

To show how the nine-point structure works and can be used as a model, Figure 5.7 depicts *Cinderella* broken down into its nine points with explanations in parentheses. I have added an antagonist to the nine points to suggest the necessary protagonist/antagonist conflict.

Notice how the suspense builds through strong first- and second-act turning points to a proper climax which resolves the problem raised by the story (namely, will Cinderella escape slavery by marrying the prince?).

In Figure 5.7 you will notice that the appearance of the fairy godmother marks the end of act one and is the first-act turning point. You will also see that the first-act turning point is made up of the surprise and the obstacle; moreover, that the surprise, which is an actual physical surprise – in this case a completely unexpected and magical appearance – turns into the obstacle. That is to say, in *Cinderella*, the action of the fairy godmother in providing clothes and transport for Cinderella is also the action that creates an obstacle for Cinderella because her finery will all disappear at midnight. Good first-act turning points are always *physical surprises* that turn into obstacles. Good examples are the murder in *Thelma and Louise* (1991), the murder in *The Player* (1992), the discovery of the portal

Event structure	Breakdown of *Cinderella*
Normality	Cinderella is working as slave to her ugly sisters and wicked stepmother. (This fills in the details of 'Once upon a time there was a character who lived in [description of her world]'.)
Protagonist	Cinderella (because she drives the action).
Disturbance (catalyst)	The household receives an invitation to the ball from the handsome prince, but Cinderella, because she is a slave and has no clothes, cannot go. (This provides Cinderella with a problem.)
Plan	To go to the ball and meet the prince. (The plan is what the protagonist first does or wants in response to the disturbance. The antagonist is in opposition to this plan.)
Antagonist	The status quo — class distinction — personified by the ugly sisters and stepmother. (Sometimes identifying the antagonist tells you more about the needs of the protagonist.)
End of set-up	
Surprise	The fairy godmother appears and provides clothes and transport. (The surprise is an actual physical surprise.)
Obstacle	Clothes and transport are provided only until midnight. (Turns the problem on its head. The surprise turns into the obstacle. The surprise + obstacle = first-act turning point.)
End of act one	
Acts two and three	
Complications, substories, more surprises, and obstacles	Cinderella goes to the ball, entrances the prince, forgets the time, has to run off at midnight when her clothes change back to rags. (Antagonist — class distinction — wins.) She leaves behind her shoe.
	In some versions she goes back to the ball several times and each time leaves in rags (Antagonist — class distinction — wins.)
	The prince announces that he will marry the woman whose foot fits the shoe. (But will he defeat antagonist — class distinction?)
	In some versions events keep preventing him from entering Cinderella's house.
	Cinderella feels he will never find or want her. (Second-act turning point — lowest moment for protagonist because the antagonist — class distinction — looks like triumphing.)
End of act two	
	The prince arrives at the household but at first Cinderella is not allowed to try on the shoe. (Class distinction wins.)
Climax	Cinderella fights back by asking to try on the shoe; it fits. The prince says he will marry her. (Thereby defeating the antagonist — class distinction — although of course Cinderella is actually "of good blood." The climax answers the problem positively or negatively — in this case positively.)
Resolution	They live happily ever after.

Figure 5.7 The nine-point plan in Cinderella

in *Being John Malkovich* and, in *Tootsie* (1982), the protagonist's decision to dress up as a woman. The first-act turning point shifts the action in a whole new direction.

The second-act turning point also shifts the action in a whole new direction. It presents itself as the lowest point in the protagonist's story. It is the point at which the protagonist is physically or metaphorically closest to death. This makes sense because the second-act turning point has to have greater jeopardy than the first-act turning point, otherwise the suspense will not build. In the Cinderella story, the second-act turning point is when Cinderella feels the prince can never find her, in other words, that her greatest desire will never come true.

The third act traditionally sees the protagonist gathering all reserves of strength to wage an actual or psychological battle, usually a last-ditch, against-the-odds stand, which culminates in a climax which answers the questions raised earlier, starting at the first-act turning point (will Dorothy in *Tootsie* be revealed as a man? Will Thelma and Louise escape prosecution for the murder? What will happen to Craig if he enters the mysterious portal?). In the case of **Cinderella**, the battle against the odds is Cinderella asserting herself to get a turn trying on the shoe. The climax is the shoe fitting – the dream come true.

Drawing up a chart like the one used here for *Cinderella* is an extremely useful planning tool for a script's structure. Like the earlier chart used for *Being John Malkovich*, it permits you to think about structure but does not lock you into a scenario before you are ready. It also physically shows you where the story's gaps are and permits you to consider different ways of filling them in.

Subplot/background story/relationship line

The nine-point plan used to break down the Cinderella story provides the spine of the script, that is, its *main plot*, which is otherwise known as the *action line* or *foreground story*. But in many films the most important story is the *subplot*, otherwise known as the *background story* or *relationship line*. The classic example is *Witness* (1985), which was specifically written to explore the emotional relationship between an Amish woman and an urbanized man. The main plot – in which the woman's son witnesses a murder and the urbanized man has to hide out on the Amish farm – is merely a means to bring the two together in a suspenseful situation. Often the main plot is a means to permit the subplot to happen, although it should be fascinating and exciting in its own right. This is so of the journey down the river in *The African Queen*. This journey brings together two people who would otherwise never have had a moment's interest in each other.

The subplot needs as much consideration as the main plot, and the main plot must have a scenario that will permit the required relationship shifts of the subplot to happen. Structurally, the subplot has its own three-act structure, with catalyst/disturbance, first-act turning point, second-act turning point and climax. It is usually set up in the first act and developed extensively in the second act, after the first-act turning point has changed the protagonist's world. In *Being John Malkovich*, the subplot (the love triangle between Maxine, Lotte and Craig) is set up in the first act (in which Craig makes unsuccessful advances to Maxine) but only really takes off in the second act when Craig's access to the portal makes Maxine take an interest in him.

Index cards

The next step for many writers is to transfer the information they have about the film onto index cards, using a different index card for each step of the plot. These cards are then set out on a table so the film can be apprehended in its entirety, with the writer able to experiment with plot changes by the simple means of moving the cards around. This is infinitely preferable to writing draft after draft. Also, this method makes plot weaknesses easy to pick.

Some plotting methods involve using different colored cards or a different numbering system for different plot lines, the idea being that the writer can instantly pick, firstly, whether or not there is enough of each plot, and secondly, whether the various plots are being intertwined in a balanced way, or whether the plots are presenting in clumps. The method also helps in checking whether the film is long enough. Traditional wisdom says ninety minutes of feature film will require about sixty plot points. By plot points I mean "steps in the plot" as opposed to scenes; for example, a plot point like "Kim goes looking for Sandy all over the house" is only one plot point although it would present on screen as a number of different short scenes. Note that some theories of screenwriting use the term "plot point" to mean "moment of high drama" or "turning point."

Without good structure, a good idea is nothing. The film industry is full of good film ideas that never reach the screen – not to mention good ideas that reach the screen so structurally flawed that they never achieve their full potential. The following chapters provide a detailed, step-by-step study of one method of constructing a simple-form three-act film, as well as explaining how to avoid common pitfalls and how, as far as possible, to be your own script doctor. For help in understanding what a specific structural element actually is, or how its absence might affect a script, see Chapter 13, "Lost in the telling." "Lost in the telling" analyzes a number of films that fail as the result of specific structural faults. While it might seem strange to learn about structural elements by looking at instances where they are flawed, in fact looking at flawed films is actually often more directly informative than looking at masterpieces, which tend to dazzle.

For a highly successful three-act narrative structure, see the structural analysis of *The Piano* (1993), on page 100.

6. Development Strategies for a traditional three-act film

D evelopment Strategies 5 to 29 are designed to help create the simplest form of rising three-act narrative. They are also useful as a starting point to check that an existing three-act screenplay has the necessary structural elements in place and remedy problems if it has not. They are not rules. They are analytical tools applied to a structure in its simplest form for you to explore and challenge.

Each new Development Strategy should be brainstormed using Development Strategy 2 to get "real but unusual" answers. You will find that you will return to some of the Development Strategies again and again in the planning as more detail comes to you.

When a new structural element is introduced, cross-references are often made to films that display a faulty version of that element. This is because it is frequently easier to understand the nature and function of a structural element when it is not working than when it is. The analyses of films that are structurally flawed are all located in Chapter 13, "Lost in the telling."

Parallel storytelling

Increasingly, mainstream films are departing from the classic three-act structure and using one or other form of parallel storytelling. The most familiar parallel story form is flashback narrative, seen as long ago as *Citizen Kane* (1941) and appearing these days in films like *The English Patient* (1996), *Shine* (1996), and *The End of the Affair* (1999), but modern filmmakers can go far beyond flashback. They can run a number of distinct but connected stories, as happens in *Magnolia* (1999). They can tell stories in sequence, jumbled or from different points of view, as happens in *Pulp Fiction* (1994) and *Go* (1999). They can use an ensemble cast to depict a range of responses to one event, as happens in *American Beauty* (1999). Or, as is happening increasingly, they can combine a number of these alternative forms. This can be seen in a film like *Crimes and Misdemeanors* (1989), which combines flashbacks and parallel stories with the result that the film not only combines two distinct stories with action and relationship lines, but operates in three time-frames. These forms of parallel storytelling are dealt with in depth in Chapters 7–12.

Parallel storytelling structure relies on three-act structure

It is worth repeating that while, at first glance, these alternative forms seem a million miles away from the traditional three-act narrative, in fact they all draw heavily on traditional three-act narrative to create rising jeopardy and closure. So an understanding of parallel storytelling really requires a good grounding in the theory and practicalities of three-act structure. You cannot understand parallel storytelling without understanding traditional three-act structure.

Getting a Good Setup
Normality and disturbance

The first movement in the main plot of a film – the first step up the mountain or signpost along the road – is the *disturbance*. This simply means that something unusual happens in the normality – the normal world – of the protagonist. The disturbance acts to give the protagonist a *problem* that the course of the film will answer, either happily or otherwise. These elements – protagonist, normality and disturbance, plus the problem which arises out of the disturbance – provide the *setup*. Since a common failing of weak films is that they do not properly set up their story and main players, this is particularly important. But how is it possible to know whether a setup is working properly?

Too much normality, too little disturbance

Setup problems are often caused by writers becoming so taken with showing the protagonist acting in character – functioning in their normal world – that the normality carries on for far too long, in some cases for the whole picture. It is surprisingly easy to write material about an ongoing normality, that is, to write different scenarios or tableaus which describe an unchanging state (for example, different aspects of life in a country town) or character (that is, the way a certain character typically behaves – say, losing their temper over trivialities) rather than creating a journey through which a character must travel.

Creating and endlessly repeating the normality is something to which actor–writers are particularly prone because their training is to create a character, rather than a character *moving through a scenario*. Repeated normality – writing endless different versions of essentially the same scene – is also often seen in films about life stories, journeys or long-term relationships, because in such cases it is easy to mistake physical movement or movement of time for movement in plot and character.

A film that displays these faults very evidently is *Mr. Saturday Night* written, directed and starring Billy Crystal. The film sets out to show an egotistical, self-destructive, but ultimately endearing comedian. But rather than create a plot which takes this character on a journey, the film ends up merely showing us different instances of the same thing, namely, a comedian being self-destructive. The film becomes boring, and it is boring because the comedian is not given a problem. Compare the film of John Osborne's play

The Entertainer (1960), in which Laurence Olivier plays an egotistical, self-destructive comedian who needs money, therefore does a series of unscrupulous things. The crucial story elements here are a problem, a goal, and a journey.

To check that your film has a problem, a goal, and a journey rather than multiple versions of essentially the same scene, imagine how the story would present as a one-sentence summary (sometimes known as a logline). *Mr. Saturday Night*'s logline would be something like 'The life of a self-destructive comedian' (an ongoing normality). *The Entertainer*'s would be something along the lines of "a self-destructive comedian tries to get money at any cost" (a problem, a goal, and a journey).

Films that are slow often have too much normality before the disturbance. If the protagonist has been properly identified and is interesting enough, this can give the film an epic or art-film quality, as in *Kiss of the Spider Woman* (1985) or *Out of Africa* (1985). But poorly handled it can be disastrous. A simple way to understand what makes a disturbance is that the story cannot start until the disturbance happens. Think of shaggy dog stories. These always start with, say, the Englishman, the Scotsman and the Irishman in a specific situation, like walking along a road. But the joke cannot start until something else occurs (for example, a lion appearing).

A useful rule of thumb is that a good disturbance cannot be described without a verb, often a verb of movement, disruption or change – the gunslinger *rides* into town, the detective *breaks* a leg, the novelist *receives* a mysterious letter, the missionaries are *attacked* by enemy soldiers. An idea for a film "about a reclusive actress living in Spain" is not yet a potential story because the statement describes only a normality. Until something happens to dramatically change the actress's normality, we still only have an idea. This rule makes up Development Strategy 5.

Development Strategy 5: Making sure the disturbance involves real change

Describe the disturbance with a verb of movement, disruption or change.

Questions to ask:

Is my disturbance "real but unusual" (Development Strategy 2)?

Is the verb to describe it a verb of movement or disruption, or is it a "passive" verb like living, feeling, or experiencing? If it's the latter, you haven't got a proper disturbance in place yet.

5

It's interesting to note that sometimes only the act of identifying the disturbance makes us understand the essence of the normality. For example, in *Being John Malkovich*, if we decide that the disturbance is Craig being forced to give up puppeteering to get a job in commerce, to get maximum dramatic effect we must do everything we can in the pre-disturbance minutes to establish Craig's normality as an unsuccessful but passionately committed puppeteer. The audience can only value the disturbance if they know how much and what it is disturbing. In practical terms this means that we must use every moment from the start of the film – titles included, if possible – to describe the normality.

Finding the action line
Movement and the chain of events

With the normality and disturbance in place, the next step is to start finding the chain of reactions that spring from the disturbance. The question to ask is "Does the film have a story yet?"

A disturbance on its own does not mean there is a story. If the reclusive actress living in Spain breaks her leg, that constitutes only a disturbance. It is the sequence of events – the twists and turns that occur in consequence of the broken leg – that will provide the story.

By "story," what is meant here is the *main plot*, also known as the *action line* or *foreground story*. "Action line" is the term that will be used from now on because the word "action"'is a helpful reminder that this particular plot line must move from action to action. "Action line" is also a better term than "main plot" because "main plot" suggests that the action line is of superior importance to other plot material. In fact, as we have seen, in many films the main plot or action line only exists to permit the relationship line (or subplot or background story) to happen. The term "relationship line" is more useful than "subplot" or "background story" because it does not imply that the plot dealing with relationships is less important than the action line and it is a helpful reminder that this plot must deal with a developing relationship.

Finding the exact content of the action line and the relationship line is the work of many Development Strategies, but the specific problem of whether the screenplay is stuck at the idea stage or whether it is starting to form an action line can be tested with Development Strategy 6.

Development Stragegy 6:
Distinguishing an idea from a story

Make sure you have distinguished your idea from your story. Remember that an idea is a normality or a normality disturbed by an unusual event, and a story is a chain of reactions to an unusual event.

Questions to ask:

Am I genuinely devising a story or am I simply devising different scenes to illustrate the same normality?

What is the normality?

What is the disturbance?

6

It's interesting to note that a film which has a poor disturbance is usually a film with a poor action line because the disturbance is the first movement of the action line. As we'll see later, a poor action line means that the film has to function on a static relationship line.

Conflict and the chain of events

The next step is to start finding the chain of events in the action line and checking that this chain of events is turning into a good basic narrative structure by means of Development Strategy 7, "Creating a simple story sentence." The story sentence is really just a modern form of the "Once upon a time …" model used above to turn the Smiley/Thompson nine-point plan into a narrative. It provides a useful fill-in-the-gaps method of checking that the idea is developing into a proper narrative; that it is something more than a logline, half idea or an ongoing normality; and that it is based on the actions of the protagonist. Already, this simple sentence is showing the protagonist facing inner conflict. Later developments of the action line and relationship line will show a range of other kinds of conflict – interpersonal, social, internal, even physical. Conflict is at the heart of all drama.

Development Strategy 7: Creating a simple story sentence

Create a simple sentence to describe your story in terms of the protagonist's sequence of actions using the following model:

[**Protagonist**] *faced with* [**problem**] *responds by* [**series of actions**] *and finally deals with* [**problem**] *by* [**climax**].

Question to ask:

Can I fit my story into this simple structure?

7

The story sentence can be expanded to a paragraph or a page as you fill in the missing parts (particularly the series of events). As more fragments of the story appear, the advanced version of the story sentence may be used, as described in Development Strategy 20. In fact the story sentence can be expanded to form an entire 30-page *treatment* (a summary of the film often required by investors). This technique of writing treatments is particularly useful because it stops writers going off the point, a perennial problem with treatment writing. A treatment based around the story sentence is actually structured around the film's action line, so writers need to include reference to relationship lines.

Action line and relationship line
The action line permits the relationship line to happen

It is important at this point to decide whether the story that is presenting itself is an action line or a relationship line. It is very common for writers to be impelled to write not because they have a strong plot idea but because they want to deal with an interesting interpersonal relationship. When this happens, particular attention must be given to the action line. *This is because the action line permits the relationship line to happen.*

The relationship line will not work properly unless it is pulled along by a strong action line, that is, a scenario that not only forces the relationship line characters together but keeps challenging them individually and incrementally *in different ways*. A good example of the action line pulling along the relationship line occurs in *The African Queen*. Here, the relationship line, that is, the developing love between Rose and Allnutt, could not happen without the action line, that is, the journey down the river. In fact close analysis of *The African Queen* will show that every incident on the journey down the river marks a movement forward in the relationship between Rose and Allnutt. For the writer, this means that every incident in the action line must be chosen not only for its relevance to the story told in the action line, but for its capacity to take the relationship line another step forward. If this is not done, the relationship line cannot move satisfactorily.

Imagine that the relationship line is a vine and the action line is the tree. The vine moves upwards by clinging to the tree. Without the growing tree, the vine can only move around on itself in circles on the ground. Character films that lack good action lines typically go round and round in circles. A good example of this is *Guarding Tess* (1994), a story about the relationship between a feisty ex-president's wife and the young bodyguard who is deputized to look after her. The action line, a kidnap, does not start to happen until well into the film, meaning that a large part of the film simply shows the two warring characters warring – in other words, it simply repeats the normality. If *The African Queen* had been approached this way, we would have had Rose and Allnutt stuck in their roles as picky spinster and happy drunk, bickering at the mission, with the mission's destruction and the journey down the river starting only towards the very end of the film, which would have made a much less satisfactory film.

In fact *Guarding Tess* is doubly flawed because the action line, when it finally comes, does not serve the purpose of the film, which was to show the deepening relationship between the bodyguard and the elderly woman. A kidnapping is not a good action line for a story that sets out to show a developing relationship because it separates the parties in the relationship rather than throwing them together so they can interact and bond. The climax, showing a tearful reunion, is not convincing because the relationship has not been shown to grow. For a kidnap to have worked as a means to permit a relationship line, both the bodyguard and the woman would have to have been kidnapped. Their developing relationship could then easily be shown against an action line in which they try to escape and succeed.

Action line and relationship line should end up inextricable

Ideally, action line and relationship line should be inextricable, each enriching the other, with the climax of each being placed in the same event. *The African Queen* again provides a good example. In the closing moments of the film, just as Rose and Allnutt, moments before their scheduled execution, are being married (climax of the relationship line), the drifting wreckage of *The African Queen* hits the side of the German ship they were seeking to destroy – and blows it up (climax of action line). Rose and Allnutt could have been married either before or after the blowing up of the ship. To combine the two increases the energy of the film.

As *Guarding Tess* shows, lack of connection between action line and relationship line is a recipe for weakened impact. Poor telemovie pilots are usually instantly recognizable by the fact that the relationship line is not connected with the action line and not resolved with it, indeed, is simply serving to set up the protagonist's endearing domestic self for visits in later episodes (for example, the protagonist's marriage is breaking up and he's fighting for access to his children; the protagonist is a single mother). Rarely do these series pilots have the same impact as a film, and that lack of impact is very much a function of a relationship line and action line that are not connected.

Conflict in relationship lines

Relationship lines are usually very concerned with conflict between characters, so another way of confirming that you are developing a relationship line is to ask yourself whether your idea involves two people forced together and quarrelling. If so, this interaction is the relationship line, and you need an action line to permit a developing relationship. Remember that quarrelling can be repetitive, hence redundant. The quarrelling must be productive, that is, it must move the relationship between the characters forward and be related to changes in the world around them provided by the action line. *Thelma and Louise* is a film with productive quarrelling well-linked to the action line.

Finding the right action line for the character

In projects that start from a character, or in a script that so far only has a protagonist repeating a normality (rather than tackling new problems caused by a disturbance), the first step towards creating a good action line is to ask what sort of story you want to tell. For example, if the character at the heart of the film is a hypochondriac cleric, what genre and scenario would best depict that? Further, would it be best to have this character as protagonist or as unknowable mentor–antagonist, inventing a protagonist for them to influence? Would an action comedy be appropriate? Would a war film be more suitable? Or would one of the forms of flashback narrative do the best job?

Good questions to ask here are: What attracted you to the character in the first place? What do you want to transmit about the character to the audience? What is hot (new, exciting, interesting) about the character? Once these issues have been clarified, genres or mixed genres can be considered, and from there the creation of an actual plot can start.

Use Development Strategy 8 to work out whether you are most interested in an action or relationship line, and return to it during the course of planning to check that incidents in the action line are not only carrying the action line story forward but doing so in a way that advances the relationship line. You will not be able to answer some of the questions in Development Strategy 8 until later in the planning process.

Development Strategy 8: Differentiating the action line and the relationship line

Differentiate between the action line and the relationship line, remembering that the relationship line deals with relationships and internal changes and is often what impels writers to write. If the story idea presents itself to you as a relationship or a change of character, you are sensing the film's relationship line and you need an action line to carry it.

Questions to ask:

Is my idea based on relationships, particularly a conflict-ridden relationship, or a character undergoing internal change?

Do I have an action line yet?

Will the action plot scenario I have chosen to carry the relationship line display it better than any other?

Is the action line starting early in the film?

Do the incidents I am planning in the action line serve to take the relationship forward, or am I duplicating the same interaction over and over again?

Is my relationship line movement tied closely to my main plot's movement?

8

At a very early stage in the planning you can start to work out whether you are sensing an action line or a relationship line. But you cannot really choose appropriate action line incidents to carry the relationship line forward until you have some sense of where you want the relationship line to go. This is an ongoing process and will continue into the second and third drafts of your screenplay. At this stage you will probably have only a general sense of the progression of the relationship line (for example, "Rose and Allnutt fall in love"). This is to be expected. More detail can be filled in later. Use Development Strategy 9 to help.

Three-act structure in the relationship line

A good relationship line displays very much the same sort of three-act structure as the action line, that is, it has its own disturbance, first- and second-act turning points and climax. This is useful to know because it builds rising suspense into the relationship. The disturbance will be the start of the relationship, the first-act turning point will be the surprise/obstacle in the path of the relationship, and the second-act will show a variety of hurdles in the way of the relationship. The relationship's lowest point will occur at a second-act turning point before the characters in the relationship come together for a final great effort in their action line struggle. In the climax of the action line they will encounter the climax of the relationship line, that is, they will encounter the moment of truth for their relationship, which is the point to which the whole film has been leading them.

It's often observed that the relationship line does not properly come into its own until the second act. This is true (*Being John Malkovitch* is a good example), and it is probably because what the film is "about" (therefore, the specific pressures that can affect relationships) is not clear until the first-act turning point.

Linda Seger's book *Making a Good Script Great* has some very useful discussion and diagrams on interweaving the action and relationship lines, and particularly on how the two three-act structures interact.

Some films need fewer plot steps

Some film genres require fewer steps in the relationship and action lines than others. This is particularly so of action films. Action films have fewer story steps or beats than others for the simple reason that they do not have time for them. While we are used to thinking of action movies as being highly plot-driven (which they are), the actual plots of most action films are very simple because so much screen time is taken up with chases, fights, amazing escapes, and the like. In plotting terms, sequences like chases and hunts stop the plot because nothing can go forward until the "will they get away?/won't they get away?" of the action sequence is resolved. Once the action sequence has concluded and the chase/entry/burglary whatever has been concluded, the plot can continue – but not until then.

The bottom line here is that an action movie does not need as many plot steps or beats as other forms, but because there is less room for complexity, what steps there are must be as original as possible. This is particularly important as far as the relationship line is concerned. In many action movies the relationship line is often as simple as a developing romance between the male hero and the woman he has to save or capture. Other forms of simple relationship line occur in "buddy movies," in which the relationship line concerns the growing friendship between two partners both involved in the physical chasing of the action plot. This is the *Lethal Weapon* (1987) format. *The Fugitive* (1993) displays a more sophisticated version of this, with the relationship line showing the antagonist (the investigating marshal) gradually starting to believe in the protagonist's innocence, thereby coming to respect him and care about him to the extent that he sets out to assist him. Conflict between the protagonist and antagonist in the relationship line is standard because it energizes the screen time that the two have together.

Poor action movies often display very clichéd relationship lines, whereas good action movies usually have interesting or witty or surprising relationship lines (after all, *The African Queen*, one of the great screen love stories, is to all intents and purposes an action movie). Relationship lines in action films need careful thought because they are restricted quite seriously by the genre's inbuilt demand that they happen on the move, as part of the chase or journey. There is simply not enough time to remove the protagonist away from the scene of the action to interact with another character – for example, a spouse at home. An interesting example of an action movie where a spouse is physically removed from home and put next to the protagonist is in the Arnold Schwarzenegger film *True Lies* (1994).

Use Development Strategy 9 to work out a simple progression for the relationship. Given that many relationship lines are about warring people finding love or friendship, be careful of clichés. Return regularly to Development Strategy 9 during the planning to fill in detail, particularly of the relationship's three-act structure.

Development Strategy 9: Defining the steps of the relationship in the relationship line

Develop a three-act structure for your relationship line, because a good relationship line needs to be planned and monitored.

Questions to ask:

What are the characters in the planned relationship like at the start of the film and what are they like at the end of the film?

What hurdles can I put in the way of them coming together (or falling out)?

What changes does each have to make – or does only one change?

Am I tracking the characters in the relationship through disturbance, first- and second-act turning points and climax?

Am I building in clichés in terms of the sort of conflict I am including in the relationship line?

9

Protagonist and antagonist
Establishing whose story it is

At this point it is necessary to confirm which character is the protagonist and which the antagonist. Both writer and audience have to know this very early on because it is essential for understanding what film we're in. Put another way, to understand what film we are in, we, both writer and audience, have to know whose story we are following. The story cannot start until the protagonist is identified and shown in their normal life (in their normality). What is more, the story cannot move forward until a disturbance fractures the protagonist's normality and forces them into a course of action – which will be the film's action line, its structural foundation.

In practical terms this means that films which do not establish their protagonists early try the audience's patience. In fact a mark of a successful film is that the protagonist is established early, often within the opening moments of the film. Conversely, a mark of a poor film is that it takes a long time establishing its protagonist. A striking example is *Jaws 3* (1983) which takes twelve minutes. Possibly, delays of this sort are related to the fact that the filmmakers involved do not really know what film they are in, so are not properly focused on whose story to follow.

Interestingly, establishing the protagonist early is the mark of successful films across all cultures. While films from some cultures often take a long while to get to their disturbance or their first-act turning point, they will almost always set up their protagonist early, so the audience knows whose story it is following. A good example is *To Live* (a.k.a. *Huozhe*, 1994), in which the protagonist, a compulsive gambler, is set up in the film's opening moments. Until the audience knows who the protagonist is, the film is in limbo.

It is important to understand that there is no extra status involved in one character rather than another being the protagonist; in fact, as will become evident below, often the star of the film (in every sense) is the antagonist. It is a technical, structural matter, important because the wrong protagonist will not only damage the action line but will also result in poor characterization. Often you will not be able to identify the protagonist until you have identified the antagonist. Consequently, this section, on the protagonist, needs to be read in conjunction with the following material on the antagonist.

Isn't it obvious who the protagonist is?

We should pause here because some writers will probably be feeling irritated. Why do we need to know who the protagonist is? Isn't this just theory for the sake of it? What is the practical application? Isn't it obvious that the major character is the protagonist and whoever is against them is the antagonist?

Defining protagonist and antagonist is not always obvious – in fact it can be surprisingly difficult. The reason we need to identify the protagonist is because giving this job to the wrong character can make plot and characterization fall apart.

Probably the easiest way to explain this is to describe a personal experience. Some years ago I was asked to write a film about a bizarre and eccentric elderly fan dancer on a mission of revenge. I couldn't understand why this woman kept turning into a 1950s-style housewife. Eventually, I realized the reason was that I had assumed that she, as the major character, was the protagonist. In trying to get inside her head to give her a normal point of view and understandable motives, I had robbed her of her personality – her eccentricity, her "differentness." The defining and interesting thing about this woman was that she was the sort of character, like Raymond in *Rain Man* (1988), who defied logic and could not change. To be depicted properly, with all the comedy and mystery that she deserved, she had to be seen *from the outside*.

The problem was solved by inventing a new protagonist who was an ordinary person (a truck driver) and making the fan dancer the antagonist who came into his life and dragged him into her comic journey of revenge, changing him but remaining unchanged herself. The fan dancer remained the major character, but she was not the protagonist.

The moral of the story is that it is very easy to mistake a mentor–antagonist for the protagonist because this sort of character is so much more interesting than the pallid, ordinary person who is their foil. But if a mentor is made protagonist, it will not only cease to be interesting as a character, it will create weak action and relationship lines.

To highlight this, let us rewrite *Scent of a Woman* (1992) with the danger-seeking blind war veteran as the protagonist. If we made the veteran the protagonist, we would have to get into his head and capture his point of view and his motives. This would make him normal and remove his danger and mystery. Having removed the mystery from the veteran by making him the protagonist, we have to cast the student who comes to look after him into the role of antagonist. But this person is not an antagonist. He is mild and ineffectual. We can understand him and relate to his consternation at being stuck with a blind man on a rampage – although it is now hard to see the "normalized" veteran as somebody who would go on a rampage.

What has happened here in making the veteran the protagonist and the student the antagonist is that we have two "normal" people – indeed, two almost identical people. There is no conflict or mystery, so the whole premise of the story starts to fall apart because it is not believable that the veteran does what he is supposed to do. *Wedlock* (1991) is a film that suffers from exactly this problem of a protagonist and an antagonist who are both "everyperson" (for a detailed study of *Wedlock,* see Chapter 13, "Lost in the telling"). Other examples are *Gods and Monsters* (1998) and *You've Got Mail* (1998).

If your film involves a character who is strikingly different from everyone else, who is possessed of a unique wisdom, who changes those around them while being incapable of change themselves, whose world view is so idiosyncratic and illogical that it is impossible to anticipate – realize that you are creating a mentor–antagonist and not a protagonist. In cases like this it might be necessary to invent a normal protagonist, to be irritated by and learn from the charismatic mentor–antagonist.

How to identify the protagonist

1. The protagonist does not die

The protagonist does not die (except occasionally at the very end of the film, as in *Thelma and Louise* (1991) or *The English Patient* (1996)) because they have to be around at the end of their own story. The film *Il Postino* (1994) has the protagonist's death followed by a sort of coda, or conclusion.

2. The protagonist is the one whose life is being made difficult

The protagonist is the person whose life is being made difficult, and the person who is consistently making it difficult for them is the antagonist.

3. The protagonist is the person whose head we are inside

The protagonist is the person whose head we are inside, the person with whom we identify, not necessarily the most interesting person in the film. The protagonist provides the point of view of a normal person.

4. The protagonist is the person who changes most

Except in adventure movies (where the point is that the hero is interesting specifically because no catastrophe can change or deter them), the protagonist is the character that changes and learns most as a result of the action. Typically, this change, often a profound one, is brought about by interaction with the antagonist, who is often a charismatic mentor figure. The change will be charted in the relationship line. This provides a useful tip: if a large personality shift is required in the relationship, the action line must be constructed so as to credibly permit this. For example, the marriage of Rose and Allnutt in *The African Queen* could not have happened without an action line that threw them together under great stress.

Be aware that there is a certain sort of relationship line antagonist who does change dramatically. This is the "prude who turns action hero." Such characters are normally women, and part of their transformation involves rejecting sexual repression and becoming openly sexual. Typical examples are Rose in *The African Queen*, Thelma in *Thelma and Louise*, Lotte, Craig's wife, in *Being John Malkovich* and, in *True Lies*, Helen, the wife of the Arnold Schwarzenegger character.

5. The protagonist usually drives the action

The protagonist usually drives the action and makes the decisions, but in films using mentor–antagonists, it is the antagonist and not the protagonist who is proactive. In mentor–antagonist films, the protagonist is:

- the character that changes, while the antagonist is less capable of change, in fact is sometimes incapable of it
- the person whose view of life is that of a normal person, while the antagonist's world view is extreme, innocent, unfathomable or heroic.

6. Whoever speaks in voiceover is the protagonist

In traditional three-act structure, if someone is talking in first-person voiceover, this person is usually the protagonist and we are to follow their story. Good examples are *Notting Hill* (1999) and *The Piano* (1993). The great advantage of this sort of voiceover is that the audience knows whose story it is following from the film's opening moments. Make sure that the character speaking in voiceover is meant to be the protagonist, because the audience will assume that it is; indeed, any character speaking in voiceover will take over the film.

However, flashback films that use voiceover have extra problems. For a start, flashback films have a number of plotlines in different time frames, and there can be different protagonists in all of them. (Working out who is the protagonist in these various plotlines of flashback films is dealt with in detail in Chapters 7–10.) It has a very practical significance because the choice of protagonist (that is, of whose head we get inside) can create two completely different effects. It can either make you understand and identify with the character whose past is being told, as happens in *Shine* and *The English Patient*, or it can make you feel you can never really understand that character at all, as happens in *Citizen Kane* (1941) and *The Usual Suspects* (1995). Before starting on a flashback narrative film, look at Chapters 7–10, particularly Chapter 8, "Varieties of narrative flashback."

7. The protagonist is the protagonist in both action and relationship lines

Except in flashback narrative, the protagonist is the same in the action and relationship lines, whereas the antagonist from the relationship line may often work with, not against, the protagonist when they are battling the enemy. This happens in *Thelma and Louise*.

8. There can be more than one protagonist

Some very successful films seem to have no single protagonist, for example, *The Big Chill*. Other highly successful films have one dominant character at the centrer but in addition possess a range of other characters whose stories are told in such detail that they also seem to be protagonists, as in *American Beauty*, or antagonists, as in *Tea with Mussolini*. These films are constructed in yet another structural form, which can be called *multiple protagonists and antagonists* form. It is dealt with in detail in Chapter 12.

Films with multiple protagonists or antagonists tell the story of a group, usually in the context of either a reunion, a siege (real or metaphorical), or a mission. The characters in the group are all versions of the same type (for example, the radical student ten years on) and the story is about the deeds and survival of the group, rather than just the journey of an individual.

If you are planning to write a story about a group reunion, siege, or mission, look at Chapter 12.

9. The protagonist is central to the film's dramatic high points

The action line cannot start until the protagonist is established and cannot move until the protagonist is hit by a disturbance and makes a plan. The plan is stymied firstly by the first-act turning point, then by obstacles leading to a final climax. The climax answers the problem raised for the protagonist by the first-act turning point.

Relationship line antagonists and action line antagonists

One protagonist, many antagonists

Antagonists become easier to understand and identify once you realize that a conventional three-act film has one protagonist but two or more antagonists. This is because there has to be one antagonist in the relationship line and at least one antagonist in the action line. Spy films show this pattern very clearly. For example, in a James Bond film the action line will typically show an arch-villain as Bond's major antagonist, with minor antagonists in the form of henchmen who appear in sequence for Bond to defeat. Meanwhile, Bond's relationship line will involve a beautiful female antagonist who usually starts out as his enemy but ends up his lover.

Development Strategy 10: Identifying the protagonist

Pick the right protagonist.

Questions to ask:

Is my protagonist the POV?

Is it the voice of normality?

Is it around at the end of its own story?

Does it make the decisions, or if not, is it being troubled by a charismatic mentor–antagonist?

Have I established this person for the audience early on?

Am I using flashbacks (in which case I need to look at chapters 7–10)?

Am I telling the story of a group reunion, mission, or siege (in which case I might need to use the multiple protagonist/antagonist form as described in Chapter 12)?

Is the character speaking in voiceover the protagonist?

Is my protagonist centrally involved in the disturbance, first- and second-act turning point, and climax?

Is my protagonist the same in the action and relationship lines?

Writers often find it difficult to work out which of a pair of characters is the antagonist and which is the protagonist because both seem to be working together to evade a common enemy. This is typical of buddy movies and can be seen in versions of the genre as different as *Thelma and Louise*, the *Lethal Weapon* series, and *Planes, Trains and Automobiles* (1987). The answer relates back to the fact that the antagonist in the action and relationship lines are different characters. In the relationship line of all such films, the antagonist (buddy 1) is the wild card, the person whom we see from the outside and the person who causes the adventure and makes life difficult for the protagonist (buddy 2). But when it comes to a battle between protagonist and action line antagonists, the relationship line antagonist (buddy 1) will assist the protagonist (buddy 2). This is so even though the relationship line antagonist is usually responsible for causing the action line problems for the protagonist in the first place and, indeed, will continue to do so for the rest of the film.

Meanwhile, the protagonist (buddy 2) displays all the normal characteristics of a person whose head we are inside – the normal point of view. So that Louise is the protagonist in *Thelma and Louise* (with Thelma as the wild-card relationship line antagonist), Danny Glover's Roger Murtaugh is the protagonist in the *Lethal Weapon* series, with Martin Riggs, the Mel Gibson character, as the wild-card relationship line antagonist. In *Planes, Trains and Automobiles*, the wild-card relationship line antagonist is John Candy's Del Griffith with Steve Martin as Neal Page, the long-suffering fastidious protagonist.

While we tend to think of antagonists as creatures of the action line, in fact the most complex antagonists are relationship line antagonists. For this reason we will look at them first. But before doing so, we can establish a number of important facts about antagonists generally.

1. As we have seen above, antagonists are not necessarily less interesting than protagonists; in fact they are often the reason the film is written. A major antagonist must be at least an equal match for the protagonist and is often stronger.
2. While antagonists need not be the protagonist's enemy (indeed, they can be friends or lovers), antagonists always cause trouble or change for the protagonist. Their job is to create a conflict situation, often a major life change for the protagonist, thereby driving the plot.
3. A rule of thumb for picking an antagonist is to look for situations in which one character is causing another problems and behaving in a way no normal or reasonable person would. The instigator will normally be the antagonist, and the person being caused problems will be the protagonist.
4. The antagonist is powerfully driven and the antagonist's wishes, at least initially, are directly opposed to the protagonist's.
5. Antagonists are characters that best serve the dramatic build of a film by being depicted from the outside. While the character might be powerfully compelling, we are in the shoes of the protagonist and we have to watch the antagonist through the protagonist's eyes. Any attempt to get inside and explain the antagonist will result in the antagonist becoming too normal and the protagonist and antagonist becoming too similar (imagine a *Thelma and Louise* in which both women are sensible and streetwise). Two very different films that lack conflict and suspense because the antagonist and protagonist are too similar are *Gods and Monsters* and *You've Got Mail*.
6. Antagonists (particularly minor antagonists) often die before the end of the film. Major antagonists die only at the end.
7. In trying to identify protagonist and antagonist beware of the *Mercutio character*, which is neither of these although, because it is so compelling, initially feels as though it might be one or the other. The name is taken from the friend of Romeo who is unexpectedly killed early on in *Romeo and Juliet*. Shakespeare is often said to have killed off Mercutio because he was potentially more interesting than Romeo, the hero. The Mercutio character is a charismatic and likeable

individual who appears early in the film and is usually a friend – sometimes a partner or spouse – of the protagonist. The death of this person – usually as a result of defending or assisting the protagonist – often forms the first-act turning point, impelling the protagonist (who is filled with remorse and/or thoughts of vengeance) to respond in a way that drives the story forward. In the Smiley/ Thompson model, this death is the surprise which becomes the obstacle. A good example of the Mercutio character is the young man who dies in *The Battleship Potemkin* (1925). A more modern equivalent is the British soldier who is killed in the first act of *The Crying Game* (1992). Here, the death is a false first-act turning point. The real first-act turning point is the moment when the protagonist finds the true identity of the dead man's girlfriend. The rule about the Mercutio character is that it dies early and its death causes a crisis that drives the protagonist in a new direction.

Relationship line antagonists

Love and friendship

Relationship lines, like all drama, require conflict, hence the antagonist and protagonist in the relationship line are typically at odds with each other for a lot of the film. Often they start out enemies and end up friends or lovers. When it comes to the action line, they usually act as allies, both fighting the action line antagonists.

The protagonist as troublemaker

A variation sometimes appears in adventure films. In *Romancing the Stone* (1984), it is the protagonist, romance novelist Joan Wilder, who initiates the adventure and causes trouble for Jack Colter, an adventurer who agrees to help her. While Joan continues to make trouble for Colter throughout the film, he remains the character we see only from the outside. We never follow him for any length of time on his own – indeed, the twist at the end of the film has him disappearing, apparently having abandoned and robbed Joan, only to appear for a surprise happy ending.

This raises an interesting issue: what is the difference between *Romancing the Stone* and *The African Queen*, since both have women who initiate adventure and cause trouble for the men they get to help them? Why is Joan a protagonist and Rose an antagonist? Joan is clearly a protagonist because we follow her from the start and because Jack is so clearly seen from the outside. With *The African Queen*, there is a problem because both Rose and Allnutt change and both are seen from the inside. Why, then, does the film work? Why aren't the characters too similar to engage? And since the film clearly works, what is the point of trying to work out who the protagonist and antagonist are?

At one level, the level of simply appreciating *The African Queen*, there is probably no need to pinpoint who is the protagonist and who the antagonist. We can just say that the film works because the two characters are so strikingly different and are cast in such powerful conflict that the film holds. The lesson in planning films that work in the same way is that the film will hold with protagonist and antagonist seen from the inside if they are different enough and if sufficient conflict about their plan of action is built into their relationship. This might explain why the two lovers in *You've Got Mail* do not work: they are simply not different enough for their conflict to be credible – they are too clearly made for each other. But there is another level, one at which it is important to understand why Rose is an antagonist. This is because, as we have seen earlier, she belongs to a category of antagonists we can call "the prude who becomes an action hero," or more precisely, "the prude who becomes a sexually unrepressed action hero." Antagonists like these normally come into their own in the second act, their extreme change causing problems for the protagonist.

Danger of cliché

The antagonist and protagonist in the relationship line are always involved in an emotional relationship, usually one involving growing respect and intimacy. Very often they fall in love, so often that this is a serious danger area for cliché, with the antagonist so sketchily drawn that they become merely the love interest. Writers have to work very hard to reinvent the antagonist–protagonist love affair and inject it with genuine suspense, particularly in action movies or romantic comedies, because the moment audiences see a warring couple engaged in a comic or dramatic adventure, they suspect the ending is going to provide reconciliation and true love. Here, "the prude who turns into an action hero" is a useful model. It could be changed to become "action hero who turns into prude," or "atheist who finds religion" – indeed, to become any dramatic character turnabout. To find a new version, simply brainstorm notions of profound character change. Always make sure that conflict between the antagonist and protagonist in a relationship line is productive and does not turn into redundant bickering.

Transmitting information to the audience

On the practical side, relationship line antagonists are very useful because their presence with the protagonist permits the protagonist's thoughts to be transmitted to the audience by way of dialogue. For the same reason it is good to have a number of antagonists in the action line – so that they can discuss their plans and feelings.

Plots involving lone protagonists often create a relationship line between the protagonist and the main action line antagonist in order to give the film some emotional content. This has the practical side-effect of allowing both to discuss their plans and feelings. Such a relationship happens in *The Fugitive*, in which the marshall starts out an enemy and gradually comes to believe in the protagonist's innocence and respect him. Other antagonists in *The Fugitive* are the one-armed man and, in an interesting twist, the doctor's friend (who looked initially like a relationship line antagonist), who turns out to be an enemy. This phenomenon also occurs in *The Juror* (1996), in which Demi Moore and the criminal hunting her become involved in an intense emotional relationship.

Capacity for change

Antagonists who start out hating the protagonist and end up in love or best friends with them clearly undergo change. Antagonists who follow "the prude who turns into action hero" change most of all. The capacity for change and growth is one of the big differences between relationship line antagonists and action line antagonists. Action line antagonists typically change little and, in extreme forms, like the robot antagonist in *Terminator II* (1989), are so focused on one aim that they are physically unstoppable. Change is typical of all relationship line antagonists, except mentor–antagonists; in fact it can help with developing relationship line antagonists to think of them as "loaded guns." In all instances apart from "prude to action hero," the protagonist undergoes more change than the antagonist. Certainly we are normally better able to understand change in a protagonist rather than an antagonist because we see the protagonist's change from the inside, and it is usually a more logical change. For example, Louise's change in *Thelma and Louise* is a logical result of what happens to the two women on their journey. Given Louise's background, her behavior is utterly logical. This is quite unlike Thelma's behavior, where the change from innocent prude to action hero could not have been predicted. In *Thelma and Louise*, Thelma's transformation causes tragedy, but tracking the deeds of "prude to action hero" antagonists is often used successfully for comedy. This happens in *The African Queen* and *True Lies*.

Mentor–antagonists

Mentor–antagonists have been dealt with in some depth in the section on protagonists above. They are usually the most interesting character in the film. They can easily be mistaken for the protagonist. Mentor–antagonists cause major changes or growth in the protagonist *but change little or not at all themselves*. Mentor–antagonists teach the protagonist new values. Sometimes they are actually teachers like Robin Williams in *Dead Poets' Society* (1989), or manic power-trippers like the Vietnam veteran in *Scent of a Woman*, but often they are an innocent, for example Raymond in *Rain Man*, Thelma in *Thelma and Louise*, Jean in *Jean de Florette* (1986), the recluse in *Man Without a Face* (1993), or the bodyguard in *The Bodyguard* (1992). They may also have values that are actively destructive of the protagonist. This is so of Abigail in *The Crucible* (1996) and Withnail in *Withnail and I* (1987). It is vital they be viewed from the outside because attempting to get inside them will normalize them and rob them of their uniqueness and unpredictability.

Mentor–antagonists often act as antagonists in both the action and relationship lines. Typically, as in *Scent of a Woman* and *Julia* (1977), they take the protagonist on an adventure (action line) while teaching them and forging an emotional bond (relationship line). In this sort of scenario there will be minor antagonists whom the protagonist and mentor evade or defeat. Sometimes antagonists who are not mentors become the antagonist in both the action and relationship lines. We have seen this above in *The Fugitive* and *The Juror* (1996).

Multiple antagonists in the relationship line

Multiple antagonists in a relationship line usually occur in films about the problems and survival of a group involved in a reunion, a mission, or a siege. Typical multiple antagonist films are *Saving Private Ryan* (1998), which has the soldiers as multiple antagonists, and *Tea with Mussolini*, in which the women prisoners of war are multiple antagonists. Multiple antagonist form is complex and needs careful study (see Chapter 12, "Multiple protagonists and antagonists").

Antagonists in flashback narrative

As we have seen above, the matter of whether a character is dealt with as protagonist or antagonist has a massive effect in films that use flashback narrative. Antagonists in flashback narrative is also a complex topic (see Chapter 8, "Varieties of flashback narrative").

Action line antagonists

Action line antagonists are normally a lot simpler than relationship line antagonists. They tend not to change, unlike many relationship line antagonists, although sometimes they turn from being the protagonist's enemy to being a friend, as in the case of the sheriff in *Thelma and Louise*; indeed, sometimes they also fulfil the role of relationship line antagonists, as in *The Fugitive*.

Action lines usually have a number of antagonists. This is particularly necessary in films where the action line keeps the major antagonist away from the protagonist (as in James Bond films, or pursuit films like *Thelma and Louise*) because the major antagonist needs agents on the ground to make trouble for the protagonist. In Bond films, these are henchmen whose job it is to hunt and destroy Bond. In more subtle films, like *Thelma and Louise*, the main antagonist, the hunter, is the sheriff, assisted by other lawmen and Thelma's husband. However, because these are at a physical distance from the women, there are other antagonists in the form of the rapist, the hitchhiker, the highway patrolman, and the boorish truck driver who appear on the road to cause Thelma and Louise trouble and impel them towards their doom.

Without secondary antagonists in films like these, the protagonist/antagonist conflict would be reduced to cutting back and forth between hunter and hunted. If your film has an antagonist at a physical distance from the protagonist, you will need either to create secondary antagonists who can cause trouble at close hand or find a way to bring the major antagonist into close physical proximity.

Non-human force as antagonist

An antagonist in an action line can be a force of nature (for example, a volcano or a hurricane) or a social force (for example, class prejudice), but it normally has human agents, actual people whose actions help the non-human force to cause the protagonist trouble. In *The African Queen* the river is an antagonist, but there are human antagonists in the form of the German army and navy. Often, films that have a non-human enemy are mission films involving a group on a quest to save humanity. In this instance, the antagonism occurs within the group so there is not as great a need for external human antagonists. Films like these are usually in multiple protagonist/antagonist form, which is dealt with in Chapter 12.

11

Development Strategy 11: Identifying the antagonist

Pick the right antagonist(s) for the relationship and action lines.

Questions to ask

General

Are my antagonists characters that make life difficult for the protagonist?

>

Am I depicting my antagonists from the outside?

Am I mistaking a Mercutio character for an antagonist?

Do my major antagonists at least equal the protagonist in strength, intelligence etc.?

Are my antagonists powerfully driven with wishes that are, at least initially, directly opposed to the protagonist's?

Flashbacks and multiple antagonist structure

Does my film use flashback narrative or have a group involved in a mission, reunion, or siege? (If so, see Chapter 8, 'Varieties of flashback narrative', and Chapter 12, "Multiple protagonists and antagonists").

Relationship line antagonist

Are my antagonist and protagonist sufficiently different from each other?

Is there conflict, emotional involvement of some kind, and increasing closeness?

If I have a love affair, is it clichéd and am I creating an antagonist that is merely a love interest?

Is the protagonist/antagonist conflict productive rather than just being redundant bickering?

Does my antagonist assist the protagonist in action line battles against a common enemy?

Are the changes my antagonist goes through interesting but credible, real but unusual? Further to this, am I using a "prude who turns into action hero" model and, if so, is it a real but unusual rendering? Should I incorporate some other massive character turnabout (for example, "atheist finds religion")?

Action line antagonists

If my action line antagonist is remote from the action, does it have agents?

Alternatively, does it start to get emotionally closer to the protagonist?

If my action line antagonist is non-human, does it have human agents?

Mentor–antagonists

Is my antagonist a mentor? If so, does it teach the protagonist new values?

Am I depicting it from the outside so that it can remain a mystery?

Should it be the antagonist in both the action and relationship lines?

Getting into character

Characterization is a complex skill requiring a lot of thought and planning. Characterization has really being going on from the earliest moments of the script's development. After all, action and relationship lines are both driven by character, and many writers have such a strong sense of the characters they are creating that they feel the process of characterization is a matter of uncovering the inner workings of an existing person rather than the business of creating a fictitious being from scratch.

Ironically, because writers feel so confident about character, they can easily spend insufficient time exploring character, with the result that their characterization contains clichés.

To find interesting characters from scratch

1. Think of a new version of a character from myth, fairytale, fable or genre (see Chapter 3, "Getting good ideas fast from fairytale, myth and fable"). Look in newspapers, especially articles and advertisements, for characters or roles that sound interesting.
2. Think of a social stereotype and pull against it.
3. Consider new versions of archetypes, for example, Christopher Vogler's archetypes in the hero's journey in chapter 3.
4. Think of putting opposite personalities in conflict.
5. Define a character through its flaws.

Close detail

A series of questions and charts involving each character's emotional and chronological history, as well as their present circumstances and emotions, will help. These let you check that your characters are interesting and, moreover, that you really understand them. The process of a writer getting into character is very like the process of an actor getting into character, except that the writer invents material rather than interprets it. Figure 6.1 shows the sort of chart that might help.

There will be overlap between public and private qualities. For example, "problems mixing" has both a public and private dimension. This is not a problem because the point of the chart is not to separate the public and private, merely to force consideration of them.

Charts work to help writers get inside the character by throwing stimuli at the lateral imagination to create real but unusual connections. Connections may not happen immediately, but persist and they will.

Character development is an ongoing process that should occur simultaneously with structural planning. It takes time. It is often only after a couple of drafts that a character's motivation will be clear, or the writer will fully understand the human foibles that are being depicted in the script.

Character demands in the script as a whole

The audience needs to know:

• where the character has come from psychologically (social and family background)

- the character's weaknesses, strengths, areas of vulnerability
- the public roles of the character – job, family, etc.
- current events driving the character.

Character demands in each scene

The audience needs to know

- what the character wants out of each scene
- what the character is trying to hide in each scene.

Laying the foundations for suspense and surprise
The first-act turning point is a physical surprise

Suspense and surprise are crucial to holding the audience's attention for the duration of the film. They need to be built in at an early stage. It is important to have a first-act

Past			Present		
Personal	**Public**	**Internal**	**Personal**	**Public**	**Internal**
Date, place of birth? Where grew up?	Class of family? Education?	Personality flaws?	Family still alive? Contact, good or bad, with family?	Job? Financial state? How good at job?	Problems at work or socially?
Family?	How family was regarded?	What secrets? What did this person hate talking about?	Has partner? Children?	How happy in job? Enjoys workplace?	Grudges? Secrets? Fears?
Relationships with family?	How character came across to others?	Emotional crises in childhood?	Where lives and lifestyle?	Fits in socially and in workplace?	Damage carried from past, if any?
Unpleasant and pleasant aspects of childhood?	What jobs? Hobbies? Political/ social beliefs?		Any personal crises at the moment?	Hobbies? Political beliefs?	What does this person hate talking about?
Major family events in childhood?	Shy or outgoing?			Passions? Pet hates?	Optimist or pessimist?
	Crucial events witnessed?			Ambitions?	
				Shy or outgoing? People most loves, hates, pities, fears?	

Figure 6.1 Character chart

Development Strategy 12: Getting into character

Devise character charts by asking who, why, and how, remembering to think "real but unusual." You need to think about the protagonist/ antagonist's background, how might it drive their motives, and how they try to fulfil their aims.

Questions to ask:

Do I understand these characters well enough?

Are they and their dilemmas real but unusual?

Am I unconsciously giving them clichéd motives or actions? If so, how can I pull against the cliché?

12

turning point at about twenty minutes into the film because at this point the audience risks losing concentration. The first-act turning point should come as a strong and actual *physical* surprise (often a death, as in *Thelma and Louise*) which turns into an obstacle for the protagonist and propels the action into the second act. While the first-act turning point often causes the protagonist to make an important decision which dictates the content of the rest of the action line, a change of mind on its own it not usually powerful enough and must be triggered by a physical surprise. If no such surprise/obstacle exists, it will be necessary to invent one. The first-act turning point causes the second act. A delayed first-act turning point can cause boredom and massively damage a film – as in *Prelude to a Kiss* (1992), where it appears about an hour into the film.

The first-act turning point is what the film is about

A good rule of thumb is that the first-act turning point is what the film is "about." For example, *The Player* (1992) is about what happens when a Hollywood executive accidentally kills a writer. *The Piano* is about what happens when a woman is separated from her means of self-definition and expression. *Tootsie* (1982) is about what happens when a male actor pretends to be female. If you know what your film is about, you probably have your first-act turning point.

Linda Seger has interesting material on turning points in *Making a Good Script Great*, in which she explains that a turning point should:

- kick the action into an unexpected direction
- push the protagonist deeper into the problem
- raise the central question again but with added, surprising complications.

Development Strategy 13: Finding the first-act turning point (surprise/obstacle)

Make sure the surprise is an actual, physical surprise – an event – and that the protagonist's change of heart or decision is triggered by this physical surprise.

Questions to ask:

Have I made the protagonist experience a physical, world-changing surprise at about twenty minutes into the film?

Does my first-act turning point have all the effects described by Linda Seger?

Does my first-act turning point cause the second act?

Is my first-act turning point what the film is "about"?

13

Second-act complications

The second act is the longest and most difficult part of the script. Its job is to show the protagonist being prevented by people and circumstances from achieving the goal, in other words, showing how their story becomes fraught with conflict and complications. The temptation in devising second-act complications is to think randomly of problems that could be included and continue redrafting until a suitable mixture is found. In fact simple logic can create a much faster method.

To get a range of interesting second-act complications, first define the protagonist's goal or problem as it presents itself in the first-act turning point, then think of as many real but unusual ways as possible that this goal or problem could be obstructed, and create conflict of an emotional or physical kind for the protagonist.

For example, in *Tootsie*, the protagonist's goal or problem at the first-act turning point is that he is impersonating a woman for professional success. If you ask what obstructions could happen to a man who is trying to pass himself off as a woman, you can get a long list of possible complications in less than a minute. For example:

- Protagonist falls in love with a woman and can't declare his love.
- Protagonist declares his love for the woman and the woman thinks he's a lesbian.
- Man who thinks protagonist is a woman falls in love with him.
- Man who thinks protagonist is a woman tries to press physical advances on him.
- Protagonist is mistaken for a cross-dresser.
- Keeping make-up and costume in order is difficult.
- Getting changed is time-consuming and protagonist is often almost discovered.

- Protagonist's friends think he has deserted them.
- Protagonist is mistaken for a homosexual.
- Homosexual man makes a pass at protagonist.
- Lesbian makes a pass at protagonist.

Apart from the last two options, the list above provides all of the plot complications that actually occur in *Tootsie*.

The same method can be used to explain the second-act complications in *The Piano*. The protagonist's problem or goal as it presents itself at the first-act turning point is that her means of expression, the piano, is stuck on the beach and therefore unavailable to her. Her need is to get the piano back. If you look at the second-act complications of *The Piano* as listed at the end of this chapter, you will see that each event is an obstruction to Ada's goal of getting back the piano to express herself. The second act ends at the second-act turning point, Ada's lowest point, which is when Stewart chops off the top of her finger, therefore apparently ruining her chances of self-expression completely.

Make sure the complications are different

When devising second-act complications, make sure that the obstructions hindering the protagonist are genuinely different rather than different versions of the same obstruction. For example, in a script where the protagonist is shut in an underground dungeon and has to get out, three different instances of the protagonist being stopped by guards and killing them are not a variety of obstructions. They are three different versions of the same obstruction: guards. On the other hand, if the protagonist was first obstructed by guards, then obstructed by fear of heights, then obstructed by a booby-trapped gate, these events would genuinely constitute different obstructions.

Different kinds of obstruction

Linda Seger has excellent material in *Making a Good Script Great* on different sorts of obstructions and other ways of creating a compelling second and third act. These include, to use her terms, *barriers*, *reversals* and *complications*; methods for choosing the right settings and scenarios; using scene sequences to bump up the pace; using *foreshadowing* and *payoff*; and many other practical and detailed methods to tackle the business of stymieing the protagonist. This is obligatory reading.

Second-act sag

It is common for scripts to display a good first act complete with fine first-act turning points and then to lose their way – lose their impetus – once this surprise/obstacle has been revealed. In cases like these it often feels as if the writer is floundering as a result of not being used to the change of direction caused by the first-act turning point. Scripts that display this "sag" often find their way after a few scenes. It is useful to check that the scenes immediately after the first-act turning point are actually driving the plot forward – if anything, picking up the pace. If they are not, they should be cut because a loss of pace at this crucial time is hard to make up.

Development Strategy 14: Devising second-act complications

To get a range of interesting second-act complications, first define the protagonist's goal or plan, then brainstorm as many real but unusual ways as possible that this goal could be obstructed. Note that the goal can change or be added to.

Questions to ask:

Do I understand the protagonist's goal?

Am I writing obstructions that are real but unusual?

Do I have a lot of different obstructions rather than many versions of the same obstruction?

Could I increase the obstructions by a clever twist to the protagonist's goal?

14

The second-act turning point

The second-act turning point is the lowest point, emotionally and often physically, for the protagonist. It the closest they come to death and despair, and is designed to pump up the suspense and the audience's anxiety. After the second-act turning point, the protagonist rallies for act three, which is the final battle towards the goal.

Finding the climax

The climax answers the problem posed by issues arising from the first-act turning point. For example, the first-act turning point in "Little Red Riding Hood" is when she meets a killer wolf which she mistakes for a dog. This poses the problem of "will it kill her?" The second-act turning point is when she is eaten, thus apparently killed, but the climax is when she is ripped out of the wolf's stomach, giving the answer "no, she survives."

It is very easy in the development or writing of any script for the story to slip into a different direction so that the climax ends up not answering the problem created by the first-act turning point. In this case, either the misdirected climax must be changed to answer the problem arising from the new first-act turning point (or its ramifications), or the story must be realigned so that it leads to the climax. Sometimes it is possible to realign the climax by inventing some crucial information or event that can be set up in the first act and pay off unexpectedly but credibly in the climax.

Sometimes the climax of a piece presents itself to us before the rest of the story. In such cases we can work backwards from the climax to find the problem, and from that

15

Development Strategy 15: Finding the second-act turning point

To find the second-act turning point, look for the step in the plot where the protagonist reaches its lowest possible point, emotionally and/or physically. This usually comes before the last big struggle, which constitutes act three.

Questions to ask:

Have I found the protagonist's lowest point?

Do I have to invent or expand one (think 'real but unusual')?

Have I created a credible and powerful lowest point?

Is this turning point bigger and more dramatic than the first-act turning point?

Does it fulfil the requirements of a turning point in restating the protagonist's problem and turning them in a new direction?

Is it leading towards the climax in act three?

the first-act turning point, that is, what the story is about.

Building to a big climax that solves the problem is very satisfactory for the audience, but anticlimax is also a possibility. It may be for stylistic reasons, or to make a point, that the "make or break" climax is rejected for a more low-key effect where there is no climax in the expected sense at all: life merely goes on. This is so in *Crimes and Misdemeanors* and the Chinese film *To Live*. In both cases it works because the non-climax is really only another answer to the original problem. The misdirected climax, as in *Guarding Tess,* is not an answer to anything, therefore is irritating.

A similar misdirected climax occurs in *Jack and Sarah* (1995) in which the first-act turning point creates the problem of how a man will emerge from chronic depression following the death of his wife in childbirth (apparently the first-act turning point of a very serious film) and the film's climax answers the romantic comedy issue of whether he is in love with his baby's kooky nanny.

The climax and resolution of the action and relationship lines should ideally occur in the same scene. If not, they should be resolved as close together as possible, and as close as possible towards the end.

The climax must be not achieved too easily. That is to say, the suspense must be maintained right up to and during the climax. The climax is, after all, the ultimate conflict

– the script's major problem condensed into one make-or-break moment. It is very easy, given the pressure of the industry, for the writer to forget that the climax must genuinely be a "do-or-die battle," the culmination of a whole third-act struggle in which the protagonist (who almost always wins) could really die/lose the fight/lose the case/lose the lover. A good example of the writer not really believing in the plot and therefore creating a weak third act and climax occurs in the action comedy *Six Days Seven Nights* (1998). This is a film about two people crashing a plane on a desert island and having adventures with drug smugglers while being assumed dead. The climax depicts the couple arriving back at their own memorial ceremony, which is being held at the resort they originally left. So little attention was given to the notion of what would really happen if a couple died like this that no grieving relatives are even shown telephoning the resort, let alone attending the memorial service. This weakens the climax because it is incredible.

Development Strategy 16:
Finding the climax

Make the climax answer the problem posed by issues arising from the first-act turning point.

Questions to ask:

Does my climax answer the problem set up by the first-act turning point?

Is the "battle" in my climax being won (or lost) too easily, that is, is it genuinely exciting?

If my climax is an anticlimax, is this deliberate and will it work (or will it make the audience feel robbed)?

Am I presenting the new normality and ending the film soon after the climax?

Are the action and the relationship lines coming to a climax in the same scene?

Am I really exploring all the possibilities for suspense in the climax, that is, am I really writing as if the protagonist could actually die/lose their partner etc.?

16

What if the climax is not working?

If the climax is not working, an easy way to check that the climax is actually appropriate is to go back to the first-act turning point of both the action line and the relationship line and find out what problems these two are creating for the protagonist. This will reveal the issues that need to be resolved in the climax.

If you are stuck with an about-face climax that seems not to be credible, you might be able to render it believable if you invent some crucial information or event that can be set up in the first act and pay off unexpectedly but credibly here. This provides a satisfying unity to the end of the piece.

17

Development Strategy 17: Establishing the first-act turning point through the final climax

If you don't have a clear idea of what the film is about, try looking at the climax. The climax defines what the work is about. You can then create a first-act turning point to present the problem that will be resolved in the climax.

Questions to ask:

What problem is my climax resolving?

What would be a good first-act turning point to set up that problem?

Is my first-act turning point a physical surprise that causes an obstacle?

Resolution and ending

Once the climax has been reached, we need to demonstrate the new normality in plot and subplot as economically as possible. Often this can be done in the same scene as the climax. But sometimes writers become so involved with the characters and story that they cannot leave them. This is particularly so with films carrying great emotional or autobiographical content from the writer or director.

Films that suffer from this syndrome often show multiple endings – that is, scene after scene following the climax, each of which feels like a farewell. These multiple endings can significantly reduce the impact of the film as a whole, and in very bad cases can actually cause the audience to laugh, thereby shattering the whole illusion. If there seem to be too many endings, consider how to blend them or choose the most pertinent.

Development Strategy 18: Coming to a resolution and ending

Make the film end soon after the climax, to avoid loss of impact and inappropriate audience response.

Questions to ask:

Is my film displaying multiple endings?

If there is autobiographical or strong personal material in the film, am I sufficiently distanced to decide which is the best sort of ending?

18

Final steps before the first draft

It is now very tempting to move straight into a first draft. But checking up on structure, depth of characterization, and appropriateness of scenario at this stage will make the writing much richer and save time later.

Check for clichés

It is normal at this stage for a few clichés to have crept in. To check, list all the potential clichés of the chosen genre and characters. For example, character clichés of horror films are the handsome hero, the wimp, the bully who is really a coward, the foolish girl etc. Brainstorm as many ways as possible of avoiding the clichés.

Could I be more original?

How could more originality be added? Is this original enough? Is this worth millions of dollars?

Maintaining the personal passion

Because it is vital to hang on to the personal passion in a film, try to analyze what precisely made you commit to this idea – so that you can build personal intensity into the script. A practical way to explore the personal connections is to identify the main theme or story idea in the script then brainstorm connections. Linda Seger calls this *clustering* and regards it as a way of increasing the commercial viability of the script by finding the universal themes. In *Lateral Thinking*, Edward de Bono calls it identifying the dominant idea, and regards the notion of making connections out from it as a way of ceasing to be dominated by it, or by the mental clichés it calls up. Here is a way of clustering for an escape movie:

• Create a mind map by writing down and circling the main theme, then adding the connections its triggers for you. Figure 6.2 shows the start of a mind map on an escape movie.

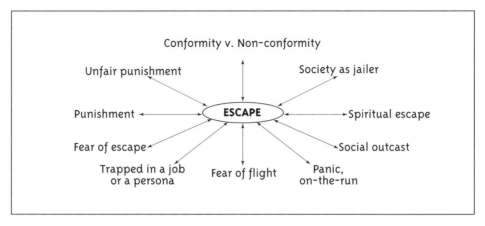

Figure 6.2 Mind map on an escape movie

- Use the mind map as a starting point to articulate as many different reasons as possible why the idea might have appealed to you. These might surprise you. For example, you might find the idea compelling because it threatens you.
- Brainstorm associations from each of the ideas thrown up in the process. For example, a theme of war might suggest rivalry, which might suggest images of chess or battle. These can be examined for their potential as symbols, or the bases for scenes.
- Examine the emotions that the ideas or images are creating in you (for example, for an escape movie, panic, stress). Let these trigger more symbols and images for possible use.
- Expect some clichés to appear, and accept that you might not fully understand your attraction to the idea until later in the writing. Be guided by intuition. If you have a strong gut feeling that a scene or character should be included, it should.

Development Strategy 19: Checking before the first draft

19

Before starting to write, check for clichés, level of originality and strength of personal passion for the idea. Explore the personal resonance of the idea via "clustering" (brainstorming subconscious connections out from a theme), moving to symbols and possible scene material.

Questions to ask:

Is the material original?

What is resonating for me in the idea?

Finding the story sentence (advanced form)

It is useful at this stage to go back to the simple story-sentence of the action line (Development Strategy 7) and expand it.

Development Strategy 20 – Creating an advanced story sentence

[**Protagonist**] *faced with* [**disturbance**] *which creates* [**problem**] *and surprised by* [**first-act turning point**] *responds and is foiled by* [**a series of action setbacks, often triggered by the antagonist but also by fate, accident, etc**] *reaches a lowest point of physical danger or despair when* [**second-act turning point**] *but fights back by* [**a series of actions in act three leading up to climax**] *and finally deals with* [**problem**] *by* [**climax**].

Question to ask:

Does the action line of my story fit into this extended narrative sentence?

20

Checking that the relationship line is moving

Films like *Mr. Saturday Night* and *Guarding Tess* show how easy it is for writers to mistake different renderings of the same normality (an elderly lady refusing to be guarded, a self-destructive comedian) for movement in the relationship line. To check that the relationship line is actually moving, apply Development Strategy 21 from time to time (see page 84).

Draw a diagram representing a road and insert the sequence of major relationship scenes or sequences, writing a descriptive signpost against each scene (this can be done in the early stages of development and added to subsequently). Make sure that each scene is a stepping stone to the next and does not duplicate it. A good way to do this is to see if any of the relationship sequences can be swapped around. If major scenes or sequences can be shuffled between acts without a problem, the relationship line is static. Note that the best scenes often contain the action and relationship lines together, so that each informs the other. If the relationship line is not moving, it could be because the action line is not permitting movement, in which case change the action line to get the possibilities of progression you required.

Close planning

There are many different ways to tell the same story, but the content of a scene is never an arbitrary matter. The function of content is to propel the film forward via plot,

Development Strategy 21: Checking that the relationship line is moving

Write a narrative sentence for the relationship line to make sure it is moving, rather than restating the same relationship point in different ways.

Questions to ask:

Does every incident in the relationship line take the relationship forward, or am I duplicating the same interaction over and again?

Could I swap around any of the relationship scenes (if so, the relationship line is not moving)?

Is my subplot's movement tied closely to the movement of my action line?

If my action line isn't helping my relationship line, do I need to change the action line?

21

characterization or a blend of the two. This means each scene must be consciously accounted for, and if a scene does not pay its way, cut it.

The first step is to decide what needs to be transmitted in terms of emotion and action, and find the right scenario to do it. One simple but very useful piece of advice about writing the individual scene is that in every scene a character must *want* something.

Before even thinking of dialogue, be sure that the setting and action of the scene will transmit the required elements of the action and relationship lines, and characterization, and be sure that it will do so in an interesting, unusual but real way. For example, take a scene in which the protagonist has lost their job and has to meet their partner and break the bad news. Although biographical and plot details about the film as a whole were decided long ago, there are a million different ways in which to write this one small piece of action. Of course, a lot will depend upon where in the script this scene is happening. If it comes early, much thought must be directed into using it to set up character. If it comes later, it will be used to depict and develop established character traits and to move the relationship and action lines forward.

A lot will also depend upon where the scene must end. If the couple needs to be at home in bed in the next scene, they cannot be boarding a plane to Africa at the end of this scene. Of course, the setting of a scene like that would have been apparent from the early planning stages of the project. But if this is not the case, brainstorm to get lateral ideas, then choose the best. Where, for example, do the two characters encounter each other? What would be the best setting? What are they doing before and during the revelation? They could be in bed, shopping, taking the dog for a walk, skiing, at a party, repairing the house, cleaning the house, at their relatives' place, at a wedding, at a funeral, at a concert, at a café, at the bus stop – the choice goes on forever.

The best setting and scenario is not necessarily obvious. To understand this, consider the famous scene in *When Harry Met Sally* (1989) where, in a crowded restaurant, Sally demonstrates how to fake an orgasm. This is a brilliantly funny and highly memorable scene. But if we consider the material that needed to be transmitted in this scene, the choice of a crowded restaurant as a setting was not obvious at all, neither was the fake orgasm. Structurally, the scene is a relationship line scene and its function is to complicate the Harry/Sally relationship, causing conflict between them (in a comical way). There is nothing in that content that dictates a crowded restaurant or, indeed, the presence of other people at all. The choice of location adds a whole extra dimension of comedy, but it was by no means built in to the content.

For a brilliant analysis of how subtext drives good scene writing see Robert McKee, *Story* (1999), "Scene Analysis."

Opening scenes

Opening scenes are particularly crucial and need much thought. These scenes must establish the protagonist's normality. The identity of the protagonist must be established as close as possible to the start, so that the audience knows who to follow, and whose story this is.

In practical terms, establishing the protagonist and their normality means transmitting a lot of facts, but doing it in an unobtrusive way via scenario, dialogue, sound and visuals. There is a need to establish the protagonist's social and personal background (their job, class, marital status, country and era they are in, etc.). It is also necessary to establish what sort of person the protagonist is, with some hints of their good points and their failings. This often also means including backstory. *Notting Hill* does all this by showing the protagonist literally walking through his normality (Notting Hill Gate, and his bookshop) and talking about himself via voiceover. Voiceover is an instant way of establishing the protagonist.

An excellent example of establishing the protagonists and their world without voiceover and with consummate economy occurs in *The Big Chill*. *The Big Chill* has six protagonists and six normalities to establish. It manages to do so in under a minute, and in the same minute also contrives to show, with a clever twist, the antagonist (the man who committed suicide) and provide the disturbance (the suicide). *The Big Chill* achieves this largely by clever choice of scenario, that is, by the selection of what plot matter goes into the opening scenes. The choice of a scenario showing each of the protagonists either re-ceiving news of the suicide or on their way to the funeral permits each protagonist to be shown, physically, in the middle of their world or normality. This is very important for later in the film because, from now on, all but two of the protagonists will be shown out of context, that is, in someone else's home. Note that the opening scenes have little or no

Development Strategy 22: Getting the right scenario for each scene

Decide what the scene needs to get across in terms of the action line, relationship line and characterization, and find the right scenario to do it. Remember that a scene is defined by what comes before and after it. A scene must have a reason to be there. The best scenes further the action line, relationship line and characterization.

Questions to ask:

What do I need to get across, plotwise and in terms of characterization?

Which character(s) want something, and what do they want?

What would be in character?

Does the setting and action of my scene grow from what comes before and trigger what comes later?

Does the setting and action of my scene fit and display the emotional make-up of my characters?

What emotional responses would these characters have in the given situation and what series of actions could depict this?

Are my setting and action real but unusual?

Do I have a genuine reason to include this scene?

What is the audience getting from this scene?

How can I make Character A do something which will make Character B react in character?

dialogue. The impact is achieved visually and aurally. The strength and economy of the opening scenes of *The Big Chill* can be felt by trying to imagine how else the film could start. Getting so much across in such a short time is a major task.

When you come to planning opening scenes, think carefully about what has to be told. Brainstorm as many scenarios as possible and think carefully about what can be told visually and aurally as well as by dialogue. Brainstorming visual and aural possibilities is also very useful. Think too about subtext.

While it is important to get a lot of information across in the opening scenes about the protagonist and their normality, it is not necessary to get in all the details about the protagonist or their backstory at this point. Sometimes showing a character behaving in a certain way but not explaining what caused this behavior provides for interest and suspense. For example, the William Hurt character in *The Big Chill* is shown swallowing a handful of drugs and gunning his car in the opening scenes, but the reasons behind this nihilism are not explained until much later in the film. Avoid using slabs of dialogue exposition.

Development Strategy 23: Creating opening scenes

Establish the protagonist and their normality in the opening scenes by carefully choosing a scenario which will permit the transmission of all the details that must be gotten across.

Questions to ask:

What information is necessary to get across in the opening scenes?

Does the scenario I have chosen do the job as well as seize the audience?

Am I using visual and aural clues as well as dialogue?

Am I putting in slabs of dialogue exposition? If so, how can I remedy it?

23

Symbolism and myth

Symbolism and myth are great weapons to increase the impact of a film. A film can be thought of as a journey through the protagonist's mental landscape. To find resonant symbolism, writers have to identify the emotional content of their material and try to find a setting which will symbolize it. This happened in the writing of Jane Campion's *The Piano*. Jane Campion says that her original idea for the film did not include a piano. She started out with an idea for a repressed woman who found her sexuality. She invented the piano as the device which could permit this to happen. The piano came at quite a late stage in the project.

Often, however, the symbolism will come first – the writer knows intuitively that a film must be set in a certain place. The task in that instance is to work out what the setting is symbolizing, in other words, what the subconscious is telling us.

Because symbolism is often strongly connected with the emotional, spiritual, and psychological content of the film, look in the relationship line to find clues to any symbols that might be appearing, and also to invent symbols if none are present.

Setting a film against a dramatic natural landscape will almost always add a seriousness and sense of universality to the plot. The desert, the mountains, the sea – all these become metaphors for life, and the characters moving across them start to become symbolic of the human race locked in battles against fate and/or the elements. We can see this in everything from *Dances with Wolves* (1990) to *Lawrence of Arabia* (1962), to *Thelma and Louise*. Even a comedy like *Priscilla, Queen of the Desert* (1994), resonates with a higher seriousness because of its desert setting. Urban settings can also have a potent symbolic quality. Both *Blade Runner* (1982) and the *Batman* (1989–97) films create a powerfully symbolic urban jungle for their background.

Both Christopher Vogler and Linda Seger hold that finding the mythical elements in scripts increases their power and, indeed, their commercial viability. To find mythical elements, simply look for similarities in the script with stories in myth, then boost the elements of myth in the script.

Development Strategy 24: Using symbolism and myth

Look for any symbolism that is appearing and develop it. Think of symbols to enforce themes and ideas, particularly in the development of the relationship line.

Questions to ask:

Are symbols and elements of myth already appearing in the script, particularly in the relationship line? If so, how can I develop them?

Can I think of symbolism that will give the relationship line greater resonance?

Have I set the film in a place that has useful symbolism?

Have I inadvertently set up symbolism that might be counterproductive (for example, set a comedy against a background with dark symbolism)?

24

Specific plotting problems: adaptation
From fiction

Adapting for the screen from prose fiction involves putting oneself into the mind of the original creator and reproducing a screen version as close as possible to the spirit of the original. This can be hard because many novelists rely heavily on prose narrative description of changing states of mind, feeling and perception. In film we cannot describe changing states of mind with any detail except through montage or surrealism, but even this is limited. Film tells its story through the word and the specific, demonstrative act. It utilizes the single crucial scene, or event, to sum up how a character is feeling at any point in time. Character on screen *is* what it *does*. Screenwriters who are looking to adapt heavily narrative-dependent novels and novelists who plan to adapt their work for the screen both need to find ways of expressing narrative content through scenario and dialogue.

There will always be more than one – and often many – possible adaptations of a film. Novelists often start in the middle of the story and get their characters to muse over the beginning. This does not have be copied to film via voiceover and flashback to provide backstory, but if flashbacks are necessary, structure them according to the rules of flashback narrative in Chapters 7–10.

Novels that tell stories in parallel can be transferred to the screen via one of the forms of parallel storytelling described in Chapters 7-12, perhaps tandem or sequential narrative.

Problem areas

Dialogue in novels may have to be completely rewritten for the screen. Novelists are often poor at dialogue. Another problem area in adaptations is the middle of the story. Novels often do not have powerful dramatic middles, or second acts, to their plots because they are not so dependent as scripted forms on action to depict character. An adaptation might require that a new second act be developed out of a minor plot point. The danger area in all scripts is the second act, or middle. With television miniseries, the second episode carries all of the dangers of the second act.

Most novels contain too much action for an average-length film and will need to be condensed. In any case, things take longer to illustrate on film, so plot content will have to be cut back. An interesting example of this is the film *Three Days of the Condor* (1975). It is based on a book called *Seven Days of the Condor*. If you are choosing a piece of fiction to adapt, a short story or novella provide about the right amount of material for a feature film. Adapting a larger work means extensive cutting.

Characters might have to be blended or new ones invented to permit the speaking aloud of what is handled in the novel via narrative. Again, the rule is that character on screen *is* what it *does*.

Be aware that many novels, like many script ideas, utilize mentor–antagonists.

From fact

Adaptation of factual/historical material involves picking out the "story steps" of a real story and creating out of it a piece of drama which will operate on the audience in the same way as a fictitious story. You need to have an attitude on the extent to which (if at all) you are going to elaborate upon the truth for dramatic effect. There can be legal problems involved in this form.

Checklist for planning adaptations of fiction, poetry or fact

1. Check whether the dominant story is an action line or relationship line (see Development Strategy 8).
2. Write a story sentence summary of the action line and the relationship line. (At this stage aim for more than one version of each.)
3. Name the protagonist(s) and antagonist(s), or list who they might be. Be aware that the most interesting character might be a mentor–antagonist. Be aware that if the source material is about different versions of the same sort of character, there could be multiple antagonists or protagonists. If so, structure accordingly.
4. Consider whether a traditional three-act structure will be most useful, or whether one of the forms of parallel storytelling would better serve the source material.
5. Answer the "who, why, how?" character motivation question. Complete character charts and pinpoint what is most important to transmit.
6. At some stage soon you will almost inevitably have to jettison some of the source material and probably add more to fill gaps. Attempt to pick out (a) some superfluous material; and (b) some gaps.
7. If you are using a traditional three-act narrative structure, start planning the structure with the help of the Development Strategies, that is, identify the action line and relationship line structures: normality, disturbance, first- and second-act turning points, complications, climax and resolution.

25

Development Strategy 25: Planning an adaptation of fiction, poetry or fact

Follow the adaptation checklist to plan the screen adaptation.

Questions to ask:

If I have a choice of source material, is this the best piece for my current aims in adaptation?

Have I moved through all the steps in the checklist, brainstorming a non-clichéd range of solutions?

Specific plotting problems: Comedy and satire

To write successful comedy and satire, you need to think up a scenario which will best show your character's foibles. To do that, you must understand very specifically what those foibles are. You need to work out what is sometimes known as the character's comic or dramatic perspective – that is, what character flaw at once defines him or her and makes them funny. This is not a new technique. The classic comic satirists like Molière and Ben Jonson actually gave their characters surnames which summed up this comic perspective and made it easier for the audience to twig quickly what comic failing they were to be amused by.

Having decided what the foible will be, you then put the character in precisely the situation where their foible will be most exercised. A misogynist has to be in a situation where he has to be nice to women. A miser has to be in a situation where money needs to be spent – and so on. The more varied and interesting ways you can think of to torment your character, the funnier. This is what happens in the John Cleese film *Clockwise*. Here, the comedy deals with an obsessively punctual man who misses a vital train. The technique is not restricted to comedy. *Hamlet* is all about an indecisive man asked to be decisive.

The bottom line is that the more out of character that events demand a character to be, the more intrigued the audience will be. If, for example, there is a character who has a comic phobia about shopping in a supermarket, classic comedy technique demands a scenario that keeps taking that character to the supermarket – with increasing mania that culminates in a funny incident. This technique appears in *A Fish Called Wanda* (1988), in which huge mileage is got out of the simple comic inversion of an animal lover who keeps accidentally killing animals. Incidentally, for some reason three is usually a good number for these sorts of comic events – two is too few and four is overkill. Notice that there are three dogs in *A Fish Called Wanda*, the comedy building to a climax with the third. The trick here is that the audience has fun in the anticipation – anticipation working here as another form of suspense.

The frequent use of three in all kinds of storytelling (for example, Chekhov's play *The Three Sisters,* and fairytales "The Three Bears" and "The Three Little Pigs," etc.) is called triplification. Triplification seems to have an innate appeal to the human mind. *The Simpsons* typically tells jokes in threes, often using visual jokes.

Specific plotting problems: the short film

Short films provide an excellent way for new filmmakers to get into the industry. But they are not easy, simply because there is so little time to impress. Short films need much thought and careful planning.

Short films can be structured as traditional three-act narratives but often they end with a surprise or twist which, in the three-act structure, is actually the first-act turning point, the surprise/obstacle. Using the Smiley/Thompson model, a short film can be structured as normality, protagonist, disturbance, plan and surprise/obstacle.

While the content of a short film can be happy, sad, intellectual, flippant, sick, bizarre – or anything else – an essential ingredient is impact. The short film must grab its audience and leave it with an overwhelmingly powerful impression or thought. Really, whether it is serious or comic, a short film is essentially one gag.

Planning a short film means extensive brainstorming of ideas, indeed, of every moment of the film so that each is as good as it can be. It means utilizing all the tools at your disposal and using them for every second. The tools are plot and style, sound

Development Strategy 26: Writing comedy satire

To create good comic characters, define their character flaws, obsessions or problems, then create an action line which will force them to deal with those character flaws.

26

Questions to ask:

Do I know my character's comic flaws (for example, miserliness)?

Have I brainstormed as many situations as possible that would force the character to deal with these flaws (for example, ways that the miser would be forced to pay out money)?

Am I using triplification to best advantage?

(dialogue, off-screen sound effects, music, voiceover), and visual elements (setting, details on the set, costumes, camera angles).

Common problems with short films

Writers of short films can often lose focus and be tempted to explore characters and ideas that are not central to the film. Often the films fizzle not because the original idea is poor, but because the film's ending does not answer the question stated or implied in the opening. If, for example, the film's topic and question is set up as "will the protagonist succeed in robbing the bank?", the climax cannot be the protagonist's discovery that she was adopted. However well written such a climax is, the film as a whole cannot work because the audience was expecting an answer to A and was given an answer to B.

Overwriting

Most short films are overwritten in first draft. Most first drafts of anything are usually overwritten, so writers should assume it will happen.

Dialogue

Too much dialogue is common. This is normal in a first draft because the writer is exploring the characters' thought progression and speech mannerisms. Writers should make a point of reading dialogue aloud and acting out scenes. This is useful for picking up redundancies and repetitions, as well as establishing pace and flow. Check that:

1. The dialogue is tight and sounds realistic with normally only one or two sentences per speech. Go for economy. Often the essence of the speech is summed up in a couple of lines and the rest can be cut.

2. The dialogue is not sounding "soapy," unless this is intentional.
3. The same thing is not being said in two ways ("I can't open the door!" "The door is jammed!").
4. The script is not stating what the audience can see for itself – unless it is to illustrate an emotional response from a character.
5. Arguing characters are engaged in productive conflict rather than redundant repetitive name-calling, or "yes, you did," "no, I didn't" type exchanges.
6. Subtext and silence are being used as tools.
7. Scenes end on a question.
8. The script is not overly concerned with getting over backstory.
9. Backstory is relevant and exposition is not clumsy.

See also Chapter 14 "Dialogue." See also Robert McKee, *Story*, "Scene Analysis."

Sound and visuals

Writers rarely make enough use of music (for comic or atmospheric effect) or visuals or action. The visual – what the camera sees and what the actors are doing – is as much a writing tool as words and silences. That said, do not feel you need to record every camera angle on the page, but have a strong sense of the camera in your head. Always visualize the scene, including moves. If an actor can think of a more sophisticated move, this is fine, but writers need to think action.

Plot and characterization

Make sure that everything on the screen is enriching and demonstrating the core idea. Do not get distracted by minor characters. Do not, for example, give long speeches or much time to characters who are only facilitating the action (the doorman whose job is simply to open the door, etc.). Stick with the protagonist and the antagonist. In a short film there is little time for action that is not specific to the main idea.

Going to second draft of a short film

First-draft stage inevitably sees the writer too close to the film. Consciously be objective and focus on basic structural issues. Before rewriting a piece, think and plan. Firstly, define what the chosen medium is supposed to do. A short film is supposed to grab its audience quickly with a striking, thought-provoking idea.

Regard the second draft as a way of lifting your game. The second draft requires the objective examination of every line of dialogue, every event and every character to see how much it is contributing towards the main idea of the film. Sum up this idea – the point of the film, its essence – in a sentence. If you are unable to do this, you do not have a clear aim. Do not proceed until you are happy with your "logline."

If the main idea of the film has shifted, there are a couple of choices. Either you can go with the new element, making sure that you change the start of the film so that the ending answers the question you set up at the start. Or, you can remove that element and store it away for another project. If you keep the new element along with the original, you will not only water down your original idea but you risk wasting the power of the new element.

New writers often feel compelled to put into their current project every element that occurs to them – the good one-liner they overheard, the weird character they saw on the bus. Be more relaxed. This is not the last thing you are going to write. If the new idea is genuinely useful in transmitting the original idea, include it. If not, put the new idea down in your notebook.

Layout

Make sure your film uses professional layout or you put yourself at a serious disadvantage. Not only does it makes you look like an amateur, but it interferes with the process of script-reading. A script is a blueprint for a movie – a plan to be read. People reading your script are attempting to visualize and hear how it would play on screen. They are reading for timing. If they have to untangle weird layout or plough through too many stage directions or camera angles they lose the pace of the film.

Possible topics for a short film

Here are some useful triggers for a short film:

- a genre, myth, or fairytale – love story, thriller, spy, science fiction
- a spoof of one of the above
- a proverb
- a cryptic phrase
- a theme
- a character
- a vice
- a motto.

Development Strategy 27: Writing short films

27

Structure the film with a view to impact, whether you are using one or three acts.

Questions to ask:

Is this the most powerful original idea and scenario I can think of?

Have I structured it properly and, if I am ending on the first-act turning point, is the twist powerful enough?

Am I answering the question I set up?

Is the dialogue overwritten?

Am I planning every moment and making best use of scenario, dialogue, characterization, sound, and visuals?

Specific plotting problems: the journey film

The journey film is such a popular form and one that so persistently fails in development that it is worth special attention. Writers are attracted to the journey film because it seems to embody action and build in opportunities for interesting encounters. This is certainly true, and it is one of the reasons why the journey is one of the oldest literary forms, where it is known as "picaresque."

While a journey may seem like a very obvious and easy means to take a character or a group of characters through an exciting story, it is fraught with difficulties. This is partly because it can so easily fragment into adventures, and partly because it is so easy for the writer to mistake physical movement on the part of the characters for movement in plot and character. It is very easy to keep creating different versions of the same scene, featuring the same unchanged protagonist.

If there is no ongoing central problem that the protagonist has to cope with in the course of the journey on the road – no incremental plot – what the writer is left to create is a hundred minutes of random adventures on the road. Creating separate adventures is actually much harder than creating a rising three-act narrative because each new character or situation on the way has to be set up from scratch. Nothing appearing earlier in the script will assist here. It is back to square one every time.

The effect of this is that each stop on the protagonist's journey becomes one gag – one sketch – and new characters almost inevitably present as stereotypes (protagonist meets shyster, protagonist meets raunchy girl, protagonist meets thug, etc.).

Monty Python and the Holy Grail (1975) – a very poor journey movie made by some of the world's most brilliant comedians – shows how the process can defeat even the very best writers. Typical of poor journey movies, *Monty Python and the Holy Grail* has brilliant moments between long stretches of boredom. It is really a series of comic sketches. It gets boring because there is no plot to follow and the film is standing or falling on the strength of each individual sketch.

Lack of action and relationship lines means that there is no story to engage and hold – nothing, as it were, to go anywhere. The effect of this is to deprive the story of any suspense or urgency – because suspense and urgency can only come out of a *sequence* of events. Take suspense and urgency out of a scripted piece and you remove the audience's ability to care about the characters.

Good journey films (like *Thelma and Louise, The African Queen*, and *Planes, Trains and Automobiles*) are pleasing not only because they have a strong action line but because each step in the action line causes a change in the central characters, a step in their emotional journey, whether comic or tragic. *The Remains of the Day* offers a variant in that while each step of the journey provides a new insight into the protagonist in the present, each step also triggers a flashback which illuminates the present. Journey stories often occur in flashback narrative (see Chapter 8).

Clockwise, another journey film out of the Python stable, is a lot more successful because it utilizes a three-act narrative with the requisite building blocks of suspense – disturbance, first- and second-act turning points, complications, and final climax. A fanatically punctual headmaster sets out on a journey to a conference. He misses his train and comic disaster builds upon comic disaster as he tries to get to the conference, culminating in his final and very late arrival, barely clothed and, to the other conference goers, apparently deranged. The film works well because each incident on the journey builds and complicates the comic disaster – in fact each incident creates the next, finishing in a comic climax. Without a structure, the film would simply have involved a character driving towards the north of England and having adventures on the way.

The best way to approach a journey film is to think of it first not in terms of its action line – that is, what physically happens on the journey – but in terms of its relationship line – that is, where the journey will take the characters emotionally and spiritually. All good journey films are actually emotional journeys.

Once you know the nature of the characters' emotional journey, you can choose a suitable kind of journey as the action line that will best display it. The next task is to select events that will happen on the journey not randomly but specifically on the basis of their capacity to move each character one emotional step forward. You will need to decide whether unfinished business at the journey's end is the point of the story as in *Priscilla, Queen of the Desert*, or whether the story of the film is contained in the journey, and what happens at the journey's end is merely the inevitable climax of what has happened before (as in *Thelma and Louise* and *Planes, Trains and Automobiles*). Films that are about unfinished business at the journey's end will make the physical journey end in the second act and use the third act to deal with the unfinished business, finalizing it in the climax, whereas films that are about the journey itself will use the third act to depict the final battle in the journey, with the climax answering the questions raised by the adventures of the journey.

Development Strategy 28: Writing journey films

Define the emotional journey you want to occur, then find a physical journey that will facilitate it.

Questions to ask:

Do I know what the characters' emotional journey is?

Is the point of the journey the incidents on the way, or the unfinished business at the journey's end?

Am I including events and characters for their own sake or for how they will impel the relationship and action lines?

Do events build on each other, or am I creating separate adventures?

28

Rewrites and problem-solving generally

By the time the script has been written to first draft, most writers are highly subjective about it and find it difficult to approach with objectivity. When going to second draft, it helps to assume that staying objective is going to be difficult and to consciously employ techniques to counteract the subjectivity and high level of emotional commitment. It helps to rerun the script through the Development Strategies right from Development Strategy 1 onwards. This is because, even with the most rigorous planning, the thrust of a film can change when it gets onto the page. This might mean, for example, that the first-act turning point is not what the film is 'about', and/or the climax is not answering the question raised by the first-act turning point. Another common problem is that a structural or character point might have been very well planned but forgotten in the actual writing.

Enriching the film can be achieved by going to Development Strategy 3, which is "genre = relevant emotion + pattern + real + unusual." Here, the idea is to look at the first draft and ask again what genre the film is, and therefore what emotions one is trying to arouse in the audience. Is the first draft succeeding in this area? Can it be improved? Is the pattern accurate but unclichéd? Finally, is the material real but unusual enough?

Development Strategy 29: Staying objective at second draft

Assume that objectivity is going to be difficult. Be prepared for the fact that the script might have changed focus in the writing and that you might have planned things that did not get successfully onto paper. Go back to the text and apply each Development Strategy, with all its questions, in turn and as objectively as possible.

Questions to ask:

Am I still in the same film?

Is my story sentence still the same?

Is it real but unusual enough?

Am I creating enough of the emotions demanded by the genre – for example, if the film is a thriller, am I creating enough excitement, suspense, anxiety, surprise, etc.?

Is the first-act turning point still what the film is about?

Does the climax still answer the question of what the film is about?

Are my action and relationship lines properly in place and functioning?

29

Many screenwriting problems do not call for great wisdom or profound mastery of technique. Rather, they call for a methodical, analytical approach that boils down to the maxim "look before you leap."

Using criticism to best advantage

When a script comes back from readers with a range of criticisms, pressure can push filmmakers to plunge straight into rewrites without diagnosing the exact nature of the criticisms or the range of possible answers. This is understandable but very dangerous because it can mean changes are locked in before problems have been properly diagnosed. Diagnosis of this kind requires a return to the basic diagnostic and brainstorming skills of Development Strategies 1 and 2.

As an example of how careful diagnosis can help in solving a faulty script, let us return to the example given earlier of a script coming back from readers with the general criticism that the female characters are too passive. The first step here is the very obvious one of *defining the task at hand* (Development Strategy 1) to pinpoint exactly what problem you are supposed to be tackling before choosing an answer and scripting scenes.

The key Development Strategy 1 questions you need to address are: Do I know the task here? What is the next step here? What is causing the problem here? Am I sure that this really is the problem, or could it be only a symptom of another problem, for example, what film we're in?

Although we know only a minimal amount about this particular script, we can open up a whole range of interesting plot and characterization possibilities just by targeting the task, in this case, by asking three questions:

1. What, precisely, is being criticized?
2. Is the readers' diagnosis accurate?
3. What solutions are possible?

1. What, precisely, is being criticized?

First of all, it is vital to know what is meant by "passive." The readers' understanding of the term might differ markedly from yours. You can't fix something until you know what it is you are supposed to fix. For example, by "passive," one reader might simply mean a character who is not doing enough on screen. That person might simply want you to give the character more action. But a militant feminist criticizing women characters as "passive" might want the film's women to be politically aware and active. Thus, for every reason (including finding out whether you and your collaborators are "in the same film"), get your readers to give you a precise definition, with examples from the text.

2. Is the readers' diagnosis correct?

The sort of definitions of "passive" you might get are things like: reactive rather than proactive, not doing enough, predictable, wooden, stereotyped, weak, irritatingly sweet, etc. But it might be that what the readers are interpreting as passivity in the female characters alone is actually a symptom of a poor and clichéd plot and characterization generally. So, a remedy would have to tackle significant plot and characterization changes throughout, rather than fine-tuning to one set of characters. The wise course is to look carefully at all possible causes of the passivity problem. It is also important to check what, if anything, is good or useful about the passivity, so you can incorporate it in some other way. For example, the passivity might be the only factor forcing a weak male protagonist to act.

3. What solutions are possible?

With this wide range of possible questions, many answers are possible. To find a good range of answers you need to use Development Strategy 2.

Using Development Strategy 2 to find a range of responses

Development Strategy 2 is about staying real but unusual. The key questions you need to address are: Is the idea credible enough? Is the idea unusual enough? Is what I am plotting credible enough? Is what I am plotting unusual enough? Have I let my lateral imagination generate enough ideas? Once I've got all the lateral ideas, am I using vertical imagination to filter out poor ones?

The task in the present instance is to find a range of possible responses to the problem of readers complaining of "passive female characters." Remember, the point at this stage is to be open to every kind of response. Do not worry if some seem to overlap.

Possible responses

Here is a list of possible responses to the charge "passive female characters."

1. Go to other readers.
2. Ditch the project.
3. Define the original themes and ideas behind the script and consider whether a different scenario would carry the ideas better, for example, using an antagonist who changes massively, as in the "prude to action hero" model.
4. If the film is a comedy, think of it as a tragedy, so as to spark ideas. If it is a tragedy, think of it as a comedy to spark ideas.
5. Remove all women from the plot.
6. Remove all men from the plot and make the entire cast female.
7. Reverse current male and female roles.
8. Combine characters to make them richer.
9. Pull against the stereotype – for example, if a female character is a stereotypical housewife, give her a non-stereotypical hobby, obsession or approach to life.
10. Make the women's passivity a comic or dramatic feature to be built upon, say, in a subplot. (For example, the women's passivity means they do not notice something vital happening or, as in *The Stepford Wives* (1975), the women's passivity is a vital clue in the plot.)
11. Make the women passive-aggressive for added conflict.
12. Scrap all current female characters completely and invent new ones.
13. Keep useful characteristics from female characters and re-use them in new characters. For example, the plot might require a new female character to have the same profession as her earlier passive version.

14. Add a new character or twist to the plot which can somehow galvanize the passive female characters into action.
15. Think of unusual ways to make the women interact more dynamically with the men. For example, turn the male protagonist's wife into his mother, sister or daughter.
16. Give a female character her own perspective on the main plot, which might be in opposition to the male protagonist's perspective. For example, make the major antagonist a proactive female.
17. Look for a model for the story in folk tale, genre, or myth that might help with new and interesting ideas for how the females could be more proactive.
18. Insert more conflict between characters generally.

Choosing a real but unusual answer

The last step of Development Strategy 2 is to choose, out of all the possibilities, a real but unusual answer. Vertical skills will have to be involved here to check not only for the best answer, but for any unforeseen consequences effect of changes. For example, will the story be completely distorted by the changes? Will new characters pull focus away from men? If so, does this need balancing? What will the audience's expectations be now that character balance has changed? Will the females have to figure much more prominently in the climax?

Notice that each of the eighteen possible responses could be used as a springboard to more detailed responses. For example, suggestion 16, 'giving a female character her own perspective on the main plot', could be brainstormed to provide a whole range of different possible perspectives, which in turn could be dramatized in a huge variety of ways. What is being tackled are the *ideas* behind any rewrites.

Note that while responses 1 and 2 ('go to other readers', and 'ditch the project') may initially seem flippant, in fact they do offer sensible alternatives. Perhaps the current reader (or producer) is simply wrong for this project. Perhaps the project is indeed not worth pursuing.

Structural analysis of *The Piano*

The Piano is a powerful and compelling film built on a fine three-act structure and containing interesting use of myth and symbolism. It is a very useful illustration of the structural components described in this chapter. Use it for reference and exercises. For example, as an exercise in understanding the narrative sentence of the hero's journey, apply them to *The Piano*.

Origins

The film *The Piano* sprang from Jane Campion's idea of writing a film about a repressed Victorian woman finding sexuality and self-expression. The plotline involving the arranged marriage and the lost piano came later. In other words, *The Piano* came from an idea for a relationship line, and the action line was invented to permit the relationship line to happen.

Structural breakdown of the action line following the nine-point plan

1. Normality
Ada's life in Scotland.

2. Disturbance
Going to New Zealand to be married.

3. Protagonist
Split between Ada and her daughter. Together they form one complete person, the protagonist. The child is both Ada's voice and her conscience. Note how Campion cuts constantly from Ada to the child, who either acts out what her mother is feeling – from dancing along the beach with joy when her mother is playing the piano with joy, to caressing the trees after her mother has caressed Baines – to cartwheeling at the end of the movie – or else acts out the opposite – most crucially, going to Stewart and not Baines with the piano key.

4. Plan
To continue her silent protest, expressing her emotions only through the piano.

5. Surprise
Ada is not allowed to bring the piano – her voice – from the beach to the house.

6. Obstacle
Because she is not allowed to bring the piano to the house, she is unfulfilled, she cannot "speak." She has to get back the piano to fulfil her plan (to express herself only through the piano). This is the problem/need that drives the rest of the film. Getting the piano back is what the film is about.

The surprise plus the obstacle form the first-act turning point.

7. Complications
Act two contains all of the obstacles which prevent Ada from fulfilling her plan to express herself through the piano:

- Stewart will not bring back the piano.
- Ada goes to Baines with a note, but he cannot read.
- When the child explains, Baines refuses to take her to the beach.
- Baines finally takes Ada to the beach to play the piano but does not bring it back.
- Baines offers Stewart some land in exchange for the piano on the condition that Ada teach him.
- The piano is dropped on its way back from the beach.
- Ada insists the piano is hers, but Stewart insists she give it up and teach Baines so he can have the land.
- Ada refuses to teach Baines because the piano must be out of tune which would distress her.

- The piano has been tuned so she teaches him.
- Baines offers the bargain – one key per visit.
- The daughter wants to come in – she might betray them, thus prevent the bargain being paid out and the piano returned.
- Baines wants her to strip for him – five keys.
- The music-lesson sham is almost exposed at the Bluebeard play.
- Baines wants more – ten keys to lie with her.
- The little girl sees and caresses the trees, stopped by Stewart – will he find out? Little girl says "I know why Mr Baines can't play the piano," but Stewart doesn't understand.
- Baines gives the piano back saying it's turning Ada into a whore and he wants her to love him.
- Stewart, thinking he'll have to pay for the piano, offers it back to Baines.
- Baines says he can keep it.
- Now that Ada has got the piano back, she suddenly finds it is not enough for her – it will no longer fully express her emotions. She now needs Baines and the piano. (Note now the complications involve not getting just the piano but getting Baines *and* the piano. Some analysts would call this act four.)
- Ada goes to Baines. He tells her to go, opens the door for her to go, so she hits him. They make passionate love.
- Stewart accidentally sees them! Will he stop them? Stop them violently?
- Stewart does not stop them. He lies under the house listening. Baines says "If you care, come back tomorrow."
- When Ada goes back the next day, Stewart catches and tries to rape her.
- Maoris are bashing at the piano. (If they destroy it, this is an obstruction.)
- Stewart barricades Ada in the house.
- Ada starts playing the piano in her sleep. (Is this impending madness? If so, it will be a very effective obstruction to getting Baines and piano.)
- Ada tries to express her sexuality with Stewart. (If she can, she won't need Baines.)
- Baines is leaving in a few days. (If he's gone, she can't have him.)
- Ada keeps trying with Stewart but won't let him touch her. (Is she falling for him? This would obstruct her need for Baines.)
- Stewart is touched by Ada's advances. He takes down the barricades. (Is Ada falling in love with him?)
- Having taken down the barricades, Stewart gets her to promise not to see Baines. (Another obstruction.)
- Ada writes "George, you have my heart," on a piano key and gives it to the child to take to Baines – but the child takes it to Stewart.

Second-act turning point: *Stewart goes crazy, chops off Ada's fingertip, which stymies her because she cannot play properly.*
> *This is Ada's lowest point, her brush with death. Will Stewart kill her?*

In act three:

- Stewart tries to initiate sex with Ada (Will she? Has he beaten her into submission?)
- Ada stops him with a strange look. He sets off with his gun to see Baines. (Will he kill Baines?)
- Stewart tells Baines that Ada's telepathy asked him to let her go with Baines. Stewart tells Baines to take her.
- Ada and Baines leave with the piano.

8. CLIMAX

Ada pushes the piano overboard, thereby rejecting it as her only instrument for expression! (Now she only has Baines.) But she catches her foot in the rope. It pulls her over into the sea where she seems destined to drown. (If she dies, she certainly won't fulfil her plan.) She decides to live. (Note, this is a brilliant double climax.)

9. Resolution

Ada is living with Baines. She is a music teacher with a silver fingertip (made by Baines), teaching herself to speak.

Action and relationship lines

The action line concerns Ada coming to New Zealand for an arranged marriage to a stiff, repressed husband. In the action line, the protagonist is Ada, plus her agent, her daughter, and the antagonist is Stewart. The non-human antagonist is Victorian morality, embodied in the Europeans (as opposed to the Maoris, who are comfortable with sexuality). Stewart, the antagonist, does not change.

The relationship line is the growing love between Ada and Baines, and the journey travelled by the protagonist Ada is a journey through sexual awakening into sexual and emotional fulfillment. Ada is the protagonist with Baines the antagonist in the relationship line. Baines is an antagonist who changes, falling in love with the protagonist. But the greatest change is in Ada, the protagonist. As commonly happens, the action line was invented to permit the relationship line to happen.

There is another minor plot about Stewart buying Maori land. This serves to show Stewart as greedy and unresponsive, a man without spirituality and intuition. The Bluebeard play is a kind of symbolic setup that pays off in the actual finger-chopping.

As normal, the second act is largely concerned with the relationship line. The climax of the action line and relationship lines occurs in the same scene, where Ada chooses life over death and silence.

Unities

The first big scene – in which Ada lands on the beach – is duplicated in the climax scene, where Ada and Baines are leaving and Ada chooses to live. Note also the unity in the script whereby Ada's first words and the opening words are "The voice you hear is my mind's voice at six years old." Ada adds later in the same scene that: "Silence affects everyone in the end'" The last words of the film are all about silence.

Symbolism

The plots and setting of a good film operate as the mental landscape of the protagonist. They are metaphors for the character's mental state.

The Piano functions against the setting of two real landscapes which have enormous metaphorical/symbolic power as symbols of sexuality. These are water (particularly the ocean, but also rain and water generally) and the wild forest. Fire is another potent symbol which Jane Campion in this instance does not use, except in the child's tall story about the death of her father, in which he is struck by lightning.

These images of storm, water, wild nature and fire are, of course, the stock in trade of Gothic fiction which, like *The Piano*, is driven by repressed sexuality. In classic Gothic style, Campion uses symbols of wild nature to externalize sexual crisis – like a storm to externalize Stewart's jealous rage just before he chops off the finger, and the pelting rain to accompany Stewart's rape. Note that the Maoris often appear naked or half-naked against water, which symbolizes their relaxed attitude towards sexuality (compared with the overdressed, repressed Europeans, whose clothes drag in the water and the mud). The Maoris actually call Stewart "old dry-balls." The uneducated Baines, who wears the Maori tattoos on his face and is powerfully driven sexually, occupies the middle ground between the two races.

The piano is another symbol, this time of western culture and the sublimated, controlled sexual passion of the nineteenth century. Jane Campion added the piano to the plot because she wanted a way to explore the dawning sexuality of a repressed Victorian woman. For Ada, the piano is her voice, her passions. Only when she is playing the piano can she speak. It is her emotional self, her passionate self, which Victorian society would seek to suppress. The juxtaposition of the piano against a raging sea operates on a powerful emotional level. The subliminal effect of these symbols – which flash up constantly and naturally in the background – is to reinforce the sexuality and passion of the plot. On a less primeval level, there is a whole symbolism of angels (western asexual creatures), which starts the moment Ada and the little girl land on the beach and the Maoris say they look like angels, to the last part of the film where the angel's wings (western asexuality) are swept back and forth through the ocean.

Myths

As we have seen above, many great films and novels link in to folk tales and myths as well as Jungian archetypes. *The Piano* links into many powerful myths, most obviously Beauty and the Beast, and Sleeping Beauty (awoken by a kiss).

To summarize, we can find elements of the following mythical/fairytale components.

- Beauty and the Beast
- Sleeping Beauty/enchanted princess
- Faustian bargain
- Folktales in which the protagonist is forced to perform onerous tasks, often nightly, to gain freedom
- Ada having a telepathic "dark power."

7. Alternative narrative structures: flashback

E arlier chapters dealt with different ways of creating a classic three-act narrative structure. These days, filmmakers are becoming increasingly interested in moving away from the standard three-act form, resulting in films that use several narratives running in parallel, films like *Pulp Fiction*, *Magnolia*, *The Green Mile*, *Shine*, *Go*, *The Sweet Hereafter*, *American Beauty*, *The End of the Affair* and many others, including most of Woody Allen's films.

These alternative structures are now so much part of mainstream cinema that it is no longer enough to study traditional narrative alone. Writers have no choice but to master the new parallel storytelling. And it is a hard task because films like these are complex, even paradoxical. Why do flashbacks in *The Remains of the Day* work to humanize and explain its central character, the stiff-backed Mr Stevens, while flashbacks in *Citizen Kane* or *The Usual Suspects* work to make the audience feel that Kane or the sleazy Verbal are ultimately unfathomable, even sinister? How does a writer go about writing a screenplay like *The Sweet Hereafter*, which uses nine different time-frames to tell eleven different stories? How do films like *The Big Chill* or *Tea with Mussolini* or *American Beauty* succeed when they are clearly following the journeys of a number of people rather than one clear protagonist? If you are trying to create a film to showcase the talents of forty actors, just where do you start?

Parallel storytelling needs serious analysis. The triumph of the three-act structure is its capacity for creating strong narrative that builds towards a suspenseful climax. Good and reliable ways to unfold character, action line and relationship line are built in to the model as the result of centuries, perhaps millennia, of experiment. Today, the form is still capable of producing films as fresh and original as *Being John Malkovich*. Any writer who rejects the classic model needs to find new ways to solve these basic storytelling problems of suspenseful narrative, good characterization, meaning, and closure. How and where can we start? Are there any rules or guidelines? What are the structural pitfalls? How can the old knowledge help us to do something new?

In fact the answers are closer than we might think. While we are used to regarding parallel storytelling as a departure from the three-act structure, in fact all of the new narrative forms rely heavily on the traditional rising three-act model to create jeopardy, unity, pace, and closure in both their individual narratives and across the film as a whole.

Parallel storytelling is a vast and exciting topic and deserves the degree of study and analysis given for years to the classic three-act model. The following chapters can only make a start, offering some observations and guidelines about the nuts and bolts of a number of different parallel storytelling structures.

Varieties of parallel narrative

There are four main categories of parallel narrative:

- There is *flashback narrative* of various kinds as used in *Shine, The Green Mile, The Sweet Hereafter,* and *Citizen Kane,* which involve a story in the present and at least one story in the past, and also in films using one recurrent flashback, such as *Catch-22.*
- There is *tandem narrative,* which uses interconnected stories running in parallel, seen in *City of Hope, Magnolia, Short Cuts,* and *Crimes and Misdemeanors.*
- There is *sequential narrative,* seen in *Pulp Fiction* and *Go,* where stories are told in sequence and a final section ties them together.
- Finally, there is *multiple protagonist–antagonist narrative,* as seen in various sorts of 'ensemble' films like *The Big Chill, The Magnificent Seven, American Beauty, Tea with Mussolini* and *Saving Private Ryan.* Here, instead of following events as experienced by one protagonist, the film uses multiple protagonists or antagonists who are all versions of the same character (for example, 'the radical student ten years on', 'the resident of Middle America', 'the English speaking lady in Italy during World War II', 'the mercenary'), and whose individual stories make up a range of possible responses to the same situation.

Within these categories there are sometimes subcategories. Studied in the following chapters are:

Flashback narrative

- Flashback as thwarted dream (for example, *Shine, The Remains of the Day*)
- Flashback as case history (for example, *Citizen Kane, The Usual Suspects*)
- Subsets of flashback narrative, including flashback as life-changing incident (for example, *Catch-22*); flashback as illustration (for example, *Crimes and Misdemeanors*); autobiographical flashback narrative (for example, *The End of the Affair, There's Something About Mary*).

Tandem narrative

For example, *Crimes and Misdemeanors, City of Hope, Magnolia, Short Cuts*

Sequential narrative

For example, *Pulp Fiction, Go*

Multiple protagonists–antagonists
- Reunion films (for example, *The Big Chill*)
- Mission films (for example, *The Magnificent Seven*, *Saving Private Ryan*)
- Siege films (for example, *Tea with Mussolini*, *American Beauty*)

Narrative told in flashbacks

Flashback narrative, seen in films like *Shine*, *The Sweet Hereafter*, *The Green Mile*, *Citizen Kane*, *The Remains of the Day*, *The English Patient*, and many others, is one of the most exciting storytelling techniques available to screenwriters. By permitting the telling of at least two stories in different time-frames in tandem, it blows open the traditional, sequential, three-act narrative structure in the most radical way. It offers writers a freedom and range that is dazzling, making possible films like *The Sweet Hereafter*, which successfully handles complex emotional stories in multiple time-frames.

Through flashback narrative, the audience can relive the past rather than just hearing about it. Flashback narrative can deliver two or more powerful films in one. It can transmit what might have been as well as what was. It can create and maintain high levels of suspense. It works equally well for comedy as for drama. It can give an epic grandeur to a film and it is unequalled in taking us inside a character's mind.

Unfortunately, narrative flashback wrongly used is a recipe for disaster. Instead of involving the audience, it irritates and alienates. Instead of giving a film more impact, it slows it down, and instead of explaining, it confuses. Poor use of flashbacks can result in a potentially fine film like *Mr. Saturday Night* reaching the screen so seriously damaged that the performances by the most skilled of actors cannot properly redeem it (see Chapter 13, 'Lost in the telling').

What causes this? Is it because the writer has chosen an unsuitable plot? Is it because flashbacks have been put in the wrong place or contain the wrong sort of material? Can we set down any rules or patterns at all to identify why and how flashback narrative works and when it can be used to best advantage?

There do seem to be certain plots, patterns, and "rules" that occur in films successfully utilizing flashback narrative. Indeed, certain films can actually act as models.

What is flashback narrative?

Firstly, we need to define what we mean by flashback narrative. In its simplest form, flashback narrative structure uses a series of flashbacks to construct an entire story in the past that runs in tandem with a story in the present. In some cases flashbacks are used to tell a number of stories in the past, and more recently the *flashforward* has appeared, which deals with stories in the future of central characters.

While flashback narrative could be defined as a form which tells a number of stories in parallel and moves between time frames, this is inadequate because there are other films that use parallel storytelling and a range of time frames but do not employ flashbacks at all, for example, *Pulp Fiction*. What sets flashback narrative apart is that it is a form crucially concerned with memories and the impact of the past upon the present. An easy way to think of this is that while normally a film is written to make the audience wonder what *will* happen, a film using flashback narrative is written to make the audience wonder *what happened in the past*.

Another significant difference between the parallel stories in films like *Pulp Fiction* and *Crimes and Misdemeanors* and the parallel stories in flashback narrative is that all the stories in *Pulp Fiction* and *Crimes and Misdemeanors* have equal importance. No one story solves the mystery of another.

In flashback narrative, as a general rule, the story in the past is much more important than the story in the present – indeed, in some cases the story in the present is skeletal or truncated, as in *Citizen Kane*. But more recent versions of flashback narrative are moving towards increasingly complex stories in the present (for example, *The End of the Affair, The Sweet Hereafter, Courage Under Fire*), and even the future (*The Sweet Hereafter*). Greater complexity is probably the way of things to come.

Other versions of flashback

Before examining flashback narrative in detail, it is necessary to say a few words about other uses of flashback which can occur within or alongside flashback as thwarted dream or flashback as case history – indeed, can even sometimes occur independently. These categories are flashback as illustration, flashback as life-changing incident and autobiographical flashback narrative.

Flashback as illustration

This is when, for example, a suspect in a detective film set in the present relates their version of what happened at the scene of the crime while the account is depicted on screen. What differentiates this sort of flashback from those that occur in flashback narrative? The main difference is the matter of focus on the past. While films using flashback narrative have the past as their main focus and usually tell a whole story, flashback as illustration is a device to make the character's dilemma in the present more vivid. An example of this sort of flashback occurs in *Crimes and Misdemeanors*, in which a man is guiltily remembering an affair. This use of flashback should not be confused with what occurs in a film like *The Usual Suspects*. In *The Usual Suspects*, flashbacks do indeed illustrate the story of a criminal who is being interviewed, but the film is much more concerned with the past than the present – indeed, it tells a whole story in the past. The latter is a significant difference. Flashback as illustration often tells only fragments of the story, and tells them out of sequence. Frequently, the function of flashback as illustration is merely to show a character's state of mind at that moment.

Flashback as life-changing incident

Flashback as life-changing incident is another device often used for showing a character's state of mind at one particular moment. This sort of flashback is seen in *Catch-22*, with the flashback about the protagonist's horrific experience on the plane. Of course, *Catch-22* contains a variety of flashback forms, but its version of flashback as life-changing incident is typical. One ominous, incomplete flashback occurs incrementally throughout the film until, at the film's climax, it appears in its shocking entirety, revealing the mysteries and motives of the protagonist. The flashback will typically appear at moments of trauma for the protagonist. For a detailed discussion of *Catch-22*, see pp. 125-126.

Autobiographical flashback narrative

This is when a narrator initiates a flashback narrative about their own life. It affects certain structural decisions. This is discussed in detail in Chapter 8, in connection with films like *The End of the Affair* and *There's Something About Mary*.

Plot requirements in flashback narrative

Films utilizing flashback narrative structure are always a kind of detective story, usually a *detective story of the heart*, exploring human passions and secrets, often over a person's entire life. This detective story is always connected with the emotional life and personal relationships of an *enigmatic outsider* figure. Typically, the film will start with the sudden appearance of such a figure, usually at a moment of serious crisis or danger in their lives. Explaining how the enigmatic outsider came to be in this situation makes up the greater part of the film, and anecdotes and memories always figure.

Frequently, the central tension of the film concerns a conflict between the enigmatic outsider's personal life or well-being and their professional duties. In autobiographical flashback narrative, the enigmatic outsider is usually the person the speaker is most concerned with, often a lost lover (this can be seen in autobiographical flashback love stories as different as *The End of the Affair* and *There's Something About Mary*). The same rules apply to this sort of outsider as to others, namely, that flashbacks deal with their appearance and history, and a conflict between desires and duty is central to their problems.

Requirements of the story in the past and the story in the present

The story in the past is usually a story of relationships and great passion, often of epic proportions. The story in the present, while typically skeletal, often features a spiritual journey or quest, and its structural role is to permit an investigation or revisiting of the traumatic past. The story in the present always contains a person or people asking questions, except in voiceover autobiographies that use flashback narrative (for example, *The End of the Affair* and *There's Something About Mary*) where nobody needs to ask questions about the past because the protagonist is talking about it voluntarily. While these days more emphasis is being put on the story in the present, the typical, traditional way that flashback narrative divides its plot material between past and present is very similar to the common division between action line and relationship line in a normal three-act structure. That is, normally, the story in the present can be thought of as being primarily the film's action line, with the story in the past – which always concerns the enigmatic outsider's personal relationships – being primarily the film's relationship line. The story in the past is pegged to the story in the present, with the story in the present being the scenario that permits it to proceed. Thus, in *The English Patient* the story in the present permits the relationship line set in the past to be told, just as the action line of *The African Queen* (the journey down the river to the great lake) enables the relationship line (love between Rose and Allnutt).

Three-act structure in flashback narrative

One of the most interesting things about flashback narrative is that while it seems to represent a complete breakaway from the three-act model, in fact, except in special cases, each of the two stories, past and present, is structured according to the traditional three-act model. Moreover, successful movement between the two stories depends on bouncing from one to the other at significant moments within the three-act structure.

Action and relationship lines

The story in the present will often have a three-act structure only in a truncated or skeletal form (this is particularly so of early flashback films like *Citizen Kane*). While the story in the present will be most concerned with action and the story in the past will be most concerned with relationships, nevertheless each of the two stories will contain an action line and a relationship line. Further, each of the two stories will feature the enigmatic outsider as either protagonist or antagonist.

This structure is clearly visible in *Shine*. *Shine*'s "film in the past" has the pianist David Helfgott as its protagonist. Its action line is the story of Helfgott's musical career from his boyhood through to his mental collapse and stay in a halfway house. The relationship line deals with his traumatic relationship with his father (in which musical success starts out being necessary for love, then becomes its enemy). *Shine*'s "film in the present" has an action line demonstrating how David gets out of the halfway house and builds a new musical career. The relationship line in the present shows that a musical career can indeed be compatible with love (this time, with a wife). The climax of both stories is the final successful concert.

The same structure is evident in films like *The Remains of the Day*, *Citizen Kane* and *The Usual Suspects*. In *The Remains of the Day*, the action line in the past is the story of Lord Darlington's naive involvement with Nazi appeasement, and how this impacts on Stevens and Miss Kenton. The relationship line in the past concerns the unspoken love between Stevens and Miss Kenton. In the present, the action line is Stevens' drive cross-country to see Miss Kenton (in which he lies about the past and allows himself to be thought of as a gentleman rather than a butler). The relationship line in the present is his voiceover correspondence and final meeting with Miss Kenton, which ends in love unfulfilled.

In *Citizen Kane*, the action line in the past is Kane's professional career. The relationship line shows his dealings with friends and wives, all of whom he loses. In the present, the action line is the journalist's quest to find documents and individuals capable of revealing the identity of "Rosebud." The relationship line in the present is very thin – in fact, we do not even see the face of Thompson, the journalist–investigator. It seems to consist of the responses – hostile, amused or irritated – of the people Thompson interviews.

In *The Usual Suspects*, the action line in the present is the police and US customs investigation of two survivors of the burnt ship. As in *Citizen Kane*, the relationship line in the present consists of the relationship between investigator and interviewee. In the past story, the action line consists of the deeds of the gang led by Keaton. The relationship line is the relationship between Keaton and Verbal.

Full circle, chronologically

Essentially, both stories unfold in chronological order (although some films will employ flashbacks to depict different versions of the same events, creating a certain overlap). The story in the present is always presented chronologically, with the flashback story pegged to it. When the past has caught up with the present, the flashbacks stop and both stories proceed together, sometimes for an extended final section, sometimes for only a brief conclusion.

More complex versions of the form may use a number of time-frames in the past, and some (like *The Sweet Hereafter,* a film about a lawyer attempting to persuade a small town it should sue for the tragic loss of its children in a school bus accident) use flashforwards, which depict stories set in the future. *The Sweet Hereafter* provides an interesting combination of flashback forms. In the course of jumping between a number of stories and time frames (nine time-frames and eleven stories), it uses both autobiographical flashback (where a protagonist describes in voiceover his experiences and deepening disillusionment as the father of a junkie), and flashback as case history (the story of the survivor of the bus crash, an enigmatic outsider), told through normal narrative.

However, the movement for each story in *The Sweet Hereafter* is still generally chronological, and the story in the present moves strictly chronologically.

The hook/triggering crisis

Like the normal three-act structure, flashback narrative utilizes a strong opening "hook" in the present. This depicts the enigmatic outsider not only as mysterious, but as lost, stranded, on the outside, or in some way shut out – perhaps even dead or dying. In *Shine*, the intriguing hook is the mature David Helfgott speaking in his typically enigmatic and laterally jumbled way – followed by a sequence in which he runs insanely through the rain and ends up banging on the window to be let into Moby's restaurant. In *The English Patient*, the hook is the crazily flying plane, with its apparently sleeping woman passenger, being shot down by German troops in the desert. This is followed by the transportation across the desert of the seriously burnt pilot, wrapped like a mummy. In *The Remains of the Day*, it is when the stately home, which has been butler Stevens' life, is to be auctioned, an event which would shut him out forever. In *Citizen Kane*, the hook and "closeness to death" is an actual deathbed scene, with an intriguing deathbed utterance. In *The Usual Suspects*, it is the dramatic death of Dean Keaton, shot on board a burning trawler.

All films need an intriguing opening hook – a crisis of some kind to get the audience interested in the story. But the hook in films using flashback narrative has a very special function. It is the trigger for two stories. It initiates the story in the present (thus it is the disturbance in the present), and is also the event that sets off the flashbacks to the past. In some films it is also the circumstance that triggers the quest for the lost dream.

Because it triggers so much, it is useful to think of the hook in flashback narrative as the "triggering crisis." The triggering crisis always appears twice, once at the start of the film and again after flashbacks have depicted the story in the past in full (always chronologically) and the past has caught up with present. After the triggering crisis has appeared a second time, there are no more flashbacks. The film either ends, or proceeds with both stories in tandem towards a climax that will resolve each.

Content of the triggering crisis

The content of the triggering crisis is very specific and cannot be chosen at random. It almost always consists of the point in the film at which the enigmatic outsider seems most without hope and closest to real or spiritual death. In films which end up showing a character trying to reclaim a thwarted dream (for example, *Shine* or *The Remains of the Day*) the triggering crisis is usually the second-act turning point, act three being the pursuit and achievement or irrevocable loss of the dream. But in films in which the outsider is dead, dying or incapable of change (for example, *Citizen Kane* or *The Usual Suspects)*, the triggering crisis is the end of the story in the past, often its climax. Flashback as case history and flashback as thwarted dream could be depicted like this:

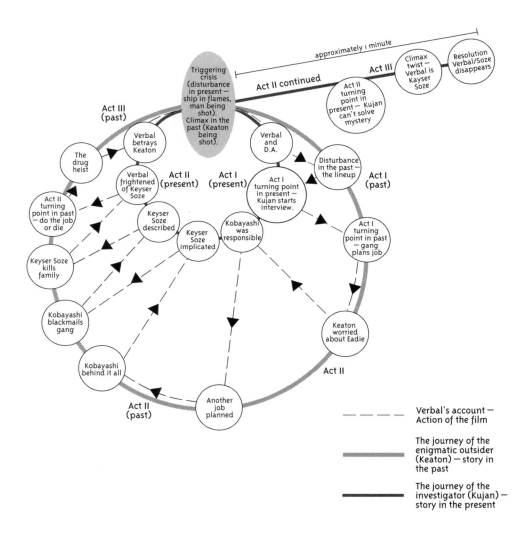

Flashback as case history: The Usual Suspects

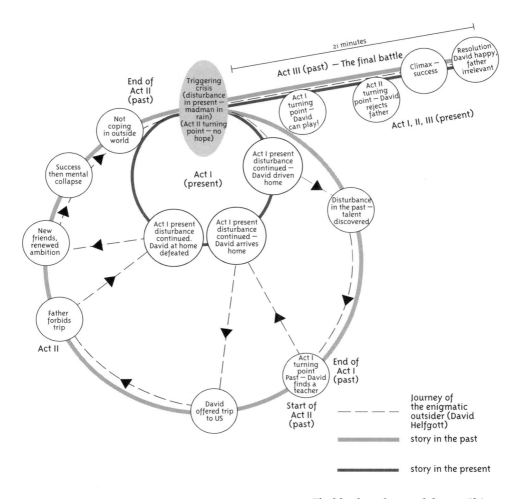

Flashback as thwarted dream: Shine

Examples of the triggering crisis in thwarted dream and case history

In *Shine*, which is about someone achieving their dream, the triggering crisis is the sequence at the start in which David, apparently insane, runs through the rain and bashes crazily on the window of Moby's restaurant, where he is befriended. In the "film in the present," this event marks the disturbance (starting the story of an apparently crazy derelict who progresses from halfway house and loneliness to happy marriage and concert hall success). In the "film in the past," this event marks the second-act turning point, that is, the point at which David is closest to spiritual death. It shows him shut away from everything he holds dear – love, approval, and a piano – with no hope of getting them and with every sign of going mad. After David's past has been explained from boyhood up to the point where the film started (at the point where he is banging on the window of

Moby's, trying to get at their piano), the 'two films' progress in tandem. The climax of both is David's successful concert, where he combines musical achievement with support from his wife, friends and the remains of his family.

But in *Citizen Kane*, a film where the enigmatic outsider is dead at the start of the film (so is unable to pursue a lost dream), the triggering crisis is actually Kane's death. His death marks the end of the story of the past, but triggers the story in the present because Kane's death is the disturbance which causes Thompson, the journalist, to be sent on a mission to find Kane the man via his last word: "Rosebud." After Kane's story has been told all the way up to his death, the story in the past concludes. The story in the present ends with the journalist, still ignorant of the meaning of "Rosebud," concluding that no one can be fully understood by their last words. The climax of the story in the present is a moment of dramatic irony in which the audience, but not the investigator, finds out what "Rosebud" meant.

In *The Remains of the Day*, a film in which the enigmatic outsider pursues the dream depicted in flashbacks, the triggering crisis is when Stevens receives a letter from his lost love – the housekeeper, Miss Kenton – consoling him about the death of his beloved Lord Darlington and the auction of Darlington Hall. This marks the disturbance in the present because it triggers Stevens' quest to bring back the housekeeper. In the "film in the past," it marks the second-act turning point because Stevens, who sacrificed everything for Darlington Hall and its treasonous master, has just lost his master and is now, it seems, about to lose the house.

Stevens sets off on a quest to bring Miss Kenton back, driving across the country to find her. During this car journey, flashbacks tell the story of the relationship between Stevens and Miss Kenton, and the story of foolish Lord Darlington's duping by the Nazis. The flashbacks end when the story in the past has been told all the way up to the point at which the housekeeper leaves to get married and Lord Darlington has aligned himself with the Nazis. In the present, the story has now reached the point where Stevens is about to meet the housekeeper. The rest of the film (which makes up the whole of the film's third act) shows him in the ultimately unsuccessful pursuit of his lost dream, the climax being when Miss Kenton rejects the chance to return to Darlington Hall.

But in *The Usual Suspects*, a film in which the triggering crisis is a death, this death is actually the climax of the story in the past (unlike the death in *Citizen Kane*, which happens some time after the climaxes of Kane's public and personal life). The film opens with the shooting, on board a burning ship, of the enigmatic outsider, the gang leader Keaton. The film is a crime mystery about the manipulation of a gang of criminals by a mysterious arch-criminal, Keyser Soze. The story is told in flashbacks by a minor gang member, Verbal Klint, as he is interviewed by US customs officer Dave Kujan. Kujan is convinced that Keaton is alive, moreover, that Keaton is in fact the arch-criminal Keyser Soze. Kujan's interrogation of Verbal forms half of the story in the present. The rest concerns the interrogation of the other survivor, a Hungarian man badly burned and in hospital. The shipboard fire and murder constitute the disturbance in the present, because they trigger the interrogation of the two survivors. In the story of the past, this event is the climax, because it marks the end of the raid on the ship (action line) and the death of the outsider, Dean Keaton. Verbal Klint's flashbacks depict the formation of the gang, their first successful job, the second job that goes wrong, and their manipulation by the arch-criminal Keyser Soze. Soze forces them to set up a drugs heist on a moored ship. The attempted heist brings the story full circle to the shipboard fire and Dean Keaton's death.

Like *Citizen Kane,* the investigator in the present (Dave Kujan) has learnt a lot about the enigmatic outsider, but by no means all. Like *Citizen Kane,* the climax in the present is a moment of dramatic irony in which, unwitnessed by Kujan, the audience sees the cripple Verbal change into the mysterious arch-criminal Keyser Soze – then melt into nowhere with his offsider, Kobayashi.

Triggering crisis at the disturbance in the past

An exception to the rule of a triggering crisis appearing at the second-act turning point of the story in the past is *The Sweet Hereafter,* in which most of the parallel narratives, past and present, are structured like one-act short films, so do not have a second-act turning point. They show a normality (life before the bus crash), then a disturbance (in all stories set in the town, the bus crash), then end with a dramatic twist on their first-act turning point (response to the bus crash). The film opens with the town immediately after the bus crash (disturbance), and a number of stories show the town's normality in flashbacks until the moment of the crash changed it all. Once the story has gone full circle and the bus crash has been shown on screen, the town's story reverts to the present and events leading up to the main witness giving her statement. So the triggering crisis is actually the disturbance in all the stories, not the second-act turning point. In other words, the circles travelled in each story are smaller, but there are many circles.

Having mostly a one-act structure for the stories is connected to the large number of stories being told (eleven, falling into nine time frames). There is simply not enough time for eleven three-act stories. For a structural breakdown of *The Sweet Hereafter,* see Chapter 10.

8. Varieties of flashback narrative

The last chapter looked at how the triggering crisis was significantly different in narrative flashback films that concluded with a quest for a thwarted dream (flashback as thwarted dream, as in *Shine*) and flashback narrative films where the enigmatic outsider dies or is beyond change (flashback as case history, as in *Citizen Kane*).

In fact this difference is only one of many between these two main sorts of flashback narrative films. Flashback as case history and flashback as thwarted dream are actually two very distinct forms. It is important to understand the differences between the forms because each has very different effects on the audience and each is very specific in terms of plot content. Choosing the right form for the planned story is vital. Never try to create a structure with flashbacks at the post-production stage because it will not work.

Differences between thwarted dream and case history

Before we look at the differences between thwarted dream flashback and case history flashback, note that films using autobiographical flashback operate rather differently and need to be looked at separately (see under the subheading "Autobiographical flashback" toward the end of this chapter). Autobiographical flashback narrative is the sort that has someone speaking in voiceover while their life story is told in flashback (for example, *The End of the Affair*).

Autobiographical flashback aside, the differences between thwarted dream and case history are:

1. Thwarted dream uses flashbacks to make the audience see the enigmatic outsider from the inside, as someone sympathetic who has been damaged by the past; in contrast, case history uses flashbacks to make the audience see the outsider from the outside, as an ultimately unknowable (and often sinister) specimen created by past trauma.

2. In case history, the enigmatic outsider is usually dead. This is a useful tip: if you are planning a flashback film about someone who is dead, you have to use case history.

3. In thwarted dream, the person having the flashbacks is the enigmatic outsider. In case history, the person having the flashbacks is a person or persons who have known the outsider. It is never the outsider because the outsider is dead or, as in *The Sweet Hereafter*, returned from the dead massively changed.

4. The flashbacks in case history give a documentary reality to the action. They make the audience a scientific observer, mystified and often appalled by the outsider, whom the flashbacks do not explain but make more mysterious. In thwarted dream, the flashbacks explain the outsider and make them appealing. They make the audience identify with the outsider.

5. Thwarted dream starts two-thirds through an unfinished story and has a final third (the third act) using new action in the present. This action is the pursuit of the lost dream. Case history starts with a story that is over except for an ironic twist.

As a rule of thumb, if the enigmatic outsider is supposed to be a normal, likeable person damaged by life, flashback as thwarted dream is used. If the outsider is supposed to be an essentially unknowable, unpredictable person, flashback as case history is used. Flashback as case history is always used if the audience is supposed to disapprove of the outsider.

Protagonist and antagonist

The striking difference in the way the audience relates to the enigmatic outsider is caused by a very simple factor: the choice of protagonist. In flashback as thwarted dream, the outsider is an unknowable antagonist in the present but an intimately known protagonist in the past – the point being to explain the outsider's strange behavior in terms of a sympathy-inducing past. In flashback as case history, the outsider is antagonist in both present and past. This is because the aim of such films is to show the outsider as a scientifically observed specimen (usually to pass comment on the strangeness of the human species), and the fact that the audience never gets into the outsider's head gives the required distancing effect.

With flashback as thwarted dream, the enigmatic outsider is capable of change. The audience very much wants them to get their lost dream and, provided this is physically possible, the outsider usually takes on the challenge. But in flashback as case history, the outsider is incapable of change. This is one of the reasons why such films have to end at the reappearance of the triggering crisis – because the outsider's incapacity for change means the film has nowhere further to go. Also, of course, flashback as case history typically deals with a story that is over bar a final ironic twist. The rules about choice of protagonist and antagonist differ in autobiographical flashback.

When to use flashback as case history

Flashback as case history is a technique commonly used in mystery or detective stories, to which its quasi-documentary feel adds a sense of reality. It is used to tell stories that are complete, except for a final ironic twist. It is seen a lot on TV. Often, a dateline is superimposed on screen in imitation of news footage. While the enigmatic outsider in flashback as thwarted dream is found to be sympathetic, and often goes on to achieve his/her lost dream and be changed by triumph, the outsider in flashback as case history is usually unchangeable and sometimes irredeemable, even evil. The protagonist learns a cautionary lesson from him/her – in fact we could describe flashback as case history as "cautionary tale."

The investigator

Flashback as case history distances the audience from the enigmatic outsider by making the outsider the antagonist in both the story in the past and the story in the present. The protagonist – that is, the person whose head we are inside – will usually be an investigator whose job it is to find out what made the outsider tick. The investigator–protagonist is often involved in crime detection of some kind, like the US customs officer in *The Usual Suspects*, or is a journalist, as in *Citizen Kane*. This role breakdown is very suitable for TV crime or mystery drama because the investigator–protagonist is, of course, already in place as the hero or one of the heroes of the series.

In films using flashback as case history, the outsider–antagonist is often the most interesting and compelling character in the film, while the investigator–protagonist is pallid and unmemorable. *Citizen Kane* is an extreme example. Here the protagonist in the present, the journalist Thompson, is literally never seen full-face. This combination of charismatic antagonist, with a protagonist who is "everyperson," is reminiscent of non-flashback films featuring a charismatic mentor, like *Rain Man* and *Scent of a Woman*. In these films, as in flashback as case history, the purpose is to show a normal person (the investigator–protagonist) being affected by someone so strange and possessed of such an odd mentality, that however much they are researched and analyzed, they will always remain a mystery.

Significantly, the investigator–protagonist is often changed by their interaction with the outsider–antagonist, but the outsider remains eternally unknowable.

Climax twist

Aside from the matter of antagonist and protagonist, the most significant structural difference between flashback as case history and flashback as thwarted dream is that there is no final, energized segment in which the enigmatic outsider pursues their dream with the audience right behind them and willing them to win. The point of flashback as case history is to present a completed story that shows the mystery of human affairs by depicting an outsider who is distant, enigmatic, and often unredeemed. Structurally, the danger of this is that films using flashback as case history will lose pace at the end because we know what happens in the end of the story in the past and the story in the present has nowhere dramatic to go.

A successful way of countering this "fizzle" effect is by giving an ironic twist to the climax of the story in the present. This happens in both *Citizen Kane* and *The Usual Suspects*, in which, using classic dramatic irony, a crucial piece of information is revealed to the audience but not to the investigator–protagonist. In *Citizen Kane*, the audience but not the investigator–protagonist is permitted to find out the meaning of "Rosebud." In *The Usual Suspects*, the audience but not the investigator–protagonist sees for sure that Verbal is Keyser Soze.

In both cases the dramatic irony gives the ending of the film a kick. It involves the audience personally while reinforcing the standard message of flashback as case history, which is that charismatic people are ultimately unknowable. An interesting exception here is *Courage Under Fire*, in which there is no need for a dose of energizing dramatic irony because the film's climax in the present is located in the protagonist's relationship line, with the protagonist putting his own ghosts to rest.

The message here is that flashback as case history needs a very striking climax in the present to make up for the fact that the audience already knows the outcome of the climax in the past.

When to use flashback as thwarted dream

The point of flashback as thwarted dream is to reveal the apparent coldness or mental imbalance of an enigmatic outsider as the understandable result of shocking personal experiences and thwarted dreams, and in doing so, to show the outsider to be normal, sensitive, and likeable. The intention and effect of flashbacks in this instance is to win the outsider enormous sympathy and goodwill from the audience, who typically feels that "there but for the grace of God go I."

This kind of flashback narrative often shows that what initially presented as mental imbalance is really a special wisdom, frequently a special wisdom born of pain as seen, for example, in *Shine* and *Forrest Gump*.

Protagonist and antagonist

As we have seen, in the story set in the present, flashback as thwarted dream usually shows the enigmatic outsider as a charismatic but unknowable antagonist, for the same reasons as we have seen in flashback as case history and films like *Scent of a Woman* and *Rain Man*. The idea is that the outsider (for example, David Helfgott in *Shine*) is so changed by the past that they can only be seen from the outside. The point of view in the present is through the "normal" people who encounter the outsider and who are changed by the association, often affected by the outsider's courage and wisdom born of pain.

Interestingly, while the relationship line of the story in the present usually has one clear protagonist to the enigmatic outsider's antagonist, the action line often has a number of protagonists, appearing in sequence, who each perform the task of asking questions. These could be described as "normal" people whose function it is to ask the questions we would ask.

This can clearly be seen in *Shine* in which, in the present, the mature David is normally antagonist, that is, he is observed rather than observing. The role of protagonist in the action line of the present is taken, one after the other, by Sylvia, Sam and, later, Gillian, all of whom ask the questions and express the reservations of a normal person. In the relationship line Gillian, who eventually marries David, is the one clear protagonist to David's antagonist. It is through the perspective of these normal people that we view the public and personal side of the mature David. Importantly, while we can deeply sympathize with the mature David and see wisdom in his tangled speeches, we are never consistently inside his head in the same way that we are inside the head of David the boy and young man.

The one moment in which we are in David's head in the present is in the scene where he meets his antagonist from the past, Peter, his father. The same phenomenon occurs in love stories like *The Remains of the Day*, the last part of which sees the enigmatic outsider once again encountering the lover–antagonist from the past. From the moment Stevens meets Miss Kenton at the hotel he is very much the protagonist, but until then, in the present, he has been very much the remote antagonist.

The English Patient presents a slight variant because there are two stories in the present, the first connected with the patient (involving the nurse looking after him in the abandoned villa) and the second involving the attempts of the war-traumatized nurse to find love and friendship with two bomb-disposal experts who come to the villa. In fact the second story fulfills the role normally played by the story in the present, in which the enigmatic outsider searches for the dream. Since the patient cannot physically move, the nurse, another traumatized person whose lover and friends were destroyed by war, pursues her own version of the same dream. She becomes the patient's surrogate. This works well, because without a strong love and redemption story in the present, the film could only deal with the silent patient being nursed. The use of a surrogate outsider in flashback as thwarted dream is a useful technique to remember for handling the problem of an outsider who is physically incapacitated.

The English Patient fits comfortably into the flashback as thwarted dream model. The patient is very much the engimatic outsider who is the protagonist in the past story and the unknowable mentor–antagonist in the present. There is a sequence of people playing investigator–protagonist, from the military authorities at the start who want to know his nationality, to the nurse and, dramatically, to Caravaggio, who comes planning to kill him as a traitor and murderer.

While the patient is unlike other enigmatic outsiders in flashback as thwarted dream in that he cannot pursue his dream and has a surrogate to do it for him, he does explain himself to Caravaggio and achieve some kind of peace before death. (It is significant that he does not ask for morphine at the start of his stay at the villa, only when he's made his peace with himself and Caravaggio.) Typical of the mentor–antagonist, he changes all around him but changes little himself.

The same pattern occurs in *Forrest Gump*. In the past Forrest is protagonist, but in the present, he is the apparently retarded but wise antagonist, with questions being asked by a range of protagonists who are normal people at the bus stop. Gump is another antagonist–mentor who changes all around with little or no change to himself.

Pursuit of the dream

A very important part of most films employing flashback as thwarted dream is the final section, set in the present, in which the enigmatic outsider, emboldened, sets out on a quest to achieve the dream thwarted earlier in life. The quest for the lost dream is often presented as a real or spiritual journey that requires the outsider to face their demons and cope with the questions of hostile strangers.

The quest actually starts at the first appearance of the triggering crisis, but acquires urgency only when the film has come full circle back to the triggering crisis. Often, the audience is unaware that the quest has started until the second appearance of the triggering crisis. This is so in *Shine*, in which David's frantic bashing on the window of Moby's

122 Scriptwriting Updated

restaurant is not recognizable as the desire for a piano until his whole past has been revealed and we are back where we started, at the triggering crisis, which is also the second-act turning point of the story in the past. The same thing happens in *The Remains of the Day.* The audience sees Mr. Stevens leave on his quest to regain Miss Kenton but, since Stevens has denied any love-relationship with her, the audience is not fully aware of the tragedy of their past. As the story in the past unfolds, so the audience begins to understand that Stevens is on a quest for lost love.

It is at the second appearance of the triggering crisis/second-act turning point that the quest takes over the film. The climax, which is the climax both of the story in the past and the story in the present, then shows whether the enigmatic outsider achieves the dream or not.

New understanding in the third act

It is interesting to compare this quest for the lost dream with what happens in the third act of standard three-act narratives. In the standard three-act narrative structure, act three is usually marked by a new energy as the protagonist finds strength to fight against the threat of the spiritual or actual death presented in the second-act turning point. Often, the start of act three shows the protagonist achieving a spiritual rebirth or a new understanding of their predicament, or of things not previously understood. This new awareness and courage typically propels the protagonist into a final "great battle," which makes up most of act three.

We can understand the pursuit of the dream in flashback as thwarted dream as a version of this classic act-three feature. In flashback as thwarted dream, the second-act turning point (that is, the triggering crisis) creates a spiritual rebirth or new understanding in the enigmatic outsider, which energizes the outsider to pursue the lost dream. Pursuing the lost dream becomes the great battle against the odds that the audience wills the outsider to win. Extra impetus and tension are added because the start of the third act (where the flashback story returns to the present) sees the audience fully informed about the outsider's terrible trauma and anxious to see them achieve their thwarted wishes.

Living the dream

The film *Titanic,* while it employs only a few flashbacks, follows the standard pattern of employing an enigmatic outsider (Rose) as protagonist in the past and antagonist in the present. Here, the lost dream is not something pursued in the final part of the film. Instead, Rose's successful life becomes a tribute to the lost dream of love with Jack, who drowned.

The ticking clock

Like the standard three-act structure, flashback as thwarted dream often adds jeopardy to the enigmatic outsider's quest by adding pressure of time to the outsider's problems. The question becomes "Is there enough time to achieve the thwarted dream, or is it too late?"

Restoring the balance

It is commonly observed of the classic three-act structure that it depicts life pushed out of balance, with balance restored at the final climax. Flashback as thwarted dream follows this pattern.

Thwarted dream becoming case history

The Sweet Hereafter has been discussed in terms of the interesting variants it provides in combining autobiographical flashback narrative as well as standard flashback narrative, and its use of one-act rather than three-act models for many of its narratives. It is also interesting because it initially feels as if both the action line of the present – the consequences of a bus crash in which most of the local children are killed – and the relationship line concerning the lawyer and his junkie daughter will be examples of flashback as thwarted dream, with the thwarted dream being "lost children redeemed," but in fact it turns out in both cases to be flashback as case history. Events prior to and after the bus crash seem to be leading to justice and peace acquired through a court case and, in the story of the lawyer's relationship with his junkie daughter, to the prodigal's return and the power of love. But in fact both stories end up being flashback as case history. In both, the dream is not achieved: instead of becoming a celebration of humanity's ability to triumph over adversity and achieve the dream, the film becomes a cautionary and mysterious tale about the unpredictability of the human heart.

In the town's story, Nicole, the sole survivor of the crash, deliberately and for unfathomable reasons, chooses to sabotage the court case and thus reject the dream. With the story of the junkie daughter, a flashforward climax reveals that the daughter is not redeemed and Mitchell Stevens' love for her has, as he admits to his fellow passenger on the plane, a schoolfriend of his daughter, been warped and destroyed by her addiction. Technically, the town's story becomes flashback as case history, while the story of Mitchell Stevens, the lawyer, becomes a rare case of flashback as thwarted dream not only ending unhappily but actually resulting in flashback as case history.

These twists have an interesting effect on the matter of protagonists and enigmatic outsider–antagonists. While the initial flashbacks of Nicole's life suggest that she is going to become a protagonist in quest of a dream (becoming a singer), her insistence on sabotaging the case and moving into a strange fantasy world concerning the lost children turns her, at the end, into a classically unknowable outsider–antagonist. In the town's story, Mitchell is a classic investigator–protagonist. He is also the protagonist in his private story – past, present, and future – but the end of his quest to achieve the thwarted dream sees the dream – of a normal loving relationship with a normal daughter – unachievable.

Interestingly, the story of Mitchell and his junkie daughter has no second or third act. It jumps straight from the first-act turning point (the revelation that the daughter has AIDS) to the second-act turning point, where we find out that the daughter is unredeemed and Mitchell admits that he cannot properly love her. We do not see the great battle to win the dream (we will see the same phenomenon of a missing third act and climax in the two stories of *Crimes and Misdemeanors* in Chapter 11).

The Sweet Hereafter is remarkable in that it uses many time-frames to tell its several stories, and includes flashforwards as well as flashbacks. It is considered in detail in

Chapter 10, but here it should be said that the film, despite its complexity and use of a one-act rather than three-act structure for most of its stories, reveals all of the standard features of flashback narrative. It involves a detective story and its main focus is what happened in the past. It opens at a triggering crisis (the bus crash) and comes full circle to end with an ironic twist (the sole survivor lying in order to sabotage the compensation suit) just after the story of the bus crash has reached its climax. It possesses in the lawyer a typical investigator–protagonist, whose job it is to ask questions.

One area in which it differs from other flashback narrative films (apart from its use of a one-act story structure) is that footage of the triggering crisis, the bus crash itself, is not seen on screen until the story of the past has been told full circle. Another difference is that the investigator–protagonist of the town's story has his own flashback narrative story which covers the past, the present (his visit to the bereaved town), and the future, two years hence. In this he is the typical enigmatic outsider being asked questions by a protagonist (Allison, his daughter's schoolfriend), with his answers, shown in flashbacks, explaining his bitterness and dark wisdom.

The Sweet Hereafter is really two flashback narrative films in one. It is as if the journalist–protagonist in *Citizen Kane* were to have had his own flashback narrative happening during and after his investigation of Kane's life story.

The flashback narrative concerning the lawyer's relationship with his junkie daughter is structurally interesting because it does not start with a triggering crisis. This is probably wise because the triggering crisis scene would be Zoe announcing that she has AIDS. Since the film already has one opening triggering crisis that is harrowing (the bus crash), an AIDS announcement would probably be over the top. The film, fascinating and moving, raises interesting questions about how many flashback narratives one film can sustain. In its use of a one-act structure for its narratives, it also provides clues as to how a number of stories can be run concurrently without audience confusion or a loss of pace.

Autobiographical flashback

Flashback as case history and flashback as thwarted dream are very specific in the use of the protagonist and antagonist to create intimacy or distance. Different rules apply in autobiographical flashback narrative, where a variety of combinations is possible because the intimacy problem is solved by a voiceover describing the narrator's life and feelings in both past and present. Sometimes the narrator is the protagonist in the present but he/she describes him/herself so objectively in the story set in the past that he/she is effectively the antagonist of that story. This is often the case in Woody Allen films.

Another interesting variant is the identity of the enigmatic outsider. Sometimes the outsider is the narrator (this is often so in Woody Allen films). Alternatively, the outsider is someone who influences the narrator, as in *The End of the Affair, There's Something About Mary* or *Sophie's Choice*.

Autobiographical flashback narrative films of this kind can either follow the flashback as thwarted dream model, in which the protagonist tries to regain the dream that was lost (as in *There's Something About Mary*), or they can follow the flashback as case history approach, in which the point, comic or dramatic, is the narrator's scientific observation of their own past, particularly of the effect on them of an enigmatic outsider (as in *Sophie's Choice*). In the latter case, the narrator is the protagonist in both stories, with the outsider as antagonist in the past.

The End of the Affair has the enigmatic outsider (Sarah) as antagonist in the past and present. *The End of the Affair* is actually flashback as thwarted dream that ends tragically. The dream is lost at the very moment it appears to have been regained. Just as Sarah has agreed to marry Maurice, they discover that she has only six months left to live. The film shows some very interesting use of flashbacks. While the general structure is flashback as thwarted dream (autobiographical form), it also uses flashback as illustration (to show Sarah's version of events when the bomb went off), blending it with flashback as life-changing incident in the repeated use of the bomb's explosion. The events that occurred at and just after the explosion are told in incremental flashbacks, and the explosion itself recurs independently, at moments of great emotion.

Like *The Sweet Hereafter*, the triggering incident in *The End of the Affair* (the breakup during the war) is not actually shown on screen until flashbacks have brought the film full circle. But the story in the present does actually start at this point which is, classically, the second-act turning point, and marks the beginning of the renewed pursuit of the dream. *The End of the Affair* follows the rule of being a detective story of the heart, and while its protagonist is not an investigator, he actually hires an investigator to pursue the enigmatic outsider (Sarah). It also, classically, involves a hunt or quest in its story set in the present.

The sophisticated use of a variety of flashback techniques is probably the way of the future, as not only filmmakers but audiences become increasingly used to its appearance.

Flashback as life-changing incident

Flashback as life-changing incident is when the events depicted in one recurring, incomplete flashback are the key to the enigmatic outsider's odd behavior in the present. In cases like this (in *Catch-22*, for example) the flashback starts by depicting a fragment of one crucial and horrifying incident in the past. As the film proceeds, more intriguing fragments are added to the flashback. The life-changing climax of the flashback is shown close to the end of the film.

In structural terms, the incident depicted in the recurrent flashback of flashback as life-changing incident is the disturbance in the story set in the present. It changes the normality of the protagonist's life and forces this character to take a new direction and make new plans. In *Catch-22*, the horrific death of the young gunner Snowdon is what makes the protagonist determined to get out of the Air Force. This plan and its frustration drives the rest of the film.

In *Catch-22*, Yossarian is the protagonist not only in the story set in the present but also in the recurrent flashbacks. However, it is perfectly possible for the character who experiences the flashbacks to be an outsider–antagonist in the story set in the present, but a sympathetic protagonist in the flashback. They could also remain a shocking antagonist. Typically, this usage occurs in films or TV drama series episodes in which an investigator of some kind is the protagonist in pursuit of a character whose behavior has been triggered by a shocking experience viewed in a recurring flashback.

As with all flashback structures, flashback as life-changing incident has elements of the detective story about it, with suspense and mystery being crucial components. The recurring flashback is a vital missing clue. The flashback usually happens whenever events in the present trigger the outsider's memory.

Other flashback uses in *Catch-22*

It should be pointed out that *Catch-22* actually contains a range of different flashbacks. It contains flashback as illustration in the form of a flashback that illustrates information just stated in dialogue (when Dreedle asks whether he is indeed decorating soldiers because they have ditched their bombs in the Mediterranean, and we see on screen the event he is describing). Similarly, when Yossarian sees the wrecked fuselage of Orr's plane floating in the sea, there is a flashback in which he remembers Orr working on a heating machine in their tent. Again, there is a dream flashback (another version of memory) where Yossarian not only dreams the life-changing flashback, but also dreams of a naked woman beckoning to him from the sea.

In fact *Catch-22* as a whole could be thought of as a variant of the flashback as thwarted dream model: the thwarted dream is Yossarian's desire to go home, which is not permitted because of Catch-22, and which he sets out to do at the end of the film.

The film actually starts just like normal flashback narrative. It opens with a typical hook cum triggering crisis – the protagonist being stabbed – to which we will later return and which, we will later discover, is actually the second-act turning point of the story in the present. While all that the audience can understand from the opening is that Yossarian is mysteriously stabbed, possibly fatally, the film will later reveal that this moment is actually his lowest point in every sense. He has just experienced a series of events that suggest all human decency has collapsed in the face of war. All of his friends are dead, missing, or insane. He has agreed, in order to go home, to become part of the corrupt system he has been opposing.

Having opened with a standard triggering crisis, the film follows typical flashback narrative structure by flashing straight back to the disturbance, namely, Snowdon's horrific death, the event that caused Yossarian's determination to leave the war. Since *Catch-22* does not have parallel stories (although, during the action set in the past, the film does twice return briefly to him immediately after the stabbing), there is only one disturbance. The film proceeds through the events that followed Snowdon's death until it reaches the stabbing which is, structurally, the second-act turning point.

Significantly, it is immediately after this repeat of the stabbing incident that we see the life-changing flashback in its entirety. We are now fully up to date on Yossarian's situation and the film can proceed into its truncated third act, in which Yossarian pursues his lost dream. The third act starts with him in his hospital bed as elaborate preparations are being made to present him with his faked bravery award. Yossarian discovers that his friend Orr not only survived a landing at sea, but rowed to Sweden, where he will sit out the war. Inspired by his example, Yossarian leaps out of the window and runs madly through the camp, finally setting off in a raft to row his way across the Mediterranean and away from the war.

Recurrent flashback as moment of calm

In films that use flashback narrative proper, that is, flashbacks to tell a story in the past and a story in the present, pace and momentum are achieved through jumping between dramatic high points in the past and dramatic high points in the present. *Catch-22* does not have two stories to sustain. It gains its pace and momentum through the increasing insanity demonstrated in both its relationship line (where Yossarian's friends all show different versions of insanity, usually connected with death and violence) and its action line (where Milo's profiteering company becomes a multinational power running all sides in the war). This means that the recurrent flashback can be used to provide moments of chilling calm amid the craziness.

9. Quick reference guide to using flashback narrative

Poor use of flashbacks is characterized by the insertion of flashbacks chosen at random and placed wherever the script seems to be flagging. But films that successfully use flashback narrative structure are actually meticulous in the placing and content of flashbacks. Placing and content are carefully linked to the demands of the three-act structure in both types of story.

Flashbacks typically occur at crucial dramatic moments of the story in the present, and depict crucial dramatic moments of the story in the past. In other words, good flashback narrative operates by jumping back and forth between cliffhangers in the past and cliffhangers in the present. Constructing and placing flashbacks like this makes good dramatic sense because it means the audience leaves each "film" on a question, and so will be interested to return.

Crucially, the cliffhangers are usually important structural components of the classic three-act structure. They can be the disturbance, the first-act turning point, complications, the second-act turning point or the climax. The first flashback of the film, placed very soon after the triggering crisis, will almost always depict the event in the past that started it all – in structural terms, the disturbance. Significantly, this event will be the disturbance in both the relationship line and the action line of the story in the past.

For example, in *Shine,* the disturbance, shown in the first flashback, is the concert where the boy David first meets the piano teacher who will initiate the conflict between family (relationship line) and musical career (action line) that lies at the core of the film. In *The Remains of the Day,* the disturbance, shown in the first flashback, is the arrival of the new housekeeper (who will trigger the relationship line) on the day of the last occasion upon which Lord Darlington (central to the action line) mixes with his English neighbors rather than Nazi sympathizers. In *The English Patient,* the disturbance, shown in the first flashback, is the arrival of Mrs. Clifford (central to the relationship line) at the same time as the plane that will help with the mapping and exploration of the desert (the action line). In *Citizen Kane,* the disturbance, shown in the first real flashback (as opposed to the newsreel obituary, which is really backstory in the present), is the arrival of Thatcher to take the boy Charlie away from his loved ones (relationship line) to further his career (action line). In *The Usual Suspects*, the disturbance, shown in the first flashback, is when the gang members are rounded up for a police identification lineup. This initiates both the relationship between Verbal and Keaton (relationship line) and the deeds of the gang (action line).

After this, the film will typically cross to a crucial moment in the present, continuing until a cliffhanger. It will then cross back to a crucial moment in the past, usually the first-act turning point. The film will continue moving between dramatic high points until it comes full circle to the scene that formed the triggering crisis which, in the case of flashback as thwarted dream, will be the second-act turning point and, in the case of flashback as case history, will be the climax (to be followed shortly afterwards by the climax twist). You can see how a number of flashback films jump between cliffhangers in Chapter 10, which provides a range of structure charts.

Plot material

Certain sorts of story do seem to lend themselves to flashback narrative. These stories have the following elements in common.

1. The past

Films using flashback narrative are typically more concerned with what happened in the past than with what could happen in the present or future, although by the end of the film the audience will often be anxious for the central character to gain their dream. As a reflection of this focus on the past, the story in the present will often be truncated. If you are planning a film with flashbacks, this difference in focus on past or present is a useful way to define whether the film in your head is flashback narrative material or whether the flashbacks you plan to use are actually just backstory.

Be aware that while the final part of your film (set in the present) might be extremely powerful and complex, the structure might still be flashback as thwarted dream. A good example is *The End of the Affair*, which is thwarted dream combined with autobiographical flashback. If your film is crucially concerned with the past, use flashback narrative. If it is crucially concerned with the present, plan the film's structure around the present and regard the flashbacks as backstory. This would be a use of flashback as memory or illustration (Chapter 7, p. 108) or flashback as life-changing incident (see Chapter 8, p. 125). *Crimes and Misdemeanors* is a good example of the use of flashback as memory or illustration (see Chapter 7). Voiceover is often used in this form.

2. Detective element

Films using flashback narrative almost always contain strong elements of the detective story, with a mystery to be solved or someone to be found. The mystery always concerns the personal relationships of an enigmatic outsider, often involving a conflict between their public and personal lives. The audience must ask "What happened?" rather than "What will happen?" You could describe flashback narrative as a detective story of the human heart.

3. The enigmatic outsider

Flashback narrative always has this character in a central role. The character appears inaccessible, mysterious, cold, crazy – or all four. The outsider is hard to categorize and is viewed with interest, sometimes suspicion, by everyone around them.

4. Thwarted dream or case history

There are two main kinds of flashback narrative. These are flashback as thwarted dream, in which the enigmatic outsider's strange behavior is shown to be the understandable outcome of horrific past experiences, and flashback as case history, in which the outsider is treated with scientific distance. Flashback as thwarted dream usually shows the outsider trying to regain the lost dream. In thwarted dream the outsider is alive. In case history the film opens with the outsider dead – or returned from the dead profoundly changed, as in the case of Nicole, the sole survivor of the bus crash in *The Sweet Hereafter*. Flashback as life-changing incident is a form that also occasionally appears (as in films like *Catch-22*). Here, one traumatic incident is shown repeatedly and incrementally until its significance is finally revealed.

Autobiographical flashback is a flashback narrative seen from the point of view of a protagonist talking in voiceover about crucial events in the past, in particular about an enigmatic outsider. The outsider changed the protagonist's life and is usually a person driven by a strong sense of duty. Sometimes this person is dead, in which case the story, like case history, starts with the outsider's death. At other times they have been lost and are found again in a third act, as in thwarted dream.

5. Protagonists and antagonists

Protagonists in the present ask questions

Flashback narrative always involves people in the present who ask questions. These people are always protagonists because they represent the normal point of view, asking the questions a normal person would ask. Frequently this person is an official investigator like a journalist, police officer, or lawyer. Sometimes there is a sequence of protagonists.

Thwarted dream has at least one and often more investigator–protagonists (for example, the people who help David Helfgott). The person they question (and often help) is always the enigmatic outsider.

Case history has only one investigator–protagonist but has at least one and often many people who are questioned (for example, all the interviewees in *Citizen Kane*). They are always questioned about a dead enigmatic outsider (or, in *The Sweet Hereafter*, someone who has returned from the dead, the sole survivor of the accident). In autobiographical flashback the protagonist is also the person asking questions, but the questions they are asking are about their own lives and they are questioning themselves (so they act as their own antagonists).

Antagonists in the present are asked questions

In all forms of flashback narrative apart from autobiographical flashback in the story set in the present, the antagonist is the person or people being asked questions. They are also the person or people causing trouble. In the relationship line they cause trouble by not answering questions, or by lying, or being enigmatic. In the action line, they are the person who has made the protagonist take their present course of action.

In thwarted dream, the antagonist in both the action and relationship lines in the present is the enigmatic outsider. They are often mentor–antagonists dragging normal people on a crazy journey, and a protagonist may take them in, even fall in love with them (as Gillian does with David).

Both case history and thwarted dream may have minor antagonists in the action line in the present. In thwarted dream the antagonist and protagonist will join forces against these minor antagonists (in *Shine*, the minor antagonists are the people who believe David is crazy). Autobiographical narrative is different because the person asking questions is the protagonist and they are asking questions of themselves.

Anyone having flashbacks is a protagonist

In all forms of flashback narrative, when the film goes into flashback, the person who is having the flashback becomes a protagonist, because we are seeing events from their point of view. In thwarted dream, we see the enigmatic outsider's flashbacks, hence, in the past, the outsider is the protagonist. In case history, we see interviewees' flashbacks, hence, in the past, they are the protagonists. You could say that autobiographical flashback breaks this rule, because the person who is having the flashback may be viewing their past self as a stranger, so their past self can be an antagonist. However, the person having the flashback is still, really, a protagonist.

Antagonists in the past cause problems

In case history flashback, the antagonist in the relationship line is always the enigmatic outsider, watched by the protagonist who is the person having the flashback. For example, in *Citizen Kane*, Kane is the outsider and he is seen through the flashbacks of people who knew him. In the past of case history, the outsider is the major antagonist in the action line. The outsider is often a mentor–antagonist, involving the protagonist in an exciting or dangerous scheme (like Kane involving his friends in the newspaper and his wife in opera singing). Often the protagonist becomes disillusioned with the scheme and suspicious of the antagonist's motives (Kane's friends becoming disillusioned with his behavior as editor, and his wife becoming disillusioned with his quest to make her an opera singer). There may be minor antagonists who cause trouble for the protagonist and the outsider against whom the two join forces (as Kane and his friends join together to triumph in the newspaper industry). Note that the outsider has to be seen from the outside as an antagonist because he is dead!

In thwarted dream flashback, the antagonist in the relationship line is the person central to the thwarted dream (like Peter Helfgott in *Shine*). As with case history, the major antagonist in the action line is often, like Peter Helfgott, a mentor–antagonist leading the protagonist on an exciting or dangerous scheme (to become a concert pianist). As with case history, the protagonist becomes disillusioned with the scheme and suspicious of the antagonist's motives (David rejecting Peter). There may be minor antagonists who cause trouble for the protagonist and the outsider and against whom the two may join forces (Peter and David against Ben Rosen and the world of conventional music training).

In the past of *The Remains of the Day*, the relationship antagonist is Miss Kenton and the action line mentor–antagonist with whom the protagonist becomes disillusioned is Lord Darlington. This is probably because the protagonist, Mr. Stevens, has two thwarted dreams, the dream of absolute service to a kind master (which turns out to be disastrous), and the thwarted dream of love.

6. Hunt, quest, or journey

Often, the story in the present (and also sometimes the story in the past) involves a hunt, quest, or journey (physical and/or metaphorical). In films using flashback as thwarted dream, the last part of the film usually involves a quest by the enigmatic outsider or surrogate to achieve the lost dream or settle unfinished business. This is a vital and energizing component of the form, and takes the place of the great battle that usually appears in the three-act structure (see below).

Structure in flashback narrative

Structure in flashback narrative is most important. For detailed structural breakdowns of flashback narrative films, see Chapter 10. The following structural components appear consistently in flashback narrative.

1. Length

Since parallel flashback contains at least two stories in one film, the film is liable to be longer than normal.

2. Three-act structure

In its basic form, flashback narrative contains one story in the past and one in the present. Both the flashback story and the story in the present follow the classic three-act structure, although the story in the present is often truncated. Both contain their own action line and relationship line, protagonist and antagonist, and could almost function as two separate films. In films like *The Sweet Hereafter*, in which there are many stories to be told, often many or all of the narratives show a one-act structure typical of short "twist-ending" films – that is, they consist of normality, disturbance and a first-act turning point (see *The Sweet Hereafter* in Chapter 10).

3. Flashbacks appear chronologically

Flashbacks typically tell the story in chronological order. The story in the present is always presented chronologically. Flashback as case history often features flashbacks which are different people's versions of the same event. This means there is overlap. This chronological rule is also followed in flashback as life-changing incident. The first appearance of the flashback shows the beginning of the incident, while later ones reveal it step by step. In flashback as illustration, events can be shown out of sequence.

4. Placing and content

The flashback story deals with the enigmatic outsider's personal relationships and self-development. There is usually a conflict between their personal desires or well-being and their professional duties.

Flashbacks do not occur at random and their content is not arbitrary. Placing and content are carefully linked to the demands of the three-act structure in both stories. Flashbacks typically occur at important dramatic moments in both stories, often at turning points. That is, they will occur at an important dramatic moment in the story set in the present, flashing back to an important dramatic moment in the past. Then, the flashback will end at an important dramatic moment in the past, rejoining the present at an important dramatic moment. In other words, they typically move from cliffhanger to cliffhanger. This can be seen clearly in the structure charts of flashback narratives presented in Chapter 10.

5. Protagonist and antagonist

In films which use flashback as thwarted dream, the story in the past will usually feature the enigmatic outsider as protagonist. The past is normally the outsider's story, and we are inside the outsider's head as the traumatic events occur. But in the film in the present, the outsider will normally be a compelling but unknowable antagonist in both the action line and the relationship line (this closely resembles the pattern in films like *Scent of a Woman* and *Rain Man* that feature charismatic mentors). The protagonist in the present – the person whose head we are inside – will be a normal person who encounters the outsider and is changed by the association, often affected by the outsider's courage and wisdom born of pain. In flashback as case history, the outsider is often the antagonist in the past and present. The exception to these rules is flashback as autobiography, in which the narrator is the protagonist in the past and present, although sometimes the narrator is the outsider or is affected by the outsider. In story terms, flashback as autobiography can happen in flashback as case history, flashback as thwarted dream, or flashback as life-changing incident.

6. The story in the present

The story in the present is a genuine ongoing story, although it might be truncated or skeletal. A character who simply sits thinking or is caught randomly at everyday tasks will not work. In other words, the story in the present must always have a proper action line culminating in a powerful climax and usually employing a three-act structure. Frequently it involves a hunt, quest, or journey of discovery in which the enigmatic outsider is threatened by hostile strangers. In flashback as case history, the relationship line in the present is often quite thin, and often consists of the relationship between investigator and witness. The story in the present always contains characters who ask questions, or who want questions answered. In autobiographical flashback narrative, the character asking questions is the narrator.

7. The story in the past

The story that is told in flashback plays the same part in the film as the relationship line in the standard three-act structure. In other words, as in the standard three-act structure, the relationship line (the story told in flashback) is pegged to the action line told in the present. The action line told in the present usually involves a real or spiritual journey of discovery.

8. Triggering crisis

The triggering crisis is where the story starts, and must be chosen with great care. This moment must be a turning point or crisis for the enigmatic outsider, and it must fulfil a number of specific requirements. The triggering crisis gets its name because it

- triggers flashbacks to the story in the past
- triggers the story in the present
- triggers the need to pursue the thwarted dream once again (if death or the inability to change does not prevent this).

9. Contents of triggering crisis

In flashback as thwarted dream, the triggering crisis is normally the second-act turning point in the enigmatic outsider's story (their lowest point, where they are often symbolically shut out or close to real or spiritual death). Meanwhile, in the story set in the present, the triggering crisis forms the disturbance, that is, it is the event which sets the story in progress.

In flashback as case history the triggering crisis is often the death of the outsider; sometimes it is actually the climax of the story. Seeing the outsider in such a crisis creates audience interest in the past, the main focus of interest in flashback narrative. Note that in some cases, particularly in flashback narrative films that have many stories, the triggering crisis can be the disturbance not only in the present but also in the flashback stories. This occurs in *The Sweet Hereafter*, in which all the stories connected with the townsfolk have the bus accident as their disturbance, with life before the bus crash as normality. Instead of having a climax occurring after three full acts, they obey the rule of many short films, ending with a twist at the first-act turning point, something that is often necessary because of time constraints.

10. Full circle

Flashbacks commence at the triggering crisis and continue until they have told the story all the way up to the triggering crisis again. They then continue – at length in flashback as thwarted dream – and briefly in flashback as case history.

11. Third-act quest

In the standard three-act structure, it is at the second-act turning point that the protagonist finds the strength to fight the final great battle. This is also true in flashback as thwarted dream. The search to fulfil the thwarted dream takes the place of the great battle. Extra impetus and jeopardy are added because the start of the third act (where the flashback story returns to the present) sees the audience fully informed about the enigmatic outsider's terrible trauma and anxious to see them achieve their lost dream. Many flashback films of this kind create even more tension by adding time pressures to the outsider's problems in resolving the unfinished business. The climax depicts the quest won or lost.

12. Stories in tandem

After the triggering crisis is encountered the second time the stories proceed in tandem, culminating in a climax which solves both. Note that if you are planning to continue your film after the reappearance of the triggering crisis, make sure that the story at this point concerns a quest for the lost dream dealt with in the first part of the film. Unless you do this, you risk the last part of the film becoming essentially a new film, stuck on at the end.

13. No pursuit of the dream

Sometimes pursuit of the dream can be actively rejected (*The Sweet Hereafter*). Sometimes a life well lived replaces the pursuit of the dream (*Titanic*).

In flashback as case history, there is no third-act search for the dream because the triggering crisis is usually the final climax of the story told in flashback or the second-act turning point of the flashback story with a very truncated third act and climax. When it is reached for the second time, it is very close to the end of the film – followed usually by resolution in the form of a piece of dramatic irony which provides a final, powerful kick.

Method for constructing flashback narrative

A good way to start constructing flashback narrative is as follows:

1. Using the information above, decide whether you should use flashback as thwarted dream, flashback as case history (autobiographical flashback will be one of the two), or flashback as life-changing incident.
2. Check that flashback narrative will best serve your writing purpose – for example, check that you are more interested in telling the story in the past than the story in the present. If the present is what interests you, only flashback as life-changing incident is likely to be of use and you should consider another narrative form.
3. Get ideas for the content of each of the stories in the past and also the present, remembering that the form is essentially a detective story of the heart. Think of thwarted dream as a story with the motto of "There but for the grace of God …" and case history as a story subtitled "A cautionary tale." If you want to use flashback as life-changing incident, plan the story in the present that is caused by the life-changing incident.
4. Plan the structure of each story separately, and assume that the story in the past will be more detailed.
5. Make sure the stories have an action line and a relationship line, even in skeletal form.
6. Identify dramatic high points in each structure (that is, the disturbance, first-act turning point, second-act turning point, and climax). If you are using many stories, consider constructing some of them as one-act narratives with the triggering climax in each story set in the past being its disturbance rather than its second-act turning point. In cases like these, the final climax will be the first-act turning point, that is, a twist or surprise.
7. Combine the stories by crossing between them at these dramatic high points.

Exercise in creating flashback narrative

To help explain how to rearrange a narrative structure for flashback narrative purposes, I have turned the action line of *Cinderella* (Figure 9.1) into the beginning of a plan for both flashback as thwarted dream (Figure 9.2) and flashback as case history (Figure 9.3). Flashback narrative often deals with Cinderella stories, presenting them with either happy or sad endings. Four films dealt with in depth in the discussion of flashback narrative (*Shine, The Remains of the Day, Citizen Kane,* and *The Usual Suspects*) are actually versions, tragic or happy, of *Cinderella*.

This is a simplified version of the Cinderella plan given in Chapter 5 to explain the Smiley/Thompson nine-point plan.

Event structure	Breakdown of *Cinderella*
Normality	Cinderella is working as a slave to her ugly sisters and wicked stepmother.
Protagonist	Cinderella.
Disturbance/catalyst	The household receives an invitation to the ball from the handsome prince, but Cinderella cannot go because she has no clothes.
Plan	To go to the ball and meet the prince.
Antagonist	The status quo — 'class distinction' — personified by the ugly sisters and stepmother.
End of set-up	
Surprise	The fairy godmother appears and provides clothes and transport.
First-act turning point	
Obstacle	Clothes and transport are provided only until midnight.
End of first act	
Second act	Cinderella goes to the ball, entrances the prince, forgets the time.
Complications, substories, more surprises, and obstacles	(In some versions there is a ball every night for a week and she goes back to the ball several times, getting away before midnight every time except the last.)
Second-act turning point	It's midnight. Her clothes turn into rags. She runs off in despair, leaving behind her shoe.
End of second act	>>

Figure 9.1 Standard Cinderella story (action line only)

Third act	Cinderella returns to her old life, despairing of ever seeing the prince again. The prince announces that he will marry the woman whose foot fits the shoe. In some versions, events keep preventing him from entering Cinderella's house. The prince arrives at the household, but Cinderella is not at first allowed to try on the shoe. Cinderella fights back by asking to try on the shoe.
Climax	The shoe fits. The prince says he will marry her.
Resolution	They live happily ever after.

Figure 9.1 (cont.) Standard Cinderella story (action line only)

Event structure	*Cinderella* (thwarted dream)
Note: the only person who has flashbacks is Cinderella	
Triggering crisis	The clock is striking twelve. Cinderella, in rags, is running away from the ball with no shoe, traumatized (second-act turning point in the story in the past).
Protagonist and antagonist	The protagonist in the past is Cinderella. In the present, it is a person or people who ask questions. (We will use as an example a person, X, who works with Cinderella in her new job in a restaurant kitchen.) In the present, Cinderella is the relationship line antagonist, possibly also action line antagonist.
Enigmatic outsider	Cinderella (exists in present only).
Normality in the present	Cinderella as enigmatic outsider working in restaurant being watched and asked questions by X, a co-worker who is protagonist.
Cinderella's flashback — to her normality and the disturbance in the past	Cinderella is working as a slave to her ugly sisters and wicked stepmother (normality) when the household receives an invitation to the ball from the handsome prince, but Cinderella cannot go because she has no clothes (disturbance). >>

Figure 9.2 Cinderella turned into flashback as thwarted dream

Return to dramatic high point in the present	Movement in relationship between Cinderella and protagonist X. Movement in action line.
Cinderella's flashback to first-act turning point (surprise + obstacle)	The fairy godmother appears and provides clothes and transport (surprise). Clothes and transport are provided only until midnight (obstacle).
Return to dramatic high point in the present	Movement in relationship between Cinderella and X. Perhaps X falls in love with her. Movement in action line.
Cinderella's flashback to start of second act. More complications, substories, surprises, and obstacles	Cinderella goes to the ball, entrances the prince, falls in love with him. (In some versions she goes back to the ball several times and gets away, but the last time her clothes change into rags.)
More flashbacks between dramatic high points in the past and present stories	
Return of triggering crisis, past and present have caught up. No more flashbacks after this	On the verge of her dream coming true, the clock strikes twelve and she is tragically transformed. She runs back to poverty, leaving behind her shoe (second-act turning point from the story in the past forming the second-act turning point of story in the present).
From now on the story is all in the present	
Act three Cinderella sets out to achieve her dream	Cinderella is now working in the restaurant kitchen with X. The prince announces that he will marry the woman whose foot fits the shoe. Cinderella, assisted by X, sets out to achieve her dream of marrying the prince. The prince arrives at the restaurant but Cinderella is not at first allowed to try on the shoe. Cinderella fights back by asking to try on the shoe, assisted by X.
Climax Achieves dream (or, in tragic version, doesn't)	The slipper fits. X, in love with her, is saddened.
Resolution	Marries prince (or perhaps X instead).

Figure 9.2 (cont.) Cinderella *turned into flashback as thwarted dream*

Event structure	*Cinderella* (case history)
Triggering crisis/disturbance	The clock is striking twelve. Cinderella, in rags, is running away from the ball with no shoe, traumatized (this is now the climax in the story set in the past).
Protagonist and antagonist	In the past, the protagonist is the person or people who knew Cinderella (in this example, we will use Buttons, the groom) and the antagonist is Cinderella. In the present, the protagonist is an investigator figure (in this example, we will use a psychiatrist investigating Cinderella's depression). The relationship line antagonist in the present is Buttons. The protagonist in the present (the psychiatrist) will be asking Buttons questions, and his answers will be the flashbacks. It will be Buttons' flashbacks that we see, and we will see Cinderella from the outside. Note that Cinderella is always an antagonist (that is, in both the past and the present). She is never seen from the inside, only through the eyes of Buttons in the past and the psychiatrist in the present.
Enigmatic outsider	Cinderella in the past and the present.
Button's first flashback to normality and disturbance in the past	As seen by the past story protagonist, Buttons, Cinderella is working as a slave to her ugly sisters and wicked stepmother (normality) when the household receives an invitation to the ball from the handsome prince, but Cinderella cannot go because she has no clothes (disturbance).
Return to dramatic high point in the present	Psychiatrist's dealings with Buttons and Cinderella.
Buttons' flashback to first-act turning point in the past	As seen by the past story protagonist, Buttons, the fairy godmother appears and provides clothes and transport (surprise). Clothes and transport are provided only until midnight (obstacle).
Return to dramatic high point in the present	Psychiatrist trying to find out more about Cinderella from Buttons. Possibly also interviewing other people. >>

Figure 9.3 Cinderella *turned into flashback as case history*

Buttons' flashback to second act complications, substories, more surprises, and obstacles	As seen by the past story protagonist, Buttons, Cinderella goes to the ball, entrances the prince, falls in love with him.
More flashbacks between dramatic high points in the past and present stories	
Return of triggering crisis, past and present have caught up. Second-act turning point and climax together. No more flashbacks after this	As seen by the past story protagonist, Buttons, Cinderella, on the verge of her dream coming true, is tragically transformed, runs back to poverty, leaving her shoe. She now has no chance of achieving her dream of marrying the prince. She drops into despair (climax). Buttons takes her to the psychiatrist.
From now on the story is all in the present	
Climax twist/resolution incorporating dramatic irony	Psychiatrist commits Cinderella to psychiatric hospital. Climax twist known to the audience but not to the protagonist (for example, why Cinderella really went mad was because she found out she was actually the prince's twin sister, abandoned at birth).

Figure 9.3 (cont.) Cinderella *turned into flashback as case history*

Using other sorts of flashback
Turning *Cinderella* into flashback as life-changing incident

Note that you could create a version of *Cinderella* using flashback as life-changing incident simply by devising and inserting a recurrent incomplete flashback into the action line, showing it in its entirety either at the second-act turning point (the protagonist's lowest moment) or the climax, depending upon what sort of story you want to tell.

Turning *Cinderella* into autobiographical flashback

The triggering crisis can occur as given. Regard the prince as the enigmatic outsider in the past and present. Make Cinderella speak in voiceover. In this sort of flashback, the prince would typically be torn between duty and desire.

Incorporating flashback as memory into *Cinderella*

You could incorporate this backstory device by inventing a list of important moments in Cinderella's past life and inserting them at points in the standard structure where they seem appropriate. You could also use a scene from the action of the later part of the story. For example, you could insert a flashback to the ball after the second-act turning point when Cinderella feels her dream cannot be achieved. Normally, flashback as memory or illustration presents flashbacks in their chronological order, starting with the disturbance.

Incorporating alternative versions of events via flashback

You could use the standard structure of *Cinderella* in combination with flashback as memory or illustration to show alternative versions of events, or even Cinderella's unbalanced delusions or fractured view of reality.

Starting flashbacks at the disturbance and ending just after the first-act turning point

This would be copying the structure of *The Sweet Hereafter*. It would involve many stories featuring Cinderella and others around her, and perhaps around the prince. The film would open with the invitation to the ball. There would be an enigmatic outsider asking questions about the invitation, this person perhaps being involved in an intense personal relationship and flashforward story of their own. The film would then use flashbacks to follow the doings of Cinderella and the other characters in the period leading up to the invitation – their normality. When the story had been told full circle, returning to the disturbance (the appearance of the invitation), the film would end with the appearance of the fairy godmother and a surprise twist. Cinderella might reject the chance to go to the ball. She might die on the way. She might meet her true love when the carriage breaks down. The outsider would be bewildered and leave, concluding their own flashback – or flashforward – story.

Detailed structural breakdowns of flashback placement in *Shine, The Remains of the Day, The Usual Suspects, Citizen Kane,* and *The Sweet Hereafter* are found in the next chapter.

10. Structure charts of flashback narrative

This chapter contains structural breakdown charts of five flashback films described in the previous chapters. There are two thwarted dream models (*Shine* and *The Remains of the Day*), two case history models (*The Usual Suspects* and *Citizen Kane*) and one film that starts out as thwarted dream and becomes case history (*The Sweet Hereafter*). The charts demonstrate how each film maintains suspense by jumping from cliffhanger in the present to cliffhanger in the past, and sometimes in the future. They show how the cliffhangers tend to be act turning points or other dramatic highpoints.

The charts for *Shine, The Remains of the Day, The Usual Suspects,* and *Citizen Kane* show how each film has two stories with complete action and relationship lines, and how each of these action and relationship lines, past or present, is constructed in three acts (although parts may be truncated). The chart of *The Sweet Hereafter* shows how the film uses mostly stories in one act, and how it manages to remain intelligible while moving between its many stories and time-frames.

The charts also show how protagonists and antagonists change between past and present, and how they are related to the enigmatic outsider.

For a detailed explanation of the various forms of flashback narrative see Chapters 7–9.

In the following charts, 1ATP represents first-act turning point and 2ATP represents second-act turning point.

Structure of *Shine* (thwarted dream)			
Story in the present		**Story in the past**	
An ex-psychiatric patient, once a famous pianist, is rescued from a halfway house, finds love and fame.		A boy pianist with a bullying father achieves success but has a nervous breakdown, is sent to a psychiatric hospital and ends up in a halfway house.	
Action line (quest)	**Relationship line**	**Action line**	**Relationship line**
Protagonist/ interviewer	**Protagonist**	**Protagonist**	**Protagonist**
Sylvia, Gillian	Sylvia, Gillian	David Helfgott	David Helfgott
Antagonist and enigmatic outsider	**Antagonist and enigmatic outsider**	**Antagonist**	**Antagonist**
Mature David	Mature David	Peter Helfgott	Peter Helfgott
Note: Everything happening in the present is really act three of the story in the past.			
Start of film			
Triggering crisis		**Triggering crisis**	
Disturbance	**Disturbance**	**2ATP**	**2ATP**
These happen simultaneously.		**These happen simultaneously.**	
David banging on window of Moby's in rain.	David banging on window of Moby's in rain.	David banging on window of Moby's in rain.	David banging on window of Moby's in rain.
David is given lift home by Sylvia and Bob. He listens to rain on the window. The sound of rain becomes applause.	David gets on well with Sylvia.		
		First flashback	
		Disturbance	**Disturbance**
		These happen simultaneously.	
		Disastrous concert. David plays Chopin on piano that slips away.	David lets down his father by losing at concert.
		Music teacher Ben Rosen offers to teach David. Peter rejects offer.	
		David picks out Rachmaninov concerto on piano.	David pleases Peter by picking out Rachmaninov concerto on piano.

Story in the present		Story in the past	
Action line (quest)	Relationship line	Action line	Relationship line
Disturbance	Disturbance	Disturbance	Disturbance
		Peter asks Ben Rosen to take on David as pupil and teach him Rachmaninov. Rosen says will teach him, but not Rachmaninov.	Peter is no longer David's teacher.
Bob's car has arrived at the halfway house where David lives. Sylvia takes David in. Sylvia notices he has a piano and asks if he can play. He says he can "kind of" play. She leaves him, staring after her, alone and miserable. He looks out into the rain.			
Second-act turning point of the story in the past (continued)		**End — first flashback First-act turning point**	
		Second flashback	
		David has won major piano competition. Isaac Stern offers him place at US music school.	Peter proud about win, but stony-faced about offer to go to America.
		Rosen suggests they raise funds by giving David a Bar Mitzvah.	Peter disapproves of religion.
		David is at fund-raiser being held by high society.	Peter highly critical of high society. Back at home, Peter talks to his wife about the importance of family, and of the family they lost in the holocaust. He looks proudly through the scrap-book he keeps of David's successes.

Story in the present		Story in the past	
Action line (quest)	Relationship line	Action line	Relationship line
		David plays at Communist Party meeting. Meets attractive young girl, then meets the novelist, Katharine Susannah Prichard.	Father disapproves of the young girl. Approves of Prichard.
		A letter arrives from family in US with whom David will stay while he studies.	
		Peter announces that David cannot go to US because it will split up the family.	Peter announces that David cannot go to US because it will split up the family.
		David, devastated, runs to Ben Rosen's house for help. Rosen isn't in.	David is devastated by Peter's refusal to let him go to America.
		David is in the bath. Peter comes in to have his bath in the same water. He sees that David has defecated in the bath. He beats him with towel, but David is almost catatonic.	Peter is furious with David for defecating in the bath.
		David has Bar Mitzvah.	
		Rosen begs Peter to let David go to US. Ends up by telling him that he must not inflict "bloody Rachmaninov" on David. Peter refuses to answer. Rosen is now no longer teacher.	

Story in the present		Story in the past	
Action line (quest)	**Relationship line**	**Action line**	**Relationship line**
			David is silent in bed. Peter gently tells him that it is a terrible thing to hate your father. He tells him that music will always be his friend, and that he must survive. He tells him that no-one will ever love him as Peter does.
		End second flashback	
David is asleep on the floor fully dressed. The TV is on. In his hand is a crumpled letter from the Royal College of Music, London.			
Second-act turning point continued of the story in the past			
		Third flashback	
		David plays for Katharine Susannah Prichard.	It is a good relationship. As he plays, she invents a story to fit the music. David gives her a photo of himself.
		David plays Rachmaninov in a major competition and loses to Roger Woodward.	Father upset at the loss. Father and Rosen exchange angry looks. David asks Katharine about her father. She tells story of his affection.
		David reveals to Katharine that he has won scholarship to Royal College of Music in London. He's worried about telling his father.	

Story in the present		Story in the past	
Action line (quest)	Relationship line	Action line	Relationship line
		David tells his father. Father beats him.	Peter tells David that if he goes he will destroy the family and will never be accepted into the family again. He tells David he will be punished. Peter burns his scrapbook of David's triumphs.
		David is at the Royal College leading a happy student life.	Father returns David's letters unopened. David corresponds with Katharine.
		David decides to play Rachmaninov's 3rd concerto for the concerto competition. Practices hard. Spends much time with teacher.	Katharine dies.
		David plays at the competition. Collapses at the end.	His father listens to tape, and has winner's medal.
		David has ECT therapy.	David, back in Australia, rings father. Father hangs up.
			David's sister comes to see him at Glendale Psychiatric Hospital. He has to be told who she is.
		David shuffles about. His fingers drum the arms of his chair. He talks silently to himself. Lays in a bath talking to himself. Keeps looking at a piano in a room in the hospital. Nurse leads him away.	

Story in the present		Story in the past	
Action line (quest)	Relationship line	Action line	Relationship line
		David sits down next to Beryl, a pianist who's playing for inmates. She finds out who he is. He tells her he isn't supposed to play the piano, on doctor's orders.	Friendship with Beryl.
		Beryl takes David home to live with her. He is very untidy. He keeps trying to touch her breasts.	
		Beryl finds a halfway house for David to live in. He'll have his own piano.	Loses Beryl.
		David plays the piano rapidly and loudly. People bang on the floor. David's piano is locked up for the day. He's advised to go out for the day and get some fresh air.	
		David goes jogging in park like a madman. Runs crazily through the rain.	
		David arrives at Moby's — the scene that opened the film.	
		Repeat of scene where David is lying on floor in front of TV with Royal College letter.	
		End third flashback. No more flashbacks. Past and present have met.	

Story in the present		Story in the past	
Action line (quest)	**Relationship line**	**Action line**	**Relationship line**
It's night. David tries to pick the lock on the piano, is unsuccessful. Grabs music and runs out. Arrives at Moby's. Sits at piano. Despite scorn from Sam, plays. Amazes everyone with his ability.			
First-act turning point **(of story in the present)**			
David playing at Moby's regularly.	David popular. Celebrity. Father reads about David playing at Moby's. Comes to see David in his flat above Moby's. Peter tries emotional blackmail on David. David rejects him. Peter gives David his Concerto Competition Medal, leaves.		
Second-act turning point **(of story in the present)**			
Gillian arrives to stay with Sylvia. David is staying. He's leaving a mess. Gillian is amused by him.			
Gillian watches David play at Moby's. She tells Sylvia she is engaged. Gillian goes to see David in his flat above Moby's. She helps him compose letter to his old professor at the College.	David and Gillian getting closer.		

Story in the present		Story in the past	
Action line (quest)	Relationship line	Action line	Relationship line
	Gillian and David go to a Roger Woodward concert together.		
	Gillian watches David swim in the ocean.		
	Gillian is leaving. David proposes. David tells her to consult the stars for advice.		
	Gillian thinks about David's offer, does astrological charts.		
	David and Gillian marry, are happy.		
David plays a concert. It's an enormous success.	David's sisters and mother are at concert, happy and proud, as is Ben Rosen.		
Climax			
	David and Gillian go to visit Peter's grave.		
The end			

Structure of *The Remains of the Day* (thwarted dream)

Story in the present		Story in the past	
A manservant drives across country to find his lost love.		A manservant devotes himself blindly to his master, a Nazi sympathizer, meanwhile rejecting the chance of love and marriage.	
Action line (quest)	**Relationship line**	**Action line**	**Relationship line**
Protagonist/ interviewer	**Protagonist**	**Protagonist**	**Protagonist**
Lewis, shopkeeper, people in pub, doctor	Stevens, the butler	Stevens	Stevens
Antagonist	**Antagonist**	**Antagonist**	**Antagonist**
Stevens	Miss Kenton	Lord Darlington	Miss Kenton
Enigmatic outsider	**Enigmatic outsider**		
Stevens	Stevens		

Note: the cross-country journey in the present (to see Miss Kenton) is really act three of the story in the past.

Triggering crisis		Triggering crisis	
Disturbance	Disturbance	2ATP	2ATP
These happen simultaneously.		**These happen simultaneously.**	
Lord Darlington disgraced as traitor, now dead. Darlington Hall and its contents up for auction. House bought by Mr Lewis. Lewis offers Stevens holiday and use of car.	Letter from Miss Kenton in voiceover. Stevens accepts offer of holiday and car in order to get Miss Kenton back. Writes to her, asking if she would see him, and name time and place. She must address letter to general delivery address.	Lord Darlington dead, house up for auction.	Miss Kenton married and not at Darlington Hall.

	First flashback	
	Disturbance	Disturbance
	These happen simultaneously.	
	Last time local friends came to Darlington Hall for hunt. Life continues as normal at Darlington Hall until ...	Miss Kenton arrives.

Story in the present		Story in the past	
Action line (quest)	**Relationship line**	**Action line**	**Relationship line**
		ıATP **These happen simultaneously**	
		Grand dinner at which Darlington warned by Lewis that Darlington is an amateur and Germany is not to be trusted.	Stevens' father dies.
		End flashback	
ıATP			
Shopkeeper says that Lord Darling-ton was a Nazi. Stevens denies knowing Lord Darlington.	Stevens collects letter from Miss Kenton saying she will meet him.		
		Second flashback	
		Lord Darlington following Nazi ideology.	Stevens declares his feelings for Miss Kenton.
		Leading British fascist comes to stay, accompanied by Blackshirt guards and his butler, Tom Dann.	
		Lord Darlington takes in two young German/Jewish refugee girls as housemaids.	Tom Dann used to work with Miss Kenton, admires her.
		Lord Darlington orders the girls to be sent away because they are Jewish. Miss Kenton threatens resignation. Girls are sent away.	Miss Kenton describes her loneliness and sense of self-disgust at not resigning. Stevens expresses his love for her in the pretence of saying how important she is to the house.

Story in the present		Story in the past	
Action line (quest)	Relationship line	Action line	Relationship line
Complications		End flashback	
Stevens runs out of petrol. At pub Stevens pretends to be gentleman involved in international affairs. Encounters the local socialist. Sleeps in the room of the son killed in the war.			
		Third flashback	
		Stevens being publicly humiliated by fascist friend of Lord Darlington, who claims that common man is too stupid to have vote.	
Complications		End flashback	
The local doctor picks Stevens as a manservant. Stevens says he did not mean to lead people astray. Stevens denies knowing Lord Darlington. Then admits it, defending Darlington. Doctor mentions that Lord D tried to make a deal with Hitler. He keeps questioning Stevens as to what his own views were. Stevens insists he was there to serve only. He says he's about to remedy his own mistake.			

Story in the present		Story in the past	
Action line (quest)	Relationship line	Action line	Relationship line
		Fourth flashback **(Events leading to the fatal mistake)**	
		2ATP	
		Lord D sorry about Jewish girls. Wants them back, but they can't be found. Nazis arrive at Darlington Hall under heavy security. Lord D's nephew Mr. Cardinal arrives to try and warn Lord D away from the Nazis. He is unsuccessful. This is the fatal mistake — after which there is no turning back.	Miss Kenton teasing Stevens. Miss Kenton finds Stevens reading. She pries the book from his fingers. Intense moment but he cannot express his feelings. Miss Kenton starts meeting Mr. Dann. He proposes. She tries to get Stevens to declare himself, but he won't. She accepts Mr. Dann's offer. Stevens devastated but won't admit it. This is the fatal mistake — after which there is no turning back
		End flashback. No more flashbacks. Past and present have met.	
Climax			
Miss Kenton is preparing to meet Mr. Stevens. Her husband appears, tells her that their daughter is pregnant. Stevens has arrived at the hotel. They meet and talk. She explains that she can't come to work at Darlington Hall. Stevens, devastated,			>>

Story in the present		Story in the past	
Action line (quest)	**Relationship line**	**Action line**	**Relationship line**
	Climax (cont.)		
	his dream lost forever, sees her off on bus, knowing they will never meet again.		
Stevens returns to Darlington Hall, throws himself into helping his new master, Congressman Lewis, the man who warned Lord Darlington against the Nazis.			
The end			

Structure of *The Usual Suspects* (case history)

Story in the present		Story in the past	
Dave Kujan, a customs officer, interviews Verbal Klint, a small-time criminal, about the involvement of Dean Keaton, a crooked cop turned businessman, in a failed drug heist.		Verbal Klint joins a group of criminals, including Dean Keaton, in stealing emeralds. The gang goes on to do another job in California, but is forced by Kobayashi, henchman of an arch-criminal Keyser Soze, to rob drugs from a ship. There is a bloodbath and the only surviving gang member is Verbal.	
Action line (quest)	**Relationship line**	**Action line**	**Relationship line**
Protagonist/ Interviewer	**Protagonist**	**Protagonist**	**Protagonist**
Dave Kujan. Plan: to get information on Dean Keaton.	Dave Kujan	Verbal Klint. Plan: to survive and make a living by crime.	Verbal Klint
Antagonist	**Antagonist**	**Antagonist**	**Antagonist**
Verbal Klint	Verbal Klint	Dean Keaton	Dean Keaton
Enigmatic outsider		**Enigmatic outsider**	
Dean Keaton (who might be the mysterious criminal Keyser Soze)		Dean Keaton (who might also be the mysterious criminal Keyser Soze)	Dean Keaton

Story in the present		Story in the past	
Action line (quest)	**Relationship line**	**Action line**	**Relationship line**
Triggering crisis		**Triggering crisis**	
Disturbance	**Disturbance**	**End of story**	**End of story**
These happen simultaneously.		**These happen simultaneously.**	
Ship burnt, many dead including Keaton.	Ship burnt, many dead including Keaton.	Ship burnt, many dead including Keaton.	Ship burnt, many dead including Keaton.
Verbal Klint, a small-time crippled criminal, is interviewed by District Attorney (DA)			
		First flashback	
		Disturbance	**Disturbance**
		These happen simultaneously.	
		A group of criminals (Keaton, Verbal, McManus, Fenster, Hockney) are rounded up for police line-up. While being held, McManus suggests they do job. Keaton says he's not interested.	Keaton tells others that he and Verbal were in jail together.
The police are investigating the ship. Meanwhile, a customs officer, David Kujan (the protagonist), persuades police to let him interview Verbal. Verbal has immunity given to him by DA. Kujan wants to make sure Keaton is dead.			
ıATP			
A burnt survivor in hospital keeps saying 'Keyser Soze'.			

Story in the present		Story in the past	
Action line (quest)	**Relationship line**	**Action line**	**Relationship line**
Kujan bullies Klint and tells him he's stupid. He asks what happened after the line-up.	Verbal Klint and Keaton were friends. Verbal refuses to believe ill of Keaton.		
		Second flashback	
		The gang leaves police station. Keaton is met by lawyer girlfriend. They all watch Keaton.	
			ıATP
			Verbal goes to Keaton's flat. He persuades Keaton to be part of the job (stealing emeralds from crooked cops) on the basis that Keaton needs money and the gang will only accept Verbal if Keaton vouches for him. Verbal says he has a plan which will mean no shooting.
		ıATP	
		Gang hijacks crooked police car containing criminal. All goes successfully. No one shot.	
		Second-act Complications	
		They all decide to go to California to hand over emeralds.	
			Keaton is very concerned for Edie, his lawyer/girlfriend. Wants to see her before they leave.

Story in the present		Story in the past	
Action line (quest)	**Relationship line**	**Action line**	**Relationship line**
Kujan says Keaton was cold-blooded killer who was only using Edie.	Verbal defends Keaton.		
Meanwhile, in the hospital a translator has been brought in. Burnt man is the only person who can give positive identification of Keyser Soze. Police ask man to describe Keyser Soze to artist, who will draw up a face for ID.			
Kujan says Keaton is using Verbal. He threatens to turn the whole criminal world against Verbal. Verbal says it was a lawyer called Kobayashi who was responsible for the burning of the ship.			
		Third flashback (continuing complication)	
		In California, Redfoot, their contact, says there is another easy job. Keaton persuaded against his will. Have to do another job.	
		The job is to steal a briefcase from some men in an underground car park. There is much shooting. Verbal shoots a man Keaton was trying to avoid shooting.	

Story in the present		Story in the past	
Action line (quest)	Relationship line	Action line	Relationship line
		Third flashback (cont.) (continuing complication)	
		They open the brief-case to find it contains dope, not money. They confront Redfoot, who says that he did not set up the job. He was asked to get them to do the job by a lawyer named Kobayashi, who will come and see them.	
Kujan reveals that Verbal never mentioned Kobayashi in his testimony to DA. Kujan is summoned to go outside. Police reveal to him that there was no cocaine on the boat, but there was a man who could positively identify Keyser Soze. Gangsters intended to sell this man to other gangsters who wanted to kill Keyser Soze. Kujan comes back to Verbal and asks him who Keyser Soze is. Verbal upset at the name.			
		Fourth flashback (continuing complications)	
		Lawyer turns up to see gang. He's Koba-yashi. He's working for Keyser Soze. Wants them to do a job for him, robbing a ship of a cocaine	

Story in the present		Story in the past	
Action line (quest)	Relationship line	Action line	Relationship line
		Fourth flashback (cont.) (continuing complication)	
		consignment. It is extremely dangerous, and some of them will die. He gives them a case containing full dossiers on the criminal life of each, to blackmail them.	
Verbal explains that Keyser Soze is a mysterious figure who may or may not exist, and is said to be ruthless.			
		Fifth flashback	
		Keyser Soze murdering his own family and the families of others, as revenge.	
Verbal says he didn't tell the DA because he thought he wouldn't be believed. He thinks Keyser Soze wants to get rid of him.			
Meanwhile, at the hospital the burnt man is giving instructions to the artist.			
		Sixth flashback	
		Fenster, one of Verbal's fellow gang members, has left the gang because he didn't want to do the new job. Kobayashi tells them where he is and they kill him.	

Story in the present		Story in the past	
Action line (quest)	**Relationship line**	**Action line**	**Relationship line**
		2ATP	
		The gang plans to kill Kobayashi. They almost do, but he tells them that terrible things will be done to their loved ones if he is killed. He goes for a meeting with Edie, Keaton's girlfriend, whom he's threatened to kill if Keaton doesn't cooperate.	
			2ATP
			Keaton doesn't kill Kobayashi because he's concerned that Edie will be murdered.
		Third act	
		The gang get ready to raid the boat. Keaton asks Verbal to stay behind to pass message on to Edie.	Keaton asks Verbal to take message to Edie.
Kujan wants to know why Keaton didn't make a run for it.			
Kujan is told by his colleagues that Edie, who is a lawyer, is defending criminals connected with the boat. He's told that there was no dope on boat. Verbal has described man in a suit and hat as the killer of Keaton. Verbal says that this man is Keyser Soze. Kujan	Verbal says he was frightened of Keyser Soze. This is why he didn't defend his friend Keaton. He let Keaton down, let Keaton, his friend, be shot dead.		

>>

Story in the present		Story in the past	
Action line (quest)	**Relationship line**	**Action line**	**Relationship line**
wants to know why Verbal didn't help Keaton. Verbal says he was frightened of Keyser Soze.			
		Seventh flashback	
		Climax	**Climax**
		Man in suit comes out to deck where Keaton is injured. He shoots him and drops cigarette on to spilt petrol. Ship lights up.	Keaton is dead.
The police tell Kujan that Edie knew that the man on the boat who could identify Keyser Soze was being sold to a Hungarian gang. Kujan bullies Verbal. Says that Keaton was using him. Kujan is convinced that Keaton didn't really die and that Keaton is really Keyser Soze. He says that Edie is dead, murdered by Keaton.	Verbal keeps defending Keaton.		
	Climax		
Kujan gets Verbal to admit that the idea for the first job was Keaton's idea. He urges Verbal to tum state's evidence. Verbal refuses.	Verbal is devastated at the revelations of Keaton's treachery. He limps off, cursing the police.		
In the hospital, the drawing of Keyser Soze is being faxed through to the police station.			

Story in the present		Story in the past	
Action line (quest)	**Relationship line**	**Action line**	**Relationship line**
Kujan feels he hasn't really learned much from Verbal.			
2ATP			
Kujan suddenly notices that names from Verbal's conversations (Redfoot, Skokie, Illinois, etc.) are actually on the police noticeboard that was in Verbal's line of vision. He notices that Kobayashi is the brand name written on the bottom of his coffee cup. He realizes Verbal has cleverly tricked him, telling him a pack of lies.			
Third act			
Kujan rushes out after Verbal. He doesn't notice the fax coming through.			
Verbal leaves the police station and walks down the street. He suddenly loses his limp and paralyzed arm and starts walking normally.			
Back in the police station, an officer looks at the faxed drawing of Keyser Soze. It is a likeness of Verbal.			
Verbal gets into a car driven by the lawyer, Kobayashi. The car drives off.			
Climax, with twist			
Nearby, Kujan has missed the event, presumably because he was still looking for a cripple.			
The End			

Structure of *Citizen Kane* (case history)

The theme of *Citizen Kane* is the classic preoccupation of case history flashback: that people are ultimately unknowable by their public or personal actions. To demonstrate this, the film presents a sequence of incomplete versions of Kane's life which, added together, tell all (and nothing). These are made up of a newsreel and the accounts of five people who knew him. The story in the present deals with the journalist who has to work out the truth about Kane.

To see how the stories in past and present are actually structured and interwoven, there are four charts. The first deals with the past, giving a chronological account of Kane's public and personal life, showing how it breaks down into action line and relationship line, each with a three-act structure. The second chart shows which interviewee tells which facts in the film. The third chart is a breakdown of the story in the present, the story of the journalist Thompson, showing how it breaks down into action and relationship lines (even though both are very slight). The fourth is a structural breakdown of the film itself, charting it from start to finish.

Note that while each of the accounts only tells part of Kane's story, each has a relationship line and action line in three acts (although certain parts are truncated). This gives each story impetus and closure. However, to maintain the mystery and interest surrounding Kane and stop the film becoming a series of short films about a man called Kane, each story starts and ends at a dramatic high point in Kane's life. This is done in such a way that Kane's story is not fully explained until the very end of the film, with Raymond, his manservant, and finally, the dramatic irony of the twist that identifies "Rosebud."

This technique of partially telling a series of stories in sequence so that they build towards a final joint climax, then rounding them off with a final twist, is very like the technique used in *Pulp Fiction*.

Breakdown of Kane's story in *Citizen Kane*		
	Action line	**Relationship line**
Disturbance	Kane taken from family.	Kane taken from family.
First-act turning point	Kane takes on a newspaper, *The Inquirer*.	Kane marries Emily.
Second-act complications	Kane commits himself to using *The Inquirer* to expose wrongs. Kane takes over rival newspaper. Kane goes into politics, runs for governor.	Kane becomes alienated from Emily. Kane takes up with Suzy. Kane and Jed fall out because Jed feels Kane is egomaniac. Emily divorces Kane. Kane marries Suzy, tries to make her an opera star. Sacks Jed Leland.
Second-act turning point	Kane's election as governor stymied by love-nest exposure. Political career in ruins.	Suzy overdoses.
Act three	Kane gives up politics, tries to make Suzy an opera star. Fails.	Kane and Suzy move into Xanadu, arguing and unhappy.
Climax	Kane goes bust as a result of the depression.	Suzy leaves Kane all alone and friendless at Xanadu.

Who tells what in *Citizen Kane?*		
	Kane's action line	**Kane's relationship line**
Note how each version ends at a dramatic highpoint in Kane's life, often an act turning point in action or relationship line.		
Newsreel version	Summary of Kane's public life, from heir to newspaper magnate, then statesman and political candidate, through to collapse of political career because of scandal followed by financial failure, life as recluse and death.	Brief mentions of first marriage, of scandal involving Suzy, of marriage to Suzy and luxurious lifestyle at Xanadu.
End of newsreel version		
Thatcher's version	**Normality and disturbance**	**Normality and disturbance**
	Working-class boy taken away to be brought up rich.	Working-class boy taken away to be brought up rich.
Second-act complications	**First-act turning point**	
	Kane takes on *The Inquirer.*	
	Climax	
	Kane's financial collapse at end of film.	
End of Thatcher's version		
Bernstein's version	**Second-act complications**	**Second-act complications**
	Kane and Jed developing newspaper empire. Jed concerned that Kane is compromising. Kane is developing socially and politically useful relationship with Emily, a politician's daughter.	
		First-act turning point
		Kane marries Emily.
End of Bernstein's version		
Jedediah's version		Kane initially happy with Emily. They have a son. Kane becoming estranged from Emily.
	Kane standing for governor.	

	Kane's action line	Kane's relationship line
	Second-act turning point	
	Kane's rival exposes him.	Kane meets Suzy. Kane starts relationship with Suzy.
	Third-act complications	
	Jed and Kane argue. Jed goes to work in Chicago. Kane tries to make Suzy an opera singer. Jed writes honest but scathing review of Suzy. Huge fight with Jed.	Jed and Kane argue. Jed goes to work in Chicago. Kane tries to make Suzy an opera singer. Jed writes honest but scathing review of Suzy. Jed sacked.
End of Jedediah's story		
Suzy's version	Kane tries to turn Suzy into an opera singer.	Suzy and Kane fighting.
		Second-act turning point
		Suzy attempts suicide.
		Third act
		Suzy and Kane at Xanadu. They live a sumptuous lifestyle but are unhappy.
		Climax
		Suzy leaves Kane, Kane flies into a rage.
		Resolution
		Kane is left all alone.
End of Suzy's story		
Raymond's version	**Climax**	
Archer's version (this is actually seen earlier in the film)	Kane financially ruined.	
Raymond's version	**Resolution**	
	Kane dies alone, remembering his childhood.	

Breakdown of Thompson's story in *Citizen Kane*		
	Action line	**Relationship line**
Disturbance	Kane dies.	Kane dies.
First-act turning point	Told to find out the truth about Kane, in particular, the identity of Rosebud.	Told to find out the truth about Kane, in particular, the identity of Rosebud.
Second-act complications	Suzy refuses to talk to him. Reads Thatcher's diaries. Interviews Bernstein. Interviews Jedediah.	Interaction with Suzy. Interaction with stiff librarian. Interaction with Jedediah.
Second-act turning point	Doesn't know what to do, decides to go back to Suzy.	Feels the job is hopeless.
Third act	Interviews Suzy. Interviews Raymond.	Interaction with Suzy. Interaction with Raymond.
Climax	Nobody can really understand who Kane was and the identity of Rosebud will remain a mystery.	Concludes that no one can fathom another human being and the identity of Rosebud will tell nothing.
Resolution (climax twist)	Rosebud is Kane's sled from childhood.	Rosebud is Kane's sled from childhood.

Flashback structure of *Citizen Kane*

Like many films using flashback as case history, each flashback gives a different version of events, in this case, of Kane's life. The story in the present has only a rudimentary three-act structure, with disturbance plan and climax twist, but no act breaks in the normal sense. Note how flashbacks start and finish at strong dramatic moments in the story of the past. Notice overlapping but essentially chronological storytelling.

Story in the present		Story in the past	
Kane, a newspaper magnate, dies and Thompson, a journalist, is sent to interview those who knew him to explain Kane, in particular, his mysterious last word "Rosebud."		Kane is adopted out of poverty, becomes an idealistic newspaper magnate, sells out morally, marries, has an affair with a singer which wrecks his chances of a political career, tries to turn the singer into an opera star, fails, dies in solitude.	
Action line (quest to discover the real Kane)	**Relationship line (meeting interviewees)**	**Action line (Kane's career)**	**Relationship line (Kanes's relationships)**
Protagonist/ Interviewer	**Protagonist**	**Protagonist**	**Protagonist**
Thompson, the journalist. *Plan:* to find Rosebud.	Thompson.	The interviewee for each version of events: Suzy, Thatcher, Bernstein,	The interviewee for each version of events: Suzy, Thatcher, Bernstein,

Story in the present		Story in the past	
		Jedediah, Raymond. *Plan:* to interact successfully with Kane.	Jedediah, Raymond. *Plan:* to interact successfully with Kane.
Antagonist	**Antagonist**	**Antagonist**	**Antagonist**
Kane	The interviewees: Suzy, Thatcher, Bernstein, Jedediah, Raymond	Kane	Kane
Enigmatic outsider		**Enigmatic outsider**	**Enigmatic outsider**
Kane		Kane	Kane
Triggering crisis		**Triggering crisis**	
Disturbance	**Disturbance**	**End of story**	**End of story**
These happen simultaneously.		**These happen simultaneously.**	
Kane dies, which will result in Thompson getting the job of finding out the truth about Kane.	Kane dies, which will lead Thompson to make contact with interviewees.	Kane dies.	Kane dies alone.
		First flashback. The newsreel version of Kane's life.	
		Newsreel of Kane's public life.	
		End flashback	
Thompson given job of finding Kane the man via the meaning of "Rosebud." Thompson goes to see Kane's second wife, Suzy, who's drunk.	Suzy refuses to talk.		
Thompson goes to library of Walter Thatcher, Kane's banker.			
	Thompson encounters grim librarian.		

Story in the present		Story in the past	
		Second flashback **(Thatcher's version of Kane's life)**	
		Thatcher arrives to take young Charlie away from his family.	Charlie fights against being taken away.
		Kane takes on newspaper.	Thatcher disapproves.
		Kane loses a lot of money in the Depression.	
		Signs over much to Thatcher's company.	Kane tells Thatcher he wishes he had been a great man of the sort Thatcher would disapprove of totally.
		End flashback	
Thompson has found nothing about "Rosebud."	Thompson asks cold librarian and guard about Rosebud. They are unpleasant.		
Thompson goes to interview Bernstein, Kane's business manager.	Bernstein makes interesting observations on life.		
		Third flashback **(Bernstein's version of Kane)**	
		Kane starts publishing *The Inquirer*, with Bernstein as business manager and Jed Leland as drama critic.	Bernstein becomes Kane's business manager at *Inquirer*. Jedediah Leland, Kane's best friend, is drama critic.
		Kane writes noble "Declaration of Principles" for *The Inquirer*.	Jed still a great friend, asks to keep the handwritten copy of "Principles."
		Circulation increases. Kane buys all the top journalists from the rival newspaper. There is a grand party.	Jed expresses fears to Bernstein that Kane will be corrupted by the new journalists.

Story in the present		Story in the past	
		Kane becomes engaged to Emily, the president's niece. He has political aspirations. Bemstein predicts she will become president's wife.	Kane becomes engaged to Emily.
		End flashback	
Bernstein recommends that Thompson talks to Jed Leland. Thompson goes to hospital to talk to Leland. Jed says he knew Emily.	Thompson inter-relates with Leland.		
		Fourth flashback (Jed's view of Kane)	
		Kane spending more time at newspaper.	Emily and Kane initially in love, become estranged as they grow older.
	Jed says Kane had no love to give.		
		End flashback	
		Fifth flashback	
			Kane meets Suzy, who has toothache. They flirt. She sings for him.
		Kane, standing for governor, giving speech, attacking political rival John Geddes.	
		John Geddes threatens Kane that he will reveal his relationship with Suzy unless Kane drops out of election.	John Geddes threatens Kane that he will reveal his relationship with Suzy unless Kane drops out of election. Kane's marriage threatened.

Story in the present		Story in the past	
		Second-act turning point	
		Kane exposed. Loses election.	Kane and Jed fight. Jed elects to work in Chicago.
			Kane marries Suzy. Tries to make her opera star. Her debut, at the Opera House he built, is a disaster.
		Jed has written savage review. Kane finishes review. Sacks Jed.	Huge fight with Jed. Jed sacked.
		End flashback	
Jed says Kane wrote to him but he never wrote back.	Jed keeps pestering Thompson for cigars. Thompson agrees to buy him cigars.		
Thompson goes to see Suzy.	Suzy is drunk, but talks.		
		Sixth flashback (Suzy's view of Kane)	
		Kane forces the opera teacher to persist with Suzy. Suzy's debut (part of which has been seen) is shown more fully, with Leland bored and Kane appalled.	
			Suzy hates review. Jed returns Kane's cheque, torn up, plus the original copy of the "Declaration of Principles."
		Susan performs in many more operas.	
			Susan overdoses, almost dies.
		Kane agrees to let Suzy give up singing. He builds Xanadu. They go there to live.	

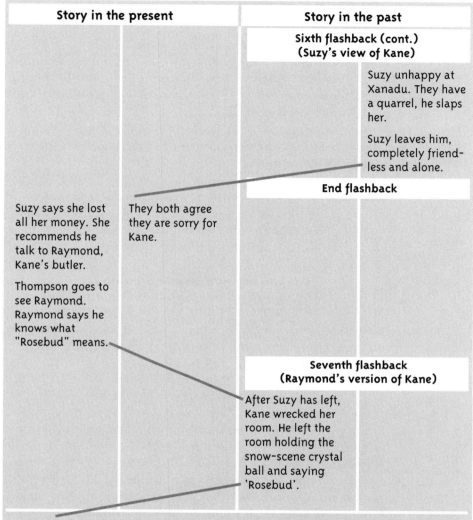

Story in the present		Story in the past	
		Sixth flashback (cont.) **(Suzy's view of Kane)**	
			Suzy unhappy at Xanadu. They have a quarrel, he slaps her.
			Suzy leaves him, completely friendless and alone.
		End flashback	
Suzy says she lost all her money. She recommends he talk to Raymond, Kane's butler.	They both agree they are sorry for Kane.		
Thompson goes to see Raymond. Raymond says he knows what "Rosebud" means.			
		Seventh flashback **(Raymond's version of Kane)**	
		After Suzy has left, Kane wrecked her room. He left the room holding the snow-scene crystal ball and saying 'Rosebud'.	

News team appears. Thompson explains that he didn't learn much. He never learnt what or who Rosebud was. He says that the word "Rosebud" is just a piece in a jigsaw puzzle and a man's life cannot be explained by one word.

Climax twist

In a distant corner of the house, workmen are burning junk. They burn an old sled, the sled Kane was playing on when Thatcher took him away from home. As it burns in the fire, the name "Rosebud" is revealed.

The end

Structure of *The Sweet Hereafter* (thwarted

A.	B.	C.	D.
Past/*Saving Baby Zoe*	Present/action line Stevens comes to town to instigate lawsuit	Present/*Stevens/Zoe relationship line*	Past/*fairground, year before crash*

A.1 Past/Saving Baby Zoe Titles over lawyer (Stevens) and wife in bed asleep with the baby daughter. **Normality.**

B.1 Present/Action line Stevens in car wash in new place. **Normality.**

C.1 Present/Relationship line *Intercut phone box in sleazy area with man in car in car wash.* Girl rushes to phone box. Lawyer takes collect

D.1 Past/Fairground, year before crash Fairground at dawn. Young girl Nicole singing with a group, accompanying

B.2 Present/Action line Back in car wash, lawyer is stuck. He struggles out of car wash, goes into garage. No one is there. Looks around. Sees a damaged bus. **Disturbance.**

D.2 Past/Fairground, year before crash Bus arriving at fair with the kids. The bus driver, Dolores, is chatting to the children as they descend from the bus. Nicole and her father,

B.3 Present/Action line Stevens' car arriving at motel. Rings bell. A woman comes out and he asks for a room. A man appears and asks whether he's a reporter. Gets a negative. Man then asks, "Are you here about the accident?" (first mention of the accident). Stevens says, "Yes, I'm a lawyer," and that it is important that he and the couple talk. Cut to couple talking about

C.2 Present/Relationship line Call is from Zoe, collect. The couple quarrel in background as Stevens talks. Zoe is not seen but Stevens'

E.1 Future/Relationship line Cut to 29 November 1997 on TV screen. Stevens is on plane. The passenger next to him is a lawyer, Allison O'Donnell, a schoolfriend

F.1 Past/Morning of crash The Ottos seeing Bear on to bus. Woman's voiceover saying Ottos always waited for bus. **Normality.**

dream becoming case history)

E. Future/Stevens/Zoe relationship line	F. Past/morning of crash	G. Past/night before crash	H. Past/Zoe's childhood

call on mobile from his daughter Zoe. Revealed that she's a junkie and unpredictable. She hangs up, storms off.

herself on the guitar. Man watching affectionately. She goes off with him, saying she's 'so happy'. He's her father. **Normality.**

Sam, are watching. Nicole watches Dolores affectionately, saying that the bus and its children are "just the biggest thing in [Dolores'] life."

neighbors as lawyer takes notes and asks questions. The man maligns his neighbors, the wife is more tolerant. Stevens wants to know which neighbors who have lost children in the crash are "good and upstanding." Wife suggests the Ottos, who are artists and whose adopted native American, Bear, was on the bus. Stevens gets a call on his mobile phone.

comments indicate that she is hostile and seeing a doctor. End on a calendar on the wall open at December 1995.

of Zoe's and daughter of his ex-partner in law firm. She asks after Zoe. He avoids answering. **Normality and disturbance in one scene.**

A.	B.	C.	D.	
Past/*Saving Baby Zoe*	Present/action line Stevens comes to town to instigate lawsuit	Present/*Stevens/Zoe relationship line*	Past/*fairground, year before crash*	

B.4 Present/Action line It's Dolores, the bus driver, talking, being interviewed by Stevens. She describes the Ottos. Her husband, Albert, in a wheelchair sits paralysed.

F.2 Past/Morning of crash Dolores' voiceover describing morning of crash. Nicole is on bus. Bus travelling along followed by a pick-up

B.5 Present/Action line Back to Dolores' kitchen. She says that Billy had no problems with law. Billy's wife Lydia died of cancer.

F.3 Past/Morning of crash Back to Billy following bus. He rings on mobile phone to talk to Risa. Intercut with Risa at the motel.

E.2 Future/Relationship line On plane with Allie. Stevens reveals that Zoe has been a drug addict for many years, going to "… clinics, halfway houses,

B.6 Present/Action line Stevens persuades the initially hostile Ottos to retain him by convincing them that crash was not caused by Dolores hitting

E.3 Future/Relationship line On plane, Stevens tells Allison: "I did everything the loving father of a drug addict is supposed to do." She would lie and scam for money. He says he's had ten years of lies. Kicking

G.1 Past/Night before crash Nicole arrives to babysit at Billy's. Billy says he will be back before nine. **Normality.**

G.2 Past/Night before crash Billy playing guitar in garage. Comes out.

G.3 Past/Night before crash Nicole reading *Pied Piper of Hamlin* to Billy's

G.4 Past/Night before crash Billy and Risa making love. **Normality.**

E.	F.	G.	H.
Future/*Stevens/Zoe* relationship line	Past/*morning* of crash	Past/*night* before crash	Past/*Zoe's* childhood

	truck driven by Billy Absell. He honks horn, waving at his kids in back of bus. He always followed bus to school. **Normality.**		
It's clear they are having an affair. He says Nicole is coming to look after his kids. He'll be over at six, will be waiting in room. Long shot of car following bus. Pan up to sky. **Normality.**			
treatment centres, detox units." He is going to see Zoe now. He changes subject then leaves seat. Goes and sits in toilet, in despair. **Stevens' normality and first-act turning point in story of the present.**			
		ice patch, but by negligence of bus company or others involved with bus and road.	
down doors, dragging her out of rat-infested apartments, etc. "Enough rage and helplessness in your life turns to something else." "What?" "To steaming piss." **Second-act turning point of Stevens/Zoe story.**			
	Comes to back of motel. Goes into end room. Waits, smoking. Risa arrives. Wendell is out. Back after ice hockey. **Normality.**		
			children. Little boy wants to ride with her on the bus. They discuss the motives of the Pied Piper. **Normality.**

A.	B.	C.	D.
Past/Saving Baby Zoe	*Present/action line Stevens comes to town to instigate lawsuit*	*Present/Stevens/Zoe relationship line*	*Past/fairground, year before crash*

A.	B.	C.	D.
		G.5 Past/Night before crash Nicole trying on dead wife's clothes. **Normality.**	
		G.6 Past/Night before crash Risa after sex. Talking about Sean not wanting to	
		G.7 Past/Night before crash Billy and Nicole discussing his dead wife's clothes.	
		G.8 Past/Night before crash Nicole is driven home by her father, Sam. Nicole's voiceover of Pied Piper, the text	
		F.4 Past/Morning of crash Panning forests, then the bus, followed by car. Dolores' voiceover says she has twenty-two kids on board. **Normality.**	
	B.7 Present/Action line (But, by the setting and costumes, this is actually a continuation of Scene b.4–5.) Stevens is talking to Dolores.		
		F.5 Past/Morning of crash Cut to voiceover about bus arriving at Risa and Wendell's motel,	
	B.8 Present/Action line Back to Dolores, upset. (This is really a continuation of scene B.4–5.)		
		F.6 Past/Morning of crash Children in bus. Bus driving along, followed by Billy in car.	

A.2 Past/Saving Baby Zoe intercut with **E.4 Future/ Relationship line** Stevens, wife (Clara) and baby Zoe in bed. Stevens' voiceover saying that whenever he goes to rescue Zoe he thinks of an event when she was three years old. The three were in their summer cottage. Stevens awakened by Zoe's labored breathing. She was sweating and swollen, and Stevens guessed she'd been bitten by an insect. Clara tried to breastfeed her while he dialed the hospital. Doctor said Zoe had been bitten by baby black widow spider. They must bring her in, keeping her calm. "Zoe loved us equally then, just as she hates us both equally now." Doctor said Stevens had to

E. Future/*Stevens/Zoe* relationship line	F. Past/*morning* of crash	G. Past/*night* before crash	H. Past/*Zoe's* childhood

go on bus. Won't want to let go of me. He has to go. **Normality.**

Lets her have them. Mustn't feel strange about wearing them. He gives her music tape containing ideas for music. **Normality.**

suggesting that the town is being punished. Nicole and Sam go off to barn. They have (incestuous) sex. Nicole's voiceover from *The Pied Piper* mentions the crippled boy left behind — how sad he is to be left behind. **Normality.**

with visuals of this. Risa bringing out Sean to the bus. Sean wants to stay with Risa. Nicole gets him to sit next to her. **Normality.**

Bus goes off the road and down on to the frozen lake. Billy stops and watches the bus sliding across ice and sinking into lake. **Disturbance.**

bring small sharp knife on the journey and do emergency tracheotomy if necessary. He would have only a minute and a half to do it. And Zoe would probably be unconscious. Doctor stressed that the parents must not let Zoe's heart beat too fast because this would spread the poison. Intercut with Zoe's face and knife beside it. They drove, waiting for Zoe's breathing to stop before making the incision. Stevens was dreading making the incision. But they made it to the hospital before the tracheotomy was necessary. Stevens: "I was prepared to go all the way." Zoe's face, with his voice singing lullaby. **This is a complete story.**

A.	B.	C.	D.	
Past/*Saving Baby Zoe*	Present/action line Stevens comes to town to instigate lawsuit	Present/*Stevens/Zoe relationship line*	Past/*fairground, year before crash*	

H.1 Past/Zoe's childhood Zoe as little girl playing with mother.

F.7 Past/Morning of crash Billy at the scene of the accident. Blanket being put over body.

B.9 Present/Action line/Flashforward? Risa and Billy in the motel. Risa asks Billy whether he is going to the funeral. He asks her whether it is true that she has retained a lawyer. (This seems to be a flashforward because Billy does not find this out until **scene B.13.**) She says she has because she feels the bus or the road safety rail might have been faulty. Billy says the bus was fine — he serviced it. She asks whether it is true that he gave Nicole one of his

B.10 Present/Action line Nicole in bed after accident.

B.11 Present/Action line Nicole's parents taking her home from hospital. She is in a wheelchair. They have installed a blue wooden ramp. Nicole

E.5 Future/Relationship line Nicole's voiceover, reading *The Pied Piper*, as Stevens sees Allison

B.12 Present/Action line Stevens coming to Nicole's house. The ramp is now painted red. He explains the legal situation and what will happen in court to Nicole. She says, emphatically, "I won't lie."

B.13 Present/Action line Dramatic haunting footage of the inside of the bus after the crash. Seems like it's Nicole's memories, but it's actually Stevens videoing bus. He runs away and hides as car approaches. It's Billy. Just staring at the bus. Takes his hat off. Stevens comes up and introduces himself to Billy. Billy hostile. Stevens gives card, Billy throws it away. Billy threatens to beat Stevens up, saying, "You can't help." Stevens persists. Billy says that Wendell and Risa "wouldn't hire a goddam lawyer." (This scene appears to be out of sequence because Billy knew in **scene B.9**

C.3 Present/Relationship line Zoe is in a phone bouth. **Disturbance.** She's savage. "Yesterday I went to sell my blood." She has AIDS.

A.3 Past/Saving Baby Zoe Flashback: Zoe's face as a child.

C.4 Present/Relationship line Zoe, as an adult: "I'm scared." Stevens: "I love you, Zoe. I'll soon be there. I'll take care of you. No matter

E. Future/*Stevens/Zoe* relationship line	**F.** Past/*morning* of crash	**G.** Past/*night* before crash	**H.** Past/*Zoe's* childhood

Rescue workers, trucks, helicopters, screaming, sobbing people. Sees his two children running towards him. **Disturbance.**

dead wife's sweaters and she was wearing it when the bus crashed — implying this might have caused crash. Billy is scathing. He says: "You know what I'm going to miss? More than making love? The nights when you couldn't get away from Wendell. The nights I'd just sit in that chair for an hour. Smoking a cigarette and remembering my life with her." **Disturbance (the crash) and first-act turning point. End of their story.**

has a new, downstairs room. There is a present from Stevens, a new computer. Nicole is told that her parents' family have retained a lawyer.

asleep on the plane. Stevens puts blanket over sleeping Allison.

that Wendell and Risa had retained Stevens.) Stevens says, "Let me direct your rage." Stevens' mobile phone rings. "It's my daughter. Or it may be the police to tell me they've found her dead." Billy: "Why are you telling me this?" Stevens: "Because we've all lost our children. They're dead to us. They're killing each other in the streets, [Billy leaves.] as they wander comatose through shopping malls. Something terrible has happened that has taken our children away. It's too late. They're gone." Phone rings again as Billy drives away. It's a collect call from Zoe.

First-act turning point (surprise/obstacle). "Welcome to hard times, Daddy." She asks for money.

what happens, I'll be there." **First-act turning point, end of one-act story.**

A.	B.	C.	D.
Past/*Saving Baby Zoe*	Present/action line Stevens comes to town to instigate lawsuit	Present/*Stevens/Zoe relationship line*	Past/*fairground, year before crash*

B.14 Present/Action line (but this seems to be a continuation of B.4–5) Morning. Back to Dolores. Dolores wants to be sure that it will be clear in court that she was only doing fifty miles an hour. Stevens says Billy has said

Flashback to B.11 Stevens remembers footage of the bus.

B.15 Present/Action line Dolores giving deposition to a judge of some kind in the town hall.

B.16 Present/Action line Billy's pick-up truck arriving at Nicole's house. Nicole sitting alone in dark. Billy wants parents to drop the lawsuit. Billy says Stevens came by garage and gave him a subpoena to make him testify

B.17. Present/Action line Father knocks on Nicole's door. She's in bed. Father says tomorrow she has to make deposition at community centre. Says it's hard to talk now. She says that in the past they didn't have to talk much.

B.18 Present/Action line Nicole and father driving to community center. He carries her to wheelchair, wheels her into hall. Voiceover from *The Pied Piper*:"When all were in to the very last, the door in the mountain side shut fast. Did I say all?" Extract from *The Pied Piper* about the crippled boy

B.19 Present/Action line Nicole in car. Stevens tells her father the case is over. Stevens says what Sam has to be concerned about is why she lied.

E.6 Future/Relationship line At an airport, Stevens is wistfully watching a playing father and child.

E.7 Future/Action line Outside airport. Getting into taxi. Sees Dolores taking tickets to get on to bus. She smiles at him. He's in cab. Nicole's voice comes in over.

B.20 Present/Action line Billy is looking at the bus. Nicole's voiceover says, "We're all citizens of a different town now. A town of people living in the sweet hereafter."

D.3 Past/Fairground, year before crash Nicole, her voiceover reading from *The Pied Piper*, is at the fair watching the big dipper.

G.9 Past/Night before crash Nicole closing book of *The Pied Piper*, the night

E. Future/*Stevens/Zoe* relationship line	F. Past/*morning* of crash	G. Past/*night* before crash	H. Past/*Zoe's* childhood

that this was so. (We have not seen this. Is it a lie or is this scene actually a later interview?) Stevens says he has to clear Dolores' name. Husband Albert gets angry and says, with difficulty, that the true jury for Dolores is the town, not strangers.

because he was behind the bus. Nicole listening. They are people employing more than one lawyer. Parents say they need the money. Billy offers to give money he'll get from insurance for his kids. Asks after Nicole. Billy sees she has been listening.

She talks about the past and being a wheelchair girl now. **Disturbance to Nicole—Sam story — the disturbance is the effects of the bus crash.**

who was left behind. Nicole answers questions. Extract from *The Pied Piper* about how sad and lonely the cripple is. Nicole starts to lie. She says that Dolores was driving at seventy-two miles an hour. Stevens closes his eyes because he knows she has wrecked the case. Everyone leaves. **First-act turning point, end of town's one-act story.**

Any child who could do that to her father is not normal. **First-act turning point, end of Nicole—Sam's one-act story.**

Allison and Stevens bid farewell to each other. Allison, the model daughter, wishes Zoe well. Stevens is nearly in tears. This is **the non-climax.**

before the crash. Kisses children goodnight. Walks away to look out of window. Headlights illuminate her silhouette. Returns to **normality prior to disturbance.**

11. Tandem narrative and sequential narrative

L ike flashback narrative, tandem narrative and sequential narrative are structures which present several different stories in the same film. At present, films contain as many as nine or ten different stories, and in future the number is likely to be even higher. Tandem narrative runs interconnected stories together in parallel and is seen in films as diverse as *City of Hope, Crimes and Misdemeanors, Short Cuts, Magnolia* and *Sliding Doors.* Examples of sequential narrative are *Pulp Fiction* and *Go.* Sequential narrative shows separate but interconnected stories one after the other, linking them at the end. In sequential narrative, each story is usually introduced with a subtitle then told uninterrupted up to a dramatic high point (a first- or second-act turning point), when the next will start. Close to the end of the film each story is revisited and concluded in a final section that explains the links between all the stories. In *Pulp Fiction,* some of the narratives are told in their entirety without interruption (as in "The Gold Watch" and "Vincent Vega and Marcellus Wallace's wife").

On occasions, both tandem and sequential narrative borrow from flashback narrative and operate in different time frames. One of the narratives in *Crimes and Misdemeanors* utilizes flashback as illustration to show both the protagonist's guilt-stricken memories of a religious upbringing and, in a separate set of flashbacks, the way he met the mistress he intends to have murdered. This means that this narrative operates in three time frames, the present, the past, and the distant past. *Pulp Fiction* tells its stories out of chronological sequence and jumps about in time so much that while the action of the film runs over three days, the film's ending actually occurs on the morning of day one. It also includes a kind of flashback in the form of a dream about childhood experienced by the boxer, Butch.

Like all forms of parallel storytelling, tandem and sequential narrative seek to paint a large canvas filled with many and different characters. Tandem narrative is usually epic in its aims and themes, seeking to portray a whole community. Sequential narrative is more interested in the individual world and viewpoint of each character in response to one event. Typically, it is structured around the same events seen from different viewpoints, or followed into different individual paths. This is useful to remember when choosing which structure to use for a parallel story film. Is the film to be epic – to go outwards and show an entire community? If so, use tandem narrative. Or is it to go inwards, to show, essentially, different views of one moment in time? In this case, choose sequential narrative.

Advantages and problems

From the writer's point of view, tandem and sequential narrative forms are very useful for large ensemble casts. The large number of different stories and different settings means the cast can be divided up into small groups and each character easily given part of the action. This is in contrast to the multiple protagonist/antagonist structure (to be discussed in Chapter 12), seen in films like *The Big Chill* or *Tea with Mussolini*, in which a large group of characters is followed through one story and each, in effect, has to compete for the limelight.

Tandem and sequential narrative have a particular advantage over the reunion and siege forms of multiple protagonist/antagonist movies because characters are not trapped in one static setting. Also, whereas reunion and siege movies often have backstory problems because they show people out of their normal context, tandem and sequential narrative tend to show people in their own environment, moreover, proactively engaged in a dynamic story which takes them back and forth into the world at large.

But tandem and sequential narrative films have particular problems in the matter of control. How does the writer control and give meaning to so many different stories? On what basis are stories chosen?

Control is really a planning problem, which is another way of saying that it is a structural problem. There are three main control or structural problems with tandem and sequential narrative, all interconnected. The first is the problem of how to give the film closure and meaning. The second is the problem of pace both within individual stories and in the film as a whole. The third is the problem of coping with length, because the longer a film becomes, the more potentially unwieldy it becomes (and also, crucially, the more expensive).

Closure and meaning

In practical terms, both closure and meaning depend on choice – choosing what meaning is to be transmitted and choosing which stories will best illustrate that meaning, both in themselves and in the way they connect initially then come together at the end.

Flashback narrative does not present this problem (of which stories to choose and how to link them) to anywhere near the same extent. An individual's story is chosen and told in full circle, with the past explaining the present and leading towards a final climax. Meaning and satisfactory closure are virtually built in. Of course, in a complex flashback narrative like *The Sweet Hereafter*, there is the problem of which stories the writer chooses to follow. But the choice is strictly limited, dictated by the central action line of the film. In the case of *The Sweet Hereafter*, it is what happens to a town when its children are killed. The choice consists only of which townsfolk will be followed through in their grief. In tandem and sequential narrative there are no obvious built in limits, no natural circular closure. The issues of choice and closure are wide open.

Films using tandem or sequential narrative tackle the problem of closure, meaning and connection in a number of ways. Usually, the various stories are linked via characters or theme. Sometimes each story has its starting point in the same event or events, for example *Go*, in which all the stories happen because one character makes a decision to work someone else's shift, or *Pulp Fiction*, in which events cover the interconnected doings of various characters connected with a criminal and his henchmen. Sometimes the action of all the stories takes place in a very limited time frame, perhaps a day (*Go* and *Magnolia*). Sometimes all the stories end in a shared event such as a wedding (in *Crimes and Misdemeanors*), a shower of frogs (in *Magnolia*), or an earthquake (in *Short Cuts*). Sometimes all the stories are linked from the start by a theme, and a "macro plot," that is, a plot that not only demonstrates the theme but shows the theme affecting different characters in different stories. This happens in *City of Hope*, in which the theme is graft and corruption, and a plot about a big development demonstrates this and has an effect on all the characters. Sometimes the link only becomes clear at the end, as in *Crimes and Misdemeanors*, in which the message "life is not like a Hollywood movie" suddenly explains the connection between two apparently unrelated narratives.

Unfortunately, few tandem or sequential story films solve the problem of closure and meaning. Most audiences complain that while the films are often extremely good, they fizzle at the end and it is hard to know what they were about' or what the point was – in other words, to what end those particular stories were chosen. This is a complaint directed at *Short Cuts, Magnolia* and *Go*. In contrast, other films that use tandem or sequential narrative have very satisfactory closure. This is so of *City of Hope, Pulp Fiction* and *Crimes and Misdemeanors*; indeed, *Pulp Fiction* has such a satisfactory although bizarre ending that it is common for audiences to applaud at the conclusion of a screening.

This points to two interesting facts. The first is that it is possible to achieve a satisfactory ending in tandem and sequential films, even highly complex ones. The second is that audiences enjoy, indeed, seem to expect, films using several narratives to present a climax in which it is made clear to what end the multiple stories have been chosen and told. One way of looking at this is that it reflects a natural need to know what film we're in. Another way to see it is that audiences seem to be seeking, effectively, a 'moral', even if that moral is bizarrely surprising (as in *Pulp Fiction*), immoral (as in *Crimes and Misdemeanors*), or depressing (as in *City of Hope*).

Some would say that audiences need to be re-educated in their expectations so that they do not expect a moral or closure, but instead believe that travelling the journey of the film is enough. Many people believe this now, and are passionate in their support of open-ended films. But at present (and this could change) most audiences come to film, as to all art, for a parable or conclusion of some kind, and feel disappointed when none is given them. Whether or not filmmakers reject or embrace majority opinion on the issue is up to them. Either way, it is useful to see what structural or thematic components can be used to create meaning and closure.

Pace and jeopardy

If closure and meaning are related to broad planning issues, pace is a matter of practical storytelling, that is, the mechanics of getting the stories onto the page. Pace problems in tandem and sequential narrative are like pace problems in other narrative structures, except multiplied by the number of stories that have to be told. Pace can be a problem in:

- the setting up of individual stories, because each requires exposition and backstory
- telling the stories, because redundant conflict or other redundant material can slow the film down
- moving between stories, where a jump at the wrong time can cause slowing.

There is also the problem of whether each story will have enough intrinsic rising jeopardy to hold the audience's attention, given the existence of all the other stories (whether it is real yet unusual enough). Finally, there is a problem unique to structures using multiple stories, which is that the concluding climax of one of the stories could feel like the end of the film, meaning that what follows could feel anticlimactic. The solution to this problem is problematical itself. In order to solve the problem of one story's climax stopping the film in its tracks, the writer must find a way to make all of the climaxes of all the stories permit a final joint climax.

Length

The final major problem in tandem and sequential stories is linked to pace and it concerns the matter of the length of the film. The longer the film, the more opportunity for the audience to feel exhausted or lose concentration – or both. The structure of the film has to address the issue of which stories – if any – to truncate and which to tell in full. This links back, of course, to the matter of meaning.

Controlling the length of the film also has major budgetary implications. Now that parallel story films are regularly coming in at three hours, they are becoming very costly. It is vital that each scene earn its keep, or multiple story films will price themselves out of existence, at least for poorer filmmakers.

Problems with closure, meaning, and pace: case studies

What follow are studies of films using tandem or sequential narrative that, despite remarkable strengths in other areas like characterization and originality, are sometimes considered to have problems with closure, meaning, or pace.

Magnolia

Magnolia is a remarkable and moving tandem narrative film containing nine complete and emotionally charged narratives linked by the fact that all of the characters have a connection, close or remote, with a television quiz show. Some characters appear in more than one narrative, and the action covers one day. As well as these nine major narratives, there is an opening section with voiceover – a kind of prologue – which, to illustrate the working of coincidence, provides two complete stories (claimed to be factual) which really have no later significance, although brief extracts from them, with voiceover, do appear later. In addition to the prologue, there is a linking device in the form of regularly appearing visuals of the sky subtitled with brief weather forecasts, mentioning the possibility of rain. These appear at regular intervals. At the end of the film there is a storm in which it literally rains frogs, an event which affects all the characters, one fatally.

The film runs for 189 minutes. Leaving aside the two self-contained stories in the prologue, the film is simple tandem narrative, that is, each story runs concurrently with the others. There are no flashbacks and only one time-frame. Each of the narratives has a three-act structure and builds to a final climax. The two opening stories with voiceover are really an elaborate hook, intriguing and interesting in themselves as well as signalling, in their very oddness, that the film is going to be different from standard fare.

Magnolia sustains its pace remarkably well given its length and number of narratives. The technical reason for this is probably that, as in *Pulp Fiction*, each narrative has interesting, unusual, and well-acted characters; high jeopardy; a strong three-act structure; and a good suspenseful build to a powerful and satisfying climax. While jeopardy in *Pulp Fiction* is to do with the threat of violence – whether characters will physically survive – the jeopardy in *Magnolia* is to do with emotional survival. All of the characters are in some way in search of love, and almost all are emotionally traumatized by parent-child betrayals. In most cases their love is rejected, or appears as if it may be rejected. In a number of stories jeopardy is increased by a "ticking clock" – Will one character die before he sees his son? Will the son agree to see his father before it is too late? Will the policeman discover the girl has drugs in the house? Will the remorseful thief return the goods undiscovered? – and so on.

The lesson from this is that a multiple narrative film can gain power when each narrative contains a powerful story, high jeopardy and a good rising suspenseful structure ending in a climax or a question. This will provide sufficiently strong turning points to keep the audience interested when the action shifts from one story to another. On the matter of pace, it is also significant that there is very little redundant character material in *Magnolia*, a common fault of multiple story films. Where it does happen it is mostly in the story of the man who was once a quiz show prodigy. On the whole, scenes move the plot onward at the same time as exploring character. This is very important in maintaining pace.

If *Magnolia* has a fault, it is its unsatisfactory ending. The film feels unresolved, as if the writer/director did not quite know where or how to stop. There are a number of attempts at linkage between stories in *Magnolia*, but none really provides satisfying closure or a sense of why the journey was made. The idea of coincidence set up in the prologue is clearly intended to provide linkage of some kind, but in fact none of the nine major narratives really provides an instance of the startling sort of coincidence demonstrated by the two opening stories. Also, there is not, as the beginning leads the audience to expect, any final startling event that links all the stories in one astonishing coincidence. All of the cast are affected in some way by the raining frogs at the end, but this still does not quite work because it is unclear what the frogs symbolize. Also, while all the main characters are affected by these raining frogs, the characters are not connected or brought together in any way by them (apart from one instance in which a policeman who appears in two stories makes an appearance in a third because he happens to see a character from another story committing a crime).

The fact that the action takes place over one day is also intended to contain the stories and the characters in some way. There is another attempt at unification through a shift into the surreal whereby every cast member sings part of the same song, but this does not go far enough and, again, its significance is not really explained.

Short Cuts

Short Cuts is a Robert Altman film, based on stories by Raymond Carver, dealing with a large group of characters in Los Angeles. These characters are connected by chance or physical proximity (like living next door to each other), or family relationships. There are ten main narratives, dealing with everything from bizarre black comedy to the tragic death of a child. Like *Magnolia*, the film is structured in tandem narrative, with no jumps between time frames and equal weight being given to all the stories. Also like *Magnolia* it runs for more than three hours and concludes with a cataclysmic natural event, in this case an earthquake.

While *Short Cuts* is a memorable film with wonderful performances, passion, and wit, it has many problems associated with structure. Unlike *Magnolia*, the narratives are not all constructed in three rising acts (or one act, for that matter) and do not all build to a suspenseful climax. There are many scenes that really only serve to repeat character material that has been seen before, and individual scenes often go on for too long. This has a slowing effect because the film has to "run in place" until more physical or emotional action makes it move again. In some cases – as in the story of the adulterous policeman and his wife, the story of the waitress and her alcoholic husband, and the story of the relationship between two couples (the doctor and his wife, and the fisherman and his clown-performer wife) – there seems to be a conscious decision to go for anticlimax, for "slice of life." Technically, this often results in these stories being internally repetitive, demonstrating an ongoing normality with redundant conflict which, predictably, has the effect of slowing the film down. In the stories that do build to a climax, there is not the same emotional impact as in *Magnolia*. This is partly because most of the stories in *Short Cuts* are not as suspenseful or harrowing as those in *Magnolia*, so the climax cannot have as much impact. It is also because the slowness of the film creates a distancing effect – it interrupts the "suspension of disbelief" and the fantasy of reality, so that rather than being emotionally involved in the story, the audience is watching the acting.

Like *Magnolia*, there is no unifying event that satisfactorily brings together and explains the choice of the film's stories. The film begins with much emphasis on a widespread insect-spraying regime being carried out by the authorities at night, when helicopters douse the city with insecticide. There is much play on the possibility of health risks and the sense of a city under siege, so much so that it feels like the setup of an event that will appear at the film's end as the explanation of what all the stories have in common and what the film is about. In fact, after the setup, the insect-spraying is not mentioned.

An attempt at a final unifying event appears in the final earthquake. Like the raining frogs in *Magnolia*, the earthquake at the end of *Short Cuts* affects all the characters but does not provide a "point" or good closure. Consequently, *Short Cuts* feels more unresolved than *Magnolia* because there is less initial connection in theme and relationships between characters. It is hard not to see the final earthquake as an easy way out.

As with *Magnolia*, the film's slowness, lack of suspenseful build in its narratives, the documentary flavor that results in the audience emotionally distancing itself, and lack of overall final resolution – all these cross over into the matter of style and, once again, the larger subjective, philosophical matter of whether a film should have a unifying message or theme, or whether travelling the journey is enough. It should be said that many people loved *Short Cuts* precisely because it did not provide closure and remained open-ended, with life just going on.

Short Cuts could have been shorter without loss – in fact cuts could have improved the film. For example, it is hard to argue for keeping material like the insect-spraying scenes, because they do not go anywhere.

Go

Go uses sequential narratives to tell six stories (three in detail) from different points of view. All of the stories happen over one night (Christmas Eve) and deal with dramatic and often bizarre events that happen to a group of friends who work in a supermarket. The events are all triggered by one character's decision to take another's shift behind the cash register. The stories overlap from the start, with different stories depicting the same scenes from different points of view, and become closely interwoven at the end.

While comparisons are often made with *Pulp Fiction* – and there are certainly stylistic links between the two, both having bizarre and violent black comedy, both dealing with double-crossing and revenge in the world of pimps and drug pushers, both telling apparently complete stories in sequence that come together with unexpected twists – there is no complicated time-jumping in *Go* as there is in *Pulp Fiction* (for example, the latter ends on day one although the film's action in fact covers three days). Also, and very significantly, while *Pulp Fiction* ends with a surprisingly traditional moral (that even criminals can find redemption), *Go* ends with no moral at all. Indeed, the film ends with normality completely restored.

Go contains high jeopardy, with each of its main characters facing death and/or prison, three for what seems initially like murder (all of the victims survive). Each of its stories has a three-act structure. For example, the central story, that of Ronna, the girl who accepts the extra shift and becomes involved with a potentially fatal drug deal, is constructed thus:

- *Disturbance:* Ronna accepts Simon's shift to pay for overdue rent and avoid eviction.
- *First-act turning point:* Agrees to get drugs for Zac and Adam in order to pay overdue rent.
- *Second-act turning point:* Left in a ditch for dead after being shot by Todd and run over by Adam and Zack.
- *Third-act:* Wakes up in hospital, discharges herself, goes to work, finds Mannie alive.
- *Climax:* Has the money for her rent and some left over.

Go succeeds very well in controlling the pace, jeopardy and length of its narratives. They all tie up cleverly. Unfortunately, it is unsatisfactory in its closure because the ending is so trite that it significantly diminishes the film. It makes no comment on the horrors of the previous night and leaves everyone alive and happy. The last words are spoken by Mannie (who almost died of an overdose the night before) to Ronna (who almost died through being shot and run over the night before) and to Clare (who had sex with a murderous drug addict and was menaced by armed criminals the night before). Mannie's question is what the three of them are going to do for entertainment on New Year's Eve. The effect is to imply that the film was merely intended as a wacky romp. It has the odd, distancing, and disappointing effect of stories that end "and it was all a dream." This is not to say that there is anything wrong with comedy. The problem with *Go* is that it is a thought-provoking film about choices, spiralling crises and the subculture of crime and drugs in the suburbs, that ends like a teen comedy. The choice of moral, of what the film is about, undersells the film, denying the audience satisfactory closure in yet another way.

Sliding Doors

Sliding Doors is a tandem narrative film that looks at two different directions a life might take. The film is a romance depicting two different versions of what might happen to a charming girl who has an unfaithful and generally unpleasant lover. The first story follows what happens when she comes home unexpectedly, discovers him with another woman, and dumps him to find an exciting new career and a nice new lover. The second version follows what happens when she does not discover the infidelity and the relationship continues. The film ends in a somewhat contrived way with the death of the girl who left the lover, but the promise that the happy story will happen anew.

Unlike many tandem narrative films, in which the central character is criminal or in some way driven, the central character in this film is not responsible for an immoral act – indeed, she is the innocent victim of one. Unfortunately, the "niceness" and passivity of the protagonist combined with the limited jeopardy involved in the plot causes serious slowing problems. There is just too little to get worried about. There is no sense of the girl getting deeper and deeper into problems. Unlike any of the desperate main players in *Pulp Fiction, Crimes and Misdemeanors, Go*, or *Magnolia,* the girl is charming, moral, beautiful, and talented – and she instantly picks up a much more endearing boyfriend.

There is a belated attempt to inject some jeopardy when the nice new boyfriend appears to be married, but this is too little too late. The film seems to assume there will be sufficient tension in the "parallel universe" device itself to carry the film. This assumption, that a parallel universe is worth looking at for its own sake, is also to blame for the sense of a lack of point or meaning in the film. Certainly the device of two alternative lives itself is interesting but, like any technical device, it can only really engage viewers on an intellectual level. By the end of the film the audience is not really emotionally engaged with the characters; instead, it is concerned with the intellectual problem of how the filmmakers will end the film when the two stories are happening independently of each other, in parallel universes. It does not really answer the question of to what end the audience is travelling the journey.

Techniques to handle closure, pace, jeopardy, and length

Tandem and sequential films that successfully handle the issues of closure, pace, jeopardy, and length do so with a variety of clever structural techniques combined with originality of ideas and characterization. Films that have problems in these areas, like those above, show clearly that, as ever in filmmaking, originality of ideas and interesting characterization alone are not enough. In fact it is probably the assumption that putting a lot of interesting characters (or actors) together and letting them create a range of parallel stories will automatically result in a good film, regardless of larger structural matters, that causes most tandem and sequential films that fail badly to do so.

Television and theatre techniques in tandem and sequential storytelling

How does a writer successfully jump between many different stories? Are there any rules? Tandem and sequential narrative is often treated as something entirely new, but structural precedents in screenwriting do exist. However, they come not so much from film as from television, which inherited them from the stage.

While the telling of equally weighted but often unconnected and very different stories alongside each other is revolutionary in mainstream film, in television it is standard. It derives from the traditional and highly successful formula of "main plot and two sub-plots" found in drama at least as far back as Shakespeare. Television drama series typically run three plots or strands, one a drama strand, the second a serial strand, and the third a truncated, often comic strand. In television, as in traditional theatre, the degree of connection between the plots can vary. In Shakespeare's plays, sometimes the doings of characters in one plot drastically affect characters in other plots (as in *A Midsummer Night's Dream*, in which Oberon's decision to get revenge on Titania affects not only Bottom but the young lovers). At other times different characters' stories are not interconnected in any serious way at all (as in *Henry V*, in which the love story and the story of the foot soldiers are from two separate worlds).

Like television drama series, television drama serials run a number of stories in tandem, but there is significantly less connection between the stories. Rarely does what happens in one story directly affect what happens in the others. The connections between stories are more tenuous, usually consisting of the social or physical connections between the characters. For example, characters may be connected by living with or near each other, or by working together. Situation comedy is similar in that the connections between stories are based on the fact that the characters live or work together, rather than on the action of one story dramatically affecting the others, although this can happen. Usually, each episode contains two unconnected comedy stories and a morality tale, each with a different member of the sitcom cast as its protagonist. Each story is resolved at the end, but while there is sometimes an overlap (for example, often the same moral is illustrated via two stories), probably more often than not the stories are quite separate. Hence a description of a sitcom will often sound something like this: "Character A finds herself stuck babysitting a precocious child. Meanwhile, character B has a date with a spy, while character C has lost his wedding ring down the sink." That this sounds remarkably like a description of many tandem narrative films is no coincidence. (The word "meanwhile" in any description, incidentally, is usually a clue to the autonomy of the stories.)

It might seem odd that tandem and sequential narrative films owe a greater or lesser debt to television, including soap opera, but it is so whether or not the filmmakers are conscious of it. At the very least, television is probably responsible for familiarizing audiences (and filmmakers) with multiple and often only remotely connected stories told in parallel. For practical purposes, its storytelling techniques – in terms of overall structure and the micro structure of each scene – can be very usefully adapted for tandem and sequential narrative in film.

Three films that solve the problems

This section looks at three very different films, two tandem narratives and one sequential narrative, that solve the issues of closure, pace, jeopardy, and length in very different ways, notably, ways that all relate to structure. The tandem narrative films are *City of Hope* and *Crimes and Misdemeanors*. The sequential narrative film is *Pulp Fiction*.

City of Hope

City of Hope is a fast, tightly structured study of corruption and the battle to maintain moral integrity. It spans an inner city community from mayor through to police, even down to children on the street. It is told through a web of interconnected stories all set in the same small physical area. All the stories in some way touch on people exploiting either the system or their official position for personal benefit. It is remarkable for the interwoven nature of its narratives and characters.

City of Hope is the most traditional of the three films being considered here. The three dominant stories are each structured in three acts and all have the corrupt mayor and/or his agents as major or subsidiary antagonists. The first concerns Nicky, an aimless young man, and his builder father, Joe. The second concerns Joe's problems trying to run his business while coping with corrupt officials. The third examines the problems of Wynn, the lone black councillor on a conservative and corrupt city council. All three deal with attempts to maintain moral integrity. Nicky, overprotected and aimless, leaves his cushy job on his father's building site to find independence (disturbance). This leads him to an abortive robbery attempt which has officialdom after him (first-act turning point) and eventually to his fatal shooting at the hands of the ex-husband of a girl with whom he falls in love at first sight. In a final scene which incorporates both second-act turning point (his lowest point) and climax, he is reunited with his father as he dies.

The second story concerns Joe who, forced to pay off corrupt city and union officials in order to continue business, tries to maintain his integrity and protect his family. He is under pressure to burn down one of his properties, a rundown apartment building so that a new development can replace it (disturbance). He resists, but finally agrees in exchange for the police dropping the attempted robbery charges against Nicky (first-act turning point). To his horror, two die in the fire and many are left homeless (second-act turning point). Later, he finds Nicky dying. They are reconciled, but it is too late to save Nicky and he dies (climax).

The third story, the story of the black councillor Wynn, concerns his problems not only with the conservative and corrupt council, but with militant black community members who despise him and try to destroy his credibility at every turn. When two black youths beat up a white teacher, then lie that he propositioned them (disturbance), Wynn has to choose between exposing the lie and keeping the black community on his side (first-act turning point). The pressure mounts on Wynn, and it seems he will have to lie and support the boys (second-act turning point). In the end, he persuades the teacher to drop the charges and unites the community against the corrupt mayor (climax).

While these three narratives are all structured in three acts, other plots that run alongside and are vital to them are either truncated or incomplete three-act structures, but all maintain the film's pace by stopping at turning points, that is, moments of high suspense. The most important of these stories is Nicky's meeting with Angela, which is a one-act structure. Nicky meets Angela on the day of the robbery (disturbance) and last sees her at the story's first-act turning point (they have sex and talk about commitment).

There is another one-act story in the account of the man who shoots Nicky, Mike Riso. Mike, already angry that Angela has left him, notices Nicky talking to her on the night they meet (disturbance). He threatens him then, later, when drunk, shoots him (first-act turning point), thereby possibly incurring a murder charge. The story of the robbery is in one-act form, stopping at the first-act turning point. The two boys undertake the robbery, roping Nicky in to help (disturbance); they are discovered by a security guard and arrested (first-act turning point).

The story of the two youths who assault Wes, the teacher, and then lie that he sexually propositioned them stops at its second-act turning point. It starts with the two boys, Desmond and Tito, irritated by police harassment, deliberately assaulting an innocent jogger, Wes (disturbance). To get out of the assault charge, they claim the man propositioned them (first-act turning point). The black community believes the boys and is horrified (from now on the story follows only Desmond, the more innocent of the two boys, and his companion disappears). Community outrage spirals. The press comes in and a community meeting is called. On the way to the meeting, Desmond's mother suspects something is wrong and asks Desmond directly whether he lied (second-act turning point). The story stops here, just as it seems Desmond is going to confess. It is not made clear whether or not he does. The next time the matter is revisited is at the community meeting, where Wynn announces he has got the charges dropped. There is a sort of epilogue where Desmond seeks out and apologizes to the teacher, and it seems there is reconciliation.

Wes's story is also concluded at its second-act turning point. The teacher is assaulted while jogging (disturbance), hears that the boys are claiming sexual assault (first-act turning point), and is told by Wynn that his reputation will be damaged regardless of whether he drops the charges or maintains them, but that there will be less damage if they are dropped (second-act turning point). He is not seen after this. Wynn provides the information that he has dropped the case.

Alongside all of these stories runs the truncated story of how the corrupt mayor and his officials manage to get a major development on track. The characters concerned are the mayor, his assistant Pauley (Joe's brother), a corrupt lawyer from the district attorney's office, and an ambitious detective, O'Brien. It consists of a disturbance (the development), followed by a first-act turning point in the news that investors will back out if building does not commence immediately; a second act showing their attempts to force Joe to burn the building down and, as third act and climax, how they discover and use Nicky's criminal act to force Joe to do their bidding.

Facilitating characters

Alongside these stories and their characters are a group of "facilitating characters" who do not have their own narratives but instead move between stories, facilitating actions and events. Primarily, there is Carl, who loans the vehicle for the robbery, arranges for the burning down of the building, and is the person who reveals to Nicky the true character of the dead brother he has deified. Another facilitating character is Wynn's wife, who influences him to get her brother the job of night watchman at the warehouse Nicky and his friends set out to rob. She is also a colleague of the teacher who is assaulted. Other facilitating characters include the ambitious detective who finds out that Nicky was the third criminal, and Mad Anthony, the owner of the electrical warehouse. He is a friend of Nicky's family and employs the night watchman (Wynn's brother-in-law) who foils the robbery attempt by Nicky and his friends. Perhaps the most interesting facilitating character is the disturbed man who, acting as a sort of chorus on the action, wanders through the stories and, at the end, is used not only to foil Joe's attempts to get help for Nicky, who is dying, but to comment on the action with his repeated howls: "We need help."

There are other, less significant facilitating characters who nevertheless help the action by moving between plots, either transmitting information to major characters or providing interesting backstory about them. Characters like this are the two builders from the site who warn Nicky about the police, Nicky's sister, the two aggressive black community members who want to discredit Wynn, and Mike Riso's police officer partner.

Meaning, connection, pace, and closure

Meaning and closure – and even pace – come from connection. While connection in *Magnolia* and *Short Cuts* rests almost entirely in theme (for example, parent–child relationships), and social and physical connections between characters (people being members of the same family or neighbors or linked through a quiz show), connection in *City of Hope* is achieved in a remarkable number of ways.

Macro story

One of the main problems of tandem and sequential narrative is explaining why the chosen stories were included and not others. It is the problem of what the film is about. While a theme alone can link stories, it is not dynamic. It is a concept, not a scenario, therefore not as dramatically compelling. One answer is what we can call a "macro story," or "macro." A macro story is an overarching plot, often truncated, that illustrates the main theme of the film. It dramatizes the common problem faced by the community of characters. It demonstrates what the film is about – in other words, it sets up meaning. In *City of Hope*, the macro, the common problem, is the attempts by the crooked council to get the new development off the ground. All of the other stories, even though they may be much longer and more complex than the macro, are versions of an individual's experience of and reaction to corruption and a system that crushes the weak. This is their common factor. This is why they were chosen and not others.

Because macro stories have to explain the responses of characters across the wide span of a community, they usually concern those in power over the community. *City of Hope* has a strong macro, in others words, a strong common threat to the community. This macro automatically provides one sort of connection between the stories and lays the foundations for jeopardy. The story of insect-spraying in *Short Cuts* starts out feeling as if it will be the macro or common problem, but then disappears. The macro in *City of Hope* immediately provides the basis for meaning and closure.

Main theme demonstrated in all narratives

Another set of connections within the film is provided by unity of theme in the narratives. The theme of corruption occurs not only in the macro plot, but in all the narratives, major and minor. Each of the three major narratives provides a different example of a protagonist's attempts to retain integrity and independence in the face of corruption and abuse of power. In the minor narratives, the story always involves the issue of individuals manipulating the system (or their power within the system) for personal gain. This even applies to the story about Nicky and Angela, in which a policeman who is abusing his power attacks and kills Nicky.

It might seem obvious to make the theme of the major narratives the same as the theme of the macro. This is not necessarily the case. It would be possible to enter the major narratives of a film via the macro, then go off on a tangent and create an entirely redundant story. For example, in *City of Hope* it would be possible to insert a story that concerned the personal relationship between the corrupt assistant district attorney and his wife (who appears once in the garage) but has nothing to do with corruption. This is what happens in *Short Cuts*, which sets out with a macro about insecticide and has to invent another, an earthquake, to finish the film.

Social and physical connections

Social and physical connections exist between the characters in different stories. They live and work near each other, are members of one of four racial groupings (black, Italian, Latin American, WASP) and sometimes members of the same family.

Scenes blending into each other

This physical closeness means that the film can move very easily between stories, and John Sayles takes advantage of this by making one scene blend into another as characters from one story literally walk past characters from another story. This is a technique frequently used in television, and its adds pace as well as maintaining contact between characters. In most tandem narrative films, the stories are kept apart and occur in different locations. This has a cumulative slowing effect because each time the film moves between stories it has to establish, firstly, that it has indeed changed stories rather than just changed locations, then it has to establish the location and get the audience up to date in the new story.

Events in one story affecting or setting up events in others

This is a technique traditionally used in theatre (as we saw above with *A Midsummer Night's Dream*) and inherited by television. In fact, in television and traditional stage drama, stories are usually chosen on the basis of how they can interconnect and knit the drama together. *City of Hope* uses this traditional technique.

It is interesting that many films using tandem and sequential narrative do not overlap plots – indeed, they isolate their stories from each other. In *Short Cuts*, the story of the couple whose child is run over is linked with the story of the long-suffering waitress only at the point where the waitress accidentally runs over the child, and there is no further connection of any kind. In *Magnolia*, the off-duty policeman from one story happens to see and catch the burglar from another story, but there was no prior connection and nothing happens between them beyond that meeting.

Both *Short Cuts* and *Magnolia* tend to use each scene to focus only on matters at hand within the story being told. Usually these matters concern the personal relationship between characters in the scene. The scene will examine how they are getting on together at the moment, or how they got on in the past. The action line, the plot, is not central – indeed, is often not there at all. There is little concern with foreshadowing later events; similarly, there is little interest in exposition (although there is often a lot of backstory) or impelling the plot forward. These character-heavy scenes often happen as the result of actors' improvisation, because actors naturally tend to focus on the emotional baggage of their character rather than the demands of the ongoing plot. Such scenes can be magnificent, but are inherently slower than scenes constructed in the traditional manner, which use action line development to pull along, indeed, permit character development.

City of Hope uses the traditional action-line led approach, which makes the scenes faster and often denser, because they transmit all sorts of plot information as well as providing insights into relationship matters. A good example is a very brief scene early in the film. Mike Riso, the jealous policeman, is driving along with his partner, Bill. Just as they are discussing Riso's refusal to stay away from his estranged wife, the ambitious, oily detective O'Brien drives by and stops (this is his first appearance). The three men talk briefly, and O'Brien asks Mike and his partner, firstly, to harass Ramirez, a local criminal, and secondly, whether they are going to the mayor's fundraising dinner. As O'Brien leaves, Bill describes O'Brien's ambitions with contempt.

This short scene transmits an extraordinary amount of information. It gives insights into Mike's jealousy (important for Nicky's story); it reveals Bill's honest and sensible character (important for when Mike shoots Nicky and Bill talks about a cover-up); it shows O'Brien's oiliness, ruthlessness and ambition (important for the macro, for Joe's story, and for Nicky's story); and it sets up the mayor's fundraising dinner, an event that is important at the end of the film (important for Wynn's story because Wynn and his followers storm the dinner to demand answers from the mayor). Thus, information vital to five plots is set up in seconds, moreover, in a credible and unobtrusive way.

Facilitating characters
City of Hope has many facilitating characters. Using characters that move across plots increases speed, adds to the impression of an interconnected community, and increases the sense of unity.

Starting and ending in the same physical and emotional place
Further unity is provided by the film opening on the building site with Nicky rejecting his father, and ending on the same building site with Nicky wanting his father to hold him as he dies.

Ending on a moral
The last moments of the film state its moral. They feature the deranged man shouting "We need help." He is actually shouting for physical help for Nicky, who is dying, but his words resonate on a symbolic level. They have extra power because they are coming from the "chorus" of the film who, disturbingly, is mad. The appearance of this appar-

ently unimportant – indeed, redundant – character as the voice of truth provides another pleasing unity, another tying-up of loose ends.

Close weave

City of Hope achieves meaning, pace, and closure by interconnecting its narratives in eight different ways. If we imagine the narratives as vertical threads in a piece of fabric, the eight different forms of connections are like horizontal threads, weaving the narratives together. This is in contrast to *Magnolia* and *Short Cuts*. These films have more vertical threads (that is, narratives) than *City of Hope* but fewer horizontal, connecting threads. They feel looser and more open than *City of Hope* because they are indeed more loosely woven.

Crimes and Misdemeanors and *Pulp Fiction*

City of Hope achieves closure, pace, and meaning through weaving horizontal connections between plots. But interweaving of this kind is clearly not what causes closure, pace, and meaning in *Crimes and Misdemeanors* and *Pulp Fiction*. The two narratives in *Crimes and Misdemeanors* are deliberately kept quite separate until the last scene of the film. There is no opportunity for interweaving at all. And *Pulp Fiction* cannot make horizontal connections because its stories are told sequentially. Clearly, other and quite different processes have been used to provide meaning, closure, and pace in these two films.

Pace

While *Crimes and Misdemeanors* seems such a quintessentially Woody Allen film that it would have to be unique, it nevertheless has striking similarities to *Pulp Fiction*, a film which at first seems from another world. Interestingly, the ways in which the two films are similar are the ways in which each film achieves pace.

Crimes and Misdemeanors is a murder–thriller told in tandem with a modern comedy–love story. These two narratives run simultaneously but are completely unconnected, apart from one minor character who takes no real part in the action and a final thematic connection to the effect that life is not like a Hollywood movie. The thriller narrative has quite a complex structure. It contains not only the murder story in the present but two separate flashback narratives. These two narratives are both flashback as memory or illustration. One depicts events leading up to the murder, and the other deals with the protagonist's boyhood.

Pulp Fiction consists of a number of crime-related stories that happen within a group of underworld figures over a period of three days. Again, each story is of equal weight. While one story is told only partially at the start of the film and completed at the end, the others, for the most part, are told in their entirety, one after the other. Characters may appear in one or more stories. Only one character appears in all. The stories move between time frames – past, present, and future – so that one character whom we have seen being shot dead in the middle of one of the stories is alive in a story set earlier in time but appearing at the end of the film. There is no one protagonist for all the stories.

Pace through jeopardy

In their murder component, both films feature high levels of jeopardy for the murderer, with murder-reprisals and destruction looming. Death and destruction seem imminent and life and death are at stake. All central characters in both films (even Cliff in the quiet comedy–romance story of *Crimes and Misdemeanors*) are guilty of immoral acts, ranging from adultery to murder.

Pace through comedy

Both films combine murder and betrayal with comedy about domestic affection and disenchantment. Both films contain complex characters who frequently behave erratically as a result of romantic entanglements, often placing themselves in serious physical danger. The comedy in *Pulp Fiction* is very black and occurs throughout, unlike the comedy in *Crimes and Misdemeanors*, which is located solely in one plot. Comedy in *Pulp Fiction* is located in the bizarre juxtaposition of mundane concerns with murder and gangland violence of all kinds. There is also, in the interaction of Jules and Vince, the gangster partners, a sense of vaudeville, with the pair interacting like a grim version of a straight man/funny man comedy duo, even down to the comic patter. In *Crimes and Misdemeanors*, comedy and tragedy are kept separate between plots until the end, when the romantic comedy has a tragic ending and the melodrama ends with everyone living happily ever after. Comedy in *Crimes and Misdemeanors* works as comic relief, providing classic catharsis from the intensity of the murder.

Pace through wit and surprise

Noticeably, both *Crimes and Misdemeanors* and *Pulp Fiction* have surprise endings, and *Pulp Fiction* is marked by many unexpected twists and turns. Like comedy and jeopardy, surprise is a means of maintaining pace.

Both films also feature witty one-liners and a range of bizarre or profound discussions about philosophical issues. The effect of this is to keep the audience engaged at a micro level, from speech to speech, as well as at the macro level of plot and characterization. *Crime and Misdemeanors* and *Pulp Fiction* achieve pace in a number of ways:

- high jeopardy
- building complexity of plot (people getting in deeper)
- comedy, including one-liners and elements of vaudevillian patter
- in individual scenes, high incidence of surprising, witty or thought-provoking acts or comments
- comic or serious philosophical comments
- a surprise ending.

Structure

In their structure, *Pulp Fiction* and *Crimes and Misdemeanors* are completely dissimilar. *Pulp Fiction* is sequential narrative and *Crimes and Misdemeanors* is tandem narrative of a very rare kind. *Crimes and Misdemeanors* consists of two completely self-contained and very different "films" shown in tandem. Unlike most tandem narrative films, the only time the two films intersect is in the very last sequence, in which the leading characters from both films meet at a wedding and talk.

The first film is a romantic comedy about an abortive love affair between Cliff, an aging, failed, married documentary film director and a glamorous film producer, Hally. The second film is a dark drama about a respectable ophthalmologist, Judah, who has a vindictive, neurotic ex-mistress murdered so she will not reveal their affair or his financial misdeeds.

The only plot crossover is a facilitating character in the form of Ben, a saintly rabbi, who is the brother-in-law of the film director and a lifelong friend of the doctor. In one sense both films are black versions of *Cinderella*. In the first, Cinderella gets murdered; in the second, the male Cinderella loses his princess to the comic villain.

Two films in one

Each of the two "films" in *Crimes and Misdemeanors* displays an action line and a relationship line. In the murder story, most of the action is taken up with the action line: the murder itself. It shows how Dolores, the ex-girlfriend, tries to interfere with Judah's family life, how he gets his hood brother to arrange a murder, and how events make him feel guilty and ready to confess. In a normal "crime and punishment" story of this kind there would be an extensive relationship line, usually with a detective or with a friend who is a confessor, or even with a collaborator. But because there is not as much time available as in an ordinary film, the relationship line is very limited. The confessor role is filled by Ben, who is really just a "talking head," delivering positive values and urging confession. The detective appears only once and the collaborator role is filled by Jack, the brother, whose role is to arrange the killing, calm Judah down, and make veiled threats of murder in the event that Judah confesses.

Judah's story uses two separate flashback narratives to dramatize the working of his guilty conscience. The first depicts how he met Dolores and started their affair, and the second shows scenes from his boyhood in a very religious and morally upright Jewish family.

Both sets of flashback are flashback as illustration. Neither is flashback as thwarted dream or flashback as case history (this could have been predicted because Judah's story is concerned much more with the present than the past). The first set of flashbacks, the story of Judah's childhood, provides different illustrations of how moral and religious the family was. There is no story about Judah's childhood as such. What is being shown is Judah's childhood normality. This is one of the rare examples in which ongoing normality is useful in building suspense.

The second set of flashbacks do have a narrative quality. They provide a truncated version of Judah's affair with Dolores. One flashback shows the disturbance (Judah meets Dolores on a plane) and the first-act turning point (Judah goes back to her apartment and kisses her). There are other flashbacks to the relationship after this (one such is experienced by Dolores), but once the audience has been shown the initial meeting there is little more. This works satisfactorily because the main questions about the past have been answered. This is significant technically because it proves that two flashbacks (one to the disturbance and one to the first-act turning point) can provide sufficient information to explain and drive the story set in the present.

Interestingly, there is also a flashback very near the start which has nothing to do with Judah's boyhood or his past with Dolores. It is very close to the start of the film and operates as a triggering crisis, a disturbance to the story set in the present. It occurs at the beginning, where Judah is receiving an award at a function held in his honor. He has a flashback to earlier in the same evening, when he came home to find an unopened letter from his mistress addressed to his wife, and burnt the letter. This event is causing him to be nervous at the award ceremony, increasing the jeopardy. What this shows is that extra tension can be obtained by showing the result of the disturbance before actually showing the disturbance itself.

Judah's story is heavy on action, Cliff's story is heavy on relationship

In contrast to the strong emphasis on action line in the murder story, the second "film" – "Cliff Loses Everything" – focuses heavily on its relationship line. The action line consists of Cliff, the filmmaker–hero, being commissioned by his sleazy television producer brother-in-law, Lester, to be director of a documentary on Lester's life. Cliff hates Lester and only agrees to the job so that he can make some money to finish his documentary on Professor Levi, a philosopher. On the shoot he meets Hally, producer on the documentary. Hally sees some of Cliff's footage on Professor Levi. She likes it, and plans to get him funding and possibly a place for it in a television documentary series. But Professor Levi dies, so that the documentary can never be finished. The final career disaster is that Lester sacks Cliff for satirizing him in the documentary he hired Cliff to make.

The relationship line consists of Cliff falling for Hally and, apparently, she for him. Cliff splits up with his wife. In a surprise ending, Hally dumps Cliff for Lester. There is also a sort of minor relationship line which deals with Cliff's relationship with his sister and niece, the latter being his confidante.

The two "films" work together in an interesting way. While all the stories in *Pulp Fiction* contain comedy, domestic overtones, violence, and high action, *Crimes and Misdemeanors* keeps these elements distinct between its two stories. All of the comedy in *Crimes and Misdemeanors*, as well as most of the human interaction, is located in Cliff's story, while all the action melodrama is located in Judah's story. Cliff's story is quiet and undramatic, and its few major dramatic turning points do not occur until Judah's story is almost finished. Thus, the death of Professor Levi, which marks the end of Cliff's major career hope, happens only well after we have followed Judah all the way through the temptation to murder, the murder night itself, and several incidents depicting his increasing guilt and terror, including him hallucinating a Seder night discussion about morality not only with dead relatives but with himself and his brother as boys.

Jumping between stories in *Crimes and Misdemeanors*

In *Crimes and Misdemeanors*, the jumps from the murder story to Cliff's story are usually greeted by a comically appropriate clip from an old Hollywood movie. Judah's story is usually left and revisited at moments of extreme crisis. Cliff's story is signally lacking in crisis or suspense. In fact the unfolding of the Cliff/Hally relationship is very low key indeed, with suspenseful moments and endings only starting to occur practically at the conclusion of the film, that is, well after the murder in Judah's story.

The quietness of Cliff's story – its quality of gradually unfolding then stopping almost before it has started – is worth considering here. It is caused, in structural terms, by the fact that neither its action line nor its relationship line have a first-act turning point of the normal surprise/obstacle kind. Nothing happens close to the start of his story to put a new twist on his plans. This is probably because Woody Allen felt there was enough jeopardy in Judah's story. If Cliff's story were to stand as a film on its own, it would probably suffer from the same lack of energy as does a film like *Falling In Love* (see Chapter 13, "Lost in the telling"). As it is, the high energy levels of Judah's story just succeed in carrying it.

Closure by a final scene reverse

Crimes and Misdemeanors achieves meaning and closure by playing tricks with the audiences' expectations of genre and structure, and revealing them in an extraordinary final scene reverse.

The moral behind the three-act structure

The moral of classic Hollywood murder melodrama is that crime does not pay, evil will be vanquished, and goodness and order will triumph. The point of Hollywood romantic comedy is that despite extraordinary barriers, the couple will come together in the end. Both melodrama and romantic comedy are committed to the idea of a narrative that permits the protagonist to change and grow (indeed, change and growth defines the protagonist), with this new growth being demonstrated in a satisfying final climax.

The classic three-act model is actually a vehicle for the moral position that humans can change and grow, that good will triumph, and that order will return out of chaos. In fact, the three-act structure as it is normally understood and taught in mainstream western cinema is really moral fable. It is *The Pilgrim's Progress* recreated for the modern age, with its morality built in to its three-act structure.

In the classic three-act structure, the protagonist typically experiences a spiritual rebirth prior to a battle for a noble goal. The rebirth does not happen until the third act – in fact it does not happen until after the protagonist has reached rock bottom, emotionally and often physically, at the second-act turning point. At the start of the third act, the protagonist experiences a spiritual rebirth in which they find new understanding and courage. After that, they spend the rest of the third act fighting to achieve what they now know to be right and appropriate. Their triumph or failure (normally triumph) will occur in a "do or die" climactic scene which is the climax of the whole film, after which the film will end.

To summarize, the third act and the climax in the classic three-act structure are concerned with the protagonist experiencing spiritual rebirth and fighting their particular good fight. But *Crimes and Misdemeanors* deliberately rejects the moral position behind this. The protagonists do not grow in moral stature or understanding. One is deserted by everyone and left completely confused, the other literally gets away with murder. For the rest, evil triumphs over good, order is not restored out of chaos, the bad guy gets the girl, and the film as a whole ends abruptly with no triumphant climax, nor indeed, with any real sense of closure at all. This rejection of the normal model is quite deliberate and is underlined by Judah's last words to Cliff, which are that if Cliff wants to see confession and punishment as the end result of murder, he should watch a Hollywood film.

Just as *Crimes and Misdemeanors* rejects the triumph of good and moral growth in the protagonist, so it rejects the normal vehicle for this triumph. Both of its narratives lack a proper third act (battle against evil) and a proper final climax (triumph). In fact, both stories end on an anticlimax shortly after the second-act turning point. For example, in Cliff's story, while the traditional Hollywood romantic comedy shows boy meeting girl, boy losing girl, boy getting girl back, Cliff does not get the girl back. The film stops at the point where he has lost his film career, his marriage, and the girl he loves. In a normal three-act structure, this would only be the film's second-act turning point. Cliff would spend the third act finding new understanding and battling successfully to get back Hally and his career. This does not happen. Instead, the film simply ends.

In Judah's story the same thing happens. It stops at its second-act turning point and ends with an anticlimax that is a reversal of the traditional scenario for the genre. Just as Judah reaches his lowest point – which involves him, now nearly insane with guilt and fear, finding out that Jack, his brother, will have him murdered if he confesses – we leave him. We leave him at the maximum point of jeopardy. The normal story progression would be a third act involving an exciting mental and/or physical battle followed either by death or confession, but this does not happen. Indeed, there are no more scenes for Judah at all until the end of the film, by which time he has lost his guilt and is living happily ever after, having committed the perfect crime.

Length

An interesting side effect of stopping at the second-act turning point is that it makes the two narratives short enough to create a film of normal length, always a problem with parallel storytelling.

The last scene

The extraordinary and total rejection of the three-act structure and the moral scheme that Hollywood typically uses it to transmit only becomes apparent in the last scene. Until then, the audience remains puzzled about connections between the two narratives and the meaning of the film as a whole, but assumes without thinking that the two narratives will end as convention demands. The last scene turns these expectations on their heads, not so as to create disappointment (as happens in *Go*), but in a highly satisfactory way, because closure and meaning are suddenly and totally revealed. All loose ends are credibly and cleverly tied. Even elements that had not seemed relevant suddenly show themselves to be part of a greater meaning. For example, the clips from Hollywood films in Cliff's story and the classic melodrama style of Judah's story, both of which had seemed mere stylistic oddities, abruptly reveal themselves as comments on the film's bleak moral – that life is not like Hollywood, that in real life the love story ends tragically and the guilty man lives happily ever after. This moral connects into the narrative dealing with Cliff and Lester, because this is also about the real world being in contrast with the world of the screen. Cliff's film-within-a-film is about life behind the scenes on a television show. It simultaneously shows life behind the scenes of documentary making.

City of Hope used a macro and interconnected stories to set up connections, meaning, and closure from its very beginning. *Crimes and Misdemeanors* is devised very much with connections, meaning, and closure in mind, but they are hidden from the audience until the final moment.

Tandem narrative in *Crimes and Misdemeanors*

Narrative 1 The murder of Dolores	Narrative 2 Cliff loses everything
Judah, a successful, respected ophthalmologist, is at a presentation ceremony with his wife, Miriam, daughter and daughter's boyfriend. He's nervous.	
Flashback to: Disturbance in present	
Earlier this evening Judah intercepted and burned a letter sent to his wife by Dolores, the mistress he has tried to dump.	
Back to ceremony. He gives a speech.	
Flashback to synagogue he went to as a boy — where God was always watching.	
In the present, Judah meets Dolores. She refuses to be dumped.	
	Footage from an old Hollywood film of a rejected mistress ranting hysterically. Cliff, an unsuccessful documentary filmmaker, is at the movies with his young niece. They hail a cab.
	Cliff arrives home. Tonight he and his wife, Wendy, are going to meet her brother, Lester, a successful TV sitcom producer, as well her other brother, Ben, a saintly rabbi.
	Disturbance
	At the function, Lester asks Cliff to be the director of a documentary to be made on Lester's life. Cliff agrees so that he can fund the making of his documentary on a philosophy professor, Professor Levi.
Disturbance in story in the past	
Driving to work, Judah has a flashback to his first meeting with Dolores. It was on a plane where she was a flight attendant.	
First-act turning point in story of the past?	
He has a flashback to a kiss very early in their relationship.	
Judah arrives at work. Receptionist says Dolores called. He calls her. She says she has to see him after work.	

Narrative 1 The murder of Dolores	Narrative 2 Cliff loses everything
Judah is testing the eyes of his friend Ben, the saintly rabbi who is Cliff's brother-in-law. He confides in Ben about Dolores. Ben advises confession to Miriam. Flashback to Dolores and Judah on the beach.	
Present. Return to Dolores at her apartment, remembering her past with Judah. Judah arrives. She wants him to take her away on holiday. He wants to end the relationship. She threatens to reveal how he embezzled charity funds. They argue.	
	Cliff is making the documentary of Lester's life. Lester is being obnoxious. Lester tries to get a date with Hally, the producer. She puts him off. Cliff introduces himself to Hally. He shows her some footage of Professor Levi. She says she can get him some funding and a place in her documentary series.
	Cliff arrives at niece's apartment with a book for her. His sister is distraught. She reveals she had a bad experience with a man she met through the personal columns. There are flashbacks to their dates. Cliff goes back to his wife. They are not sleeping together.
Judah meets his brother Jack, a small-time criminal. Jack tells Judah that Dolores could be murdered for him. Judah is appalled.	
	Footage of a melodramatic old Hollywood movie in which two men are discussing murder. Cliff and Hally are watching the movie when they should be working on the documentary.
It's Judah's birthday. His family have given him an exercise bike. Dolores rings. She's at a nearby gas station and will come over unless he comes to meet her. They are in her car, talking. She is starting to get tired of his delay.	

Narrative 1	Narrative 2
The murder of Dolores	**Cliff loses everything**

First-act turning point in present	
Alone, in the middle of the night and in a thunderstorm, Judah is talking aloud to himself and Ben about his options with Dolores. He makes up his mind to get her killed. He rings his brother and arranges it.	
	Cliff is filming Lester at work. At one point, talking to his team of comedy writers about his theories of comedy, he introduces a bimbo who is to appear in the series.
	Footage of Professor Levi talking about what people look for when they fall in love. Cliff and Hally are watching. They share a bottle of champagne. Hally still wears her wedding ring. Lester phones Hally, wanting her to come to the office late at night. He's interested in producing some of her work. Cliff warns her that Lester is being predatory. They watch *Singing in the Rain* together, eating Indian food.
Dolores is followed home by a man who tells her through the intercom that he has a delivery of flowers.	
Back at Judah's place a dinner party is in progress. The phone rings and it's Jack. Judah takes the call and is told that Dolores is dead. Judah is shocked. He makes an excuse to leave the dinner party and go to her apartment to pick up incriminating items. Her corpse shocks him.	
Past. He has a flashback to himself as a child with his religious father.	
	Cliff, Wendy, Lester, and Hally are having dinner together. Lester is flirting with Hally. When Cliff and Wendy get home, Wendy says that Hally is romantically interested in Lester. Cliff denies it. He rings Hally's home to make sure she's there. She is, but Lester is with her.
	Cliff has just been to the movies with his niece. He tells her that he is in love with Hally. He says that Ben is rapidly going blind.

Narrative 1 The murder of Dolores	Narrative 2 Cliff loses everything
Judah is examining Ben's eyes.	
Judah has flashback to his first visit to Dolores' apartment.	
Ben asks Judah if his personal difficulties have been resolved. Judah says they have.	
Judah, driving through a dark tunnel, has flashbacks to the synagogue of his youth.	
Present. Judah goes back to the house where he grew up. In the house he has a flashback of a Seder night in his childhood, with all his family there. The family is arguing about moral responsibility and getting away with crimes. Judah asks about murder. His father says that murder will out.	
Judah gets back to his surgery to find that a detective has called to see him.	
	Footage from an old movie of a woman singing a frenetic comic song about murder. Cliff and his niece come out of the cinema. Cliff says he is about to make his move on Hally. He rings his voicemail. Professor Levi has committed suicide.
	Footage of Professor Levi watched by Hally and Cliff. Hally has come over to comfort Cliff. Mention is made that the documentary probably won't get a place in the series now. Cliff can never now finish it. Cliff kisses Hally. She says she is not ready for a relationship and is very ambitious. She then kisses him back but leaves, saying, "Don't confuse me."
The detective arrives to see Judah. The records show that Dolores rang him at home. Judah talks his way through it.	
Judah, panicked and on the edge of a breakdown, meets Jack. Jack tells him to calm down. Jack implies that if Judah looks like implicating him, he, Jack, will have him murdered.	
Judah sits in his car outside Dolores' flat.	

Narrative 1	Narrative 2
The murder of Dolores	**Cliff loses everything**
Second-act turning point	
At lunch in a restaurant with Miriam and his daughter, he behaves erratically. Miriam reveals that he is drinking heavily. He bellows at his daughter, then walks out. He looks on the edge of a nervous breakdown.	
	Footage of Cliff's documentary on Lester. Cliff has intercut footage of Mussolini ranting. Lester sacks Cliff from the documentary.
	Cliff is walking through a park with Hally. He asks her to marry him. She says she's going to London for four months. Cliff says he feels as if he's been handed a prison sentence.
	Clip of Hollywood prison film with the word "Months" superimposed.

Subtitle: "Four months later." It is Ben's daughter's wedding. Ben is now completely blind, but as benevolent as ever. Cliff and Judah are both at the wedding. It is revealed that Cliff and Wendy are splitting up. Judah is very happy, "celebrating enough for two people." Guests reveal that Lester paid for the wedding. Cliff is appalled to see Hally and Lester together. He is devastated when he hears Lester explaining to some guests that Hally is to marry him. Hally sees Cliff alone and explains that she fell in love with Lester, who is a really nice man. She returns a love letter to Cliff. Cliff is devastated.

Judah finds Cliff sitting alone, miserable. This is the first time they have met. Cliff says he was planning the perfect murder. Judah replies that he has a good murder story for a filmmaker like Cliff. It is a murder story with a twist. Elsewhere at the party, Wendy tells Lester that she has met someone else. Judah tells Cliff his story in the third person. He explains he was on the edge of mental collapse and about to confess. Then one day he woke up and the crisis was over. He was happy. A man charged with other murders has been charged with Dolores' murder. He will now get on with his life, happy. Cliff says that his version would show the man turning himself in, because "then you have tragedy." Judah comments, "If you want a happy ending, you should see a Hollywood movie." He goes off happily with his wife, leaving Cliff miserable, having lost everything.

Pulp Fiction: closure by portmanteau plot

Pulp Fiction achieves closure and meaning with a surprise ending, but it uses a method completely unlike anything seen in *City of Hope* or *Crimes and Misdemeanors*. *Pulp Fiction* is innovative in the stories it tells and highly innovative in its structure. It rejects not only the classic three-act structure but also alternative structures like flashback narrative and tandem narrative. Really, *Pulp Fiction* should not work. It jumps about in time to tell a number of interconnected but autonomous stories in self-contained chunks (some of which are short, self-contained films with titles). It starts and ends in the middle of the action. It kills off what appears to be its protagonist, Vincent, in a dramatic aside in the middle of someone else's story. It is extremely long. Yet, despite all these potential recipes for disaster, it is strikingly powerful, fast, suspenseful, full of well-drawn characters, and grimly comical.

Doubtless, as has been suggested above, some of this is to do with the large amount of jeopardy, surprise, and quirky, often shocking, comedy – comedy delivered by two gangsters who much of the time interact like a comedy duo, even down to the patter. But jeopardy and comedy normally only work within a building structure, that is, within a structure that is rising to a climax. How does *Pulp Fiction* hold? Does it have a new "building structure" – or even an "anti-structure" – that could be used as a model?

The action in *Pulp Fiction*

It is useful here to summarize the action of *Pulp Fiction*, the story material that is actually told.

The film covers events of a criminal and often extremely violent kind occurring to a group of people connected with a Los Angeles gang over a period of three days. Only one character, Vincent, played by John Travolta, appears in all of the stories. The film jumps about, time-wise, within the three-day span of the action.

Jumping about in time is not something new. It has been done in flashback films for many years. What is startlingly new is, firstly, that the jumps in time are not between events of emotional significance or connection (indeed, they seem to happen just to tell a good story), and secondly, that the action in *Pulp Fiction* does not amount to a three-act narrative as we normally understand it, either in terms of traditional three-act structure or in flashback narrative. The traditional three-act structure and flashback narrative both obey the rule that all stories climb a mountain, starting at a certain point in time, just before a disturbance, and ending at the last chronological moment of the film, at the top of the mountain. Flashback narrative only differs here in that there are two or more

Figure 11.1 Chronological vs. viewing order of scenes in *Pulp Fiction*

Chronological order

1. Two gangsters, Vincent and Jules, go to wreak revenge on some young men who have tried to steal a briefcase full of gold bars from Marcellus, their boss. On the way Vincent reveals that Marcellus has asked him to take Mia, his wife, out for the evening. Jules relates that Marcellus is extremely jealous and had a man thrown out of a building just for giving Mia a foot massage. Vincent and Jules confront the young men. Jules shoots two of them, reciting a favorite passage from the bible as he shoots the second.

2. A third young man bursts out of the bathroom and shoots six bullets at Vincent and Jules from point-blank range. He misses. Jules is convinced that this indicates divine intervention. Jules and Vincent take the fourth young man, Marvin, with them in the car. Vincent accidentally shoots Marvin in the face, making blood and brains splatter everything inside the car. Jules and Vincent go to the home of Jules' friend Jimmy to clean up. Jimmy is furious, telling them that there must be no trace of them or   >>

stories in orbit, one progressing chronologically in the present and the other, or others, starting close to their end then returning to the start and proceeding, chronologically, in a full circle until they return to where they started. Put simply, the earliest point in time is the start and the last point in time is the end. But if *Pulp Fiction*'s action is untangled and put together in chronological order, the action has no shape at all.

Chronological sequence in *Pulp Fiction*

Here is the action in *Pulp Fiction* set out in simple chronological sequence.

1. *Day 1, morning:* The shooting of boys who tried to steal Marcellus's money. Jules and Vincent are not hit at point-blank range – divine intervention? Accidental shooting of Marvin, the last of the boys, and decision to go to Jimmy's to get rid of the corpse and clean up. Mr. Wolf arrives at Jimmy's and they all clean up.

   Breakfast at restaurant where Jules decides to become God's servant because he feels the bullets missing him is divine intervention and a message from God.

   Attempted robbery by Pumpkin and Honey Bunny foiled by Jules. Jules lets Pumpkin and Honey Bunny go.

   Jules and Vincent return to bar where Butch is getting instructions about fixing the fight from Marcellus.
2. *Day 1, evening:* Vince takes Mia out. She nearly overdoses. He saves her.
3. *Day 2, evening:* Butch wins the fight.
4. *Day 3, morning:* Butch goes back to his apartment to collect wristwatch. Shoots Vince. He and Marcellus are kidnapped by rapists. Butch rescues Marcellus. Marcellus forgives him. Butch leaves town with girlfriend.

Figure 11.1 compares the chronological order of scenes in *Pulp Fiction* with the order in which the scenes are actually viewed.

Viewing order

In a restaurant, Pumpkin and Honey Bunny, an affectionate young couple who make a living by robbing liquor stores, are having breakfast.

The young couple decide to rob the restaurant, pulling out guns and screaming at the clientele.

Chronological order

(cont.) Marvin when his wife, Bonny, gets home from work, which is imminent. Jules phones Marcellus, who gets a "Mr. Fixit" called Wolf to attend the scene. Wolf gets Jules and Vincent to put Marvin in the boot, then clean the interior of the car and cover it with bedding. He makes them wash themselves and dress in clothes provided by Jimmy. He then drives the car to a junkyard where it can be disposed of, with Jules and Vincent driving behind.

3. In a restaurant, Pumpkin and Honey Bunny, an affectionate young couple who make a living by robbing liquor stores, are having breakfast.

4. Jules and Vincent are having breakfast in the same restaurant as Pumpkin and Honey Bunny. Jules explains to Vincent that the divine intervention incident has made him decide to give up being a gangster to do God's work, which God will eventually reveal to him. He will tell Marcellus today. Vincent goes to the toilet.

5. The young couple decide to rob the restaurant, pulling out guns and screaming at the clientele.

6. Pumpkin, the young man, demands Jules' wallet at gunpoint and makes Jules open the briefcase full of gold bars. Jules gets Pumpkin off-guard and turns a gun on him. Honey Bunny gets hysterical but Jules, newly reformed and a man of God, sees it as his mission to let Pumpkin and Honey Bunny go. Vincent reappears from the toilet ready to shoot the young couple, but Jules prevails. He gives them the money from his wallet and tells them to leave, which they do. Vincent and Jules leave the restaurant. (End of the film.)

7. Butch, a boxer, is at Marcellus' club being given money and instructions to take a fall in a forthcoming fight. He agrees.

Viewing order

Two gangsters, Vincent and Jules, go to wreak revenge on some young men who have tried to steal a briefcase full of gold bars from Marcellus, their boss. On the way Vincent reveals that Marcellus has asked him to take Mia, his wife, out for the evening. Jules relates that Marcellus is extremely jealous and had a man thrown out of a building just for giving Mia a foot massage. Vincent and Jules confront the young men. Jules shoots two of them, reciting a favorite passage from the bible as he shoots the second.

Butch, a boxer, is at Marcellus's club being given money and instructions to take a fall in a forthcoming fight. He agrees.

Vincent and Jules arrive at Marcellus's club.

That night, at the house of Lance, a drug dealer, Vincent buys some high-grade heroin. He goes to Marcellus' house to pick up Mia and take her out for the evening. From the start the atmosphere is loaded with sexual tension. They go to a restaurant, win a dancing competition, and come home. Mia finds the heroin in Vincent's coat pocket and snorts it. She drops into a coma. Vincent drives her to Lance's place to get her an adrenalin shot. Lance makes Vincent give the adrenalin shot. He does so and Mia survives. Vincent drops Mia home and they agree Marcellus is not to be told about the overdose.

Butch the boxer dreams of the time when he was a small boy and a prisoner-of-war friend of his father's came to his house to give him his father's wristwatch, which had not only been in the family for generations, but which had been concealed from the Viet Cong for seven years by being hidden in the anus first of Butch's father, then of the friend.

Butch wakes up with a start in the dressing room prior to the fight where he is to take a fall. Butch does not take a fall, but instead deliberately beats his opponent in order to pick up money laid in bets. Butch escapes through a window, taking a taxi driven by a woman taxi driver who not only knows his identity, but is fascinated by the fact that his opponent died in the ring. At the venue, Marcellus, with Vincent and Mia nearby, is furious and vows to scour the earth for Butch.

Butch arrives at the motel where he and is his girlfriend, Fabienne, are hiding. Next >>

Chronological order

8. Vincent and Jules arrive at Marcellus' club.

9. That night, at the house of Lance, a drug dealer, Vincent buys some high-grade heroin. He goes to Marcellus' house to pick up Mia and take her out for the evening. From the start the atmosphere is loaded with sexual tension. They go to a restaurant, win a dancing competition, and come home. Mia finds the heroin in Vincent's coat pocket and snorts it. She drops into a coma. Vincent drives her to Lance's place to get her an adrenalin shot. Lance makes Vincent give the adrenalin shot. He does so and Mia survives. Vincent drops Mia home and they agree Marcellus is not to be told about the overdose.

10. Butch the boxer dreams of the time when he was a small boy and a prisoner-of-war friend of his father's came to his house to give him his father's wristwatch, which had not only been in the family for generations, but which had been concealed from the Viet Cong for seven years by being hidden in the anus first of Butch's father, then of the friend.

Butch wakes up with a start in the dressing room prior to the fight where he is to take a fall. Butch does not take a fall, but instead deliberately beats his opponent in order to pick up money laid in bets. Butch escapes through a window, taking a taxi driven by a woman taxi driver who not only knows his identity, but is fascinated by the fact that his opponent died in the ring. At the venue, Marcellus, with Vincent and Mia nearby, is furious and vows to scour the earth for Butch.

Butch arrives at the motel where he and is his girlfriend, Fabienne, are hiding. Next morning, they are about to leave town when Butch discovers that Fabienne left his father's wristwatch back at their apartment. Butch goes back to get it. Vincent   >>

Viewing order

(cont.) morning, they are about to leave town when Butch discovers that Fabienne left his father's wristwatch back at their apartment. Butch goes back to get it. Vincent is in the toilet. Butch shoots him and escapes by car. He stops for a pedestrian to cross — and the pedestrian is Marcellus. Marcellus sets off in pursuit.

After a car crash and some shooting, they stagger, fighting, into a weapons shop. The owner holds them both up at gunpoint. They are tied up and placed in a cellar. The shop owner's friend, Zed, arrives, and proceeds to rape Marcellus. Butch escapes, but comes back and saves Marcellus. Marcellus tells Butch that he will forget Butch's scam if Butch leaves town and tells nobody about the rape. Butch leaves and goes back to Fabienne, a free man.

A third young man bursts out of the bathroom and shoots six bullets at Vincent and Jules from point-blank range. He misses. Jules is convinced that this indicates divine intervention. Jules and Vincent take the fourth young man, Marvin, with them in the car. Vincent accidentally shoots Marvin in the face, making blood and brains splatter everything inside the car. Jules and Vincent go to the home of Jules' friend Jimmy to clean up. Jimmy is furious, telling them that there must be no trace of them or Marvin when his wife, Bonny, gets home from work, which is imminent. Jules phones Marcellus, who gets a "Mr. Fixit" called Wolf to attend the scene. Wolf gets Jules and Vincent to put Marvin in the boot, then clean the interior of the car and cover it with bedding. He makes them wash themselves and dress in clothes provided by Jimmy. He then drives the car to a junkyard where it can be disposed of, with Jules and Vincent driving behind.

Jules and Vincent are having breakfast in the same restaurant as Pumpkin and Honey Bunny. Jules explains to Vincent that the divine intervention incident has made him decide to give up being a gangster to do God's work, which God will eventually reveal to him. He will tell Marcellus today. Vincent goes to the toilet.

Pumpkin, the young man, demands Jules' wallet at gunpoint and makes Jules open the briefcase full of gold bars. Jules gets Pumpkin off-guard and turns a gun on him. Honey Bunny gets hysterical but Jules, newly reformed and a man of God, sees it as his mission to let Pumpkin and Honey Bunny go. Vincent reappears from the toilet ready to shoot the young couple, but Jules prevails. He gives them the money from his wallet and tells them to leave, which they do. Vincent and Jules leave the restaurant. **(End of the film.)**

Chronological order

(cont.) is in the toilet. Butch shoots him and escapes by car. He stops for a pedestrian to cross – and the pedestrian is Marcellus. Marcellus sets off in pursuit.

After a car crash and some shooting, they stagger, fighting, into a weapons shop. The owner holds them both up at gunpoint. They are tied up and placed in a cellar. The shop owner's friend, Zed, arrives, and proceeds to rape Marcellus. Butch escapes, but comes back and saves Marcellus. Marcellus tells Butch that he will forget Butch's scam if Butch leaves town and tells nobody about the rape. Butch leaves and goes back to Fabienne, a free man.

Two things are clear from these breakdowns. The first is that there is no apparent logic behind the way the action unfolds on screen, although some of the stories are presented as self-contained stories with titles. The second is that there is no one story that runs from the chronological beginning of the film's action on day one to its chronological end on day three. Instead, the film consists of a range of stories, all of equal importance, which jump in time for no apparent reason and which are connected only by theme and character. The only unifying plot strand seems to be the story of Jules, the gangster who finds God. This runs across a number of the stories and helps create a pleasing closure in a film that otherwise ends, literally, in its chronological middle.

These aspects of *Pulp Fiction* are truly remarkable because what they seem to indicate is that it is possible to create a strong dramatic structure that is not linked to one major story with a beginning, middle, and end; moreover, that it is possible to create a film with a pleasing sense of closure in which the film's climax and pleasing closure occur not at the end of the time it spans, but in the middle.

Jules's story as a traditional three-act narrative

While there is clearly no one major story that runs from start to finish in *Pulp Fiction*, surprisingly, the story of Jules's redemption actually constitutes a traditional three-act narrative of perfectibility, with Jules, in model protagonist style, being changed by his experiences. A narrative sentence of Jules' redemption would run like this:

The *protagonist* Jules, a ruthless gangster, *faced with the disturbance of* having to execute men who double-crossed his boss and *surprised by* what seems to be divine intervention (*first-act turning point*) *is stopped from* investigating the implications of this by the accidental shooting by Vincent of a hostage and the dangerous and complicated disposal of the corpse. *He plans to* reform, but *reaches a lowest point of physical and moral danger (second-act turning point) when* he is held up at gunpoint by a robber who normally he would execute. In the *climax*, he *solves the problem by* choosing the path of good, sending the robbers away unharmed.

Note that the film starts with the moments prior to the second-act turning point and climax of Jules's story, and ends back at the restaurant with the second-act turning point and climax seen in their entirety. It is interesting that the opening of the film, the start of the robbery, is very much like the triggering crisis in flashback narrative. It is the

Viewing order

disturbance in the story of Pumpkin and Honey Bunny, and the second-act turning point of Jules story (as in flashback as thwarted dream).

After the teaser opening (Pumpkin and Honey Bunny starting the robbery attempt), the film goes straight to the disturbance of Jules' story (the visit to the boys who will provide Jules with the chance for divine intervention). It then leaves Jules's story to tell all the other stories. When Jules's story returns, it is at crucial first-act turning point (divine intervention). The story then proceeds uninterrupted to its conclusion: Jules chooses God and leaves the world of gangsters to pursue his dream, which is also the conclusion of the film. Really, Jules's story follows the same pattern and has the same theme, at heart, as flashback as thwarted dream.

A portmanteau structure?

What might be happening here is that the film as a whole is being held together and given its shape – its rising structure – by being enclosed within the standard three-act narrative structure of Jules's story (see Figure 11.2), with its pointed and bizarrely

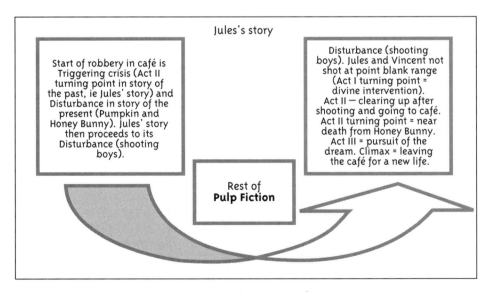

Figure 11.2 Pulp Fiction *portmanteau structure*

unexpected moral, namely, that redemption is available to all and that even a sinner can go and pursue his dream.

Could it be a new rule that, as long as the movie starts with and concludes by following a classic three-act story, presenting the narrative uninterrupted from first-act turning point through to its end, all the structural benefits of that three-act structure – built suspense, character identification, and closure – will still accrue? Are we looking at a structure that works like a carry-bag or *portmanteau*, in which one three-act narrative can contain a range of other stories?

This raises interesting questions about the other stories in *Pulp Fiction*, the stories of Vincent and Mia, and Butch and Marcellus, which are given equal weight to Jules's story. These, too, are structured as classic – if short-form – three-act narratives. Could they act equally well as the portmanteau? Here are narrative sentences for each.

Vincent Vega and Marcellus Wallace's wife

A gangster, Vincent (*protagonist*), faced with having to take out Mia, the sexy wife of his jealous gangster boss (*disturbance*), is surprised by Mia snorting his stash of high-grade heroin and starting to die (*first-act turning point which compounds the problem*). He responds by taking her to the home of Lance, the drug dealer. He is foiled (*second-act setbacks*), firstly by Lance's delay in answering the phone, then his strong reluctance to help, then by bickering between Lance and his wife, then by Lance being unable to find his medical book. He reaches his lowest point of physical danger or despair (*second-act turning point*) when his only chance of saving Mia is to stab her in the chest with a hypodermic full of adrenalin. He manages it and she revives (*climax*).

The gold watch

Butch, a boxer (*protagonist*), faced with accepting a bribe from Marcellus to rig a fight (*disturbance which creates a problem*), double-crosses Marcellus and is set to run away with the money. He is surprised (*first-act turning point which compounds the problem*) by the fact that his girlfriend, Fabienne, has left a watch of great sentimental value at his apartment. He goes back to get it and is foiled initially by Vince, who he shoots dead, then by Marcellus, who pursues him, causing him first to have a serious car crash, then to be shot at and wrestled with (*second-act series of action setbacks, often triggered by the antagonist, but also by fate, accident, etc.*) until, at his lowest point of physical danger or despair (*second-act turning point*) he ends up with Marcellus in a cellar with three sexual perverts who plan to rape him. He fights back, managing to escape. In the *climax*, he goes back to help Marcellus, the man he hated, robbed, and was about to fight to the death. He saves Marcellus, who lets him off the hook. He goes off happily, keeping his freedom, the money, and his girlfriend.

Which portmanteau?

Would the film still have worked if either of these stories had been used to open and conclude the film, using the structural breakdown shown by the Jules story – that is, pre-climax scene followed by disturbance, then, after all the other stories have been told, the first-act turning point appears and the film proceeds uninterrupted to the end? Would the film have had the same satisfactory closure? Here is how each of the stories could have been used as the portmanteau.

With *the gold watch* as the portmanteau, the film could have opened with the per-verted gunshop owner and his friend, Zed, getting the gimp out of the cage. It could then have gone back to the disturbance – where Butch is given his instructions by Marcellus – then be put aside until all the other stories had been told, to return in its entirety starting at the first-act turning point – that is, the point at which Butch discovers the watch has been left behind. The closure would have been Butch walking free.

Alternatively, using Vincent Vega and Marcellus Wallace's wife as the portmanteau, the film could have opened with Lance, the drug dealer, and his wife bickering over the missing medical book and then getting out a syringe. It could then have returned to Vincent and Jules talking about the foot massage prior to their morning reprisal raid. Then, after all the other stories had concluded, it could return to the restaurant and the first-act turning point, which is when Mia takes the heroin at her home. It could then proceed uninterrupted until the climax, in which Vincent stabs Mia with the hypodermic and she revives. The pleasing closure would be when she and Vincent return to Marcellus' house and Mia tells Vincent the tomato joke from her pilot television show, "Fox Force Four." These two alternatives for a portmanteau do not seem impossible at all. Each provides a structure with satisfying closure. It is hard to say whether either could have been made to work as well as Jules's story which, with its moral edge, passes interesting commentary on living and dying by the sword, and presents a larger moral for the film as a whole.

Portmanteau = closure via one story

Pulp Fiction seems to have found a way of containing many diverse stories of equal weight within the structure of one. Instead of relying on one major story progressing more or less chronologically like a journey up a mountain or, as in the hero's journey model, in a circle to the depths of hell and back, it seems we can now do the impossible and contain the greater within the lesser.

Of course, it would be wrong to underestimate the energizing effect on *Pulp Fiction* of its high levels of jeopardy, surprise, and black comedy, along with its elements of vaudeville, its soundtrack, and its startling juxtaposition of the mundane and domestic with the profoundly violent. But the structure of *Pulp Fiction* is something very new, something that opens up a whole range of possibilities within parallel storytelling.

Pulp Fiction is a film held together and explained by the internal structure and pleasing traditional theme (the thwarted dream achieved) of one of its stories, not by a larger unifying story that contains all the stories within a time-frame or a theme. The portmanteau is one story that comes full circle.

City of Hope, *Crimes and Misdemeanors*, and *Pulp Fiction* as models

City of Hope, *Crimes and Misdemeanors* and *Pulp Fiction* achieve meaning and closure by very different means. *City of Hope* relies on weaving a variety of horizontal connections, including a macro plot that demonstrates an overarching theme or common problem. *Crimes and Misdemeanors* uses a final twist to provide a coherent meaning and thematic connections between two apparently dissimilar narratives. *Pulp Fiction* uses a portmanteau narrative to contain and give meaning to its diverse stories. All of these methods can be useful models for tandem and sequential films. Significantly, all of the methods involve thinking about meaning and closure for all the multiple narratives then carefully factoring them in. The lesson seems to be that interesting multiple stories alone are not enough.

Actor improvisation and the macro

Stories in tandem and sequential narrative films are often put together with the help of improvisational work from actors. While the idea of a macro might seem to preempt this process, in fact it can stimulate it.

Since the macro consists of a plot demonstrating a common problem, actors can simply be asked to help create a macro plot and connected stories. For example, if the film were to be about pollution, the macro plot would in some way concern a pollution threat to the community. The actors would start their improvisational work from the theme of characters affected by or in some way connected to pollution. This could result in figurative treatments (for example, a relationship poisoned – polluted – by jealousy), or physical treatments (for example, a character suffering from an asthma attack induced by the pollution, or a worker employed by the authorities to dump pollutants). Actors can be asked to contribute towards the macro plot (that is, the overarching plot that shows pollution affecting the wider community, the common problem) and to tailor their stories to end in a climax that links each individual story with the macro and with other stories to create meaning and closure.

A postscript: recent parallel narrative films

Publication of this book coincides with the release of the excellent multiple-story film *Traffic*. While pressure of time prevents detailed analysis, *Traffic* is a tandem narrative (typically epic), and structured very much like *City of Hope*. It quickly sets up its macro plot (the judge leading the war against drugs) then runs a range of high jeopardy, classically-structured stories, each of which shows the macro affecting individuals across the community, with the climax being the judge rejecting his mission. Pace, meaning and connection (not to mention emotional and intellectual impact) are achieved through interwoven themes, interconnected plots, and the device of characters literally walking across each others' stories. Other recent parallel narrative films are *Run Lola Run* (sequential narrative – "different versions of the same event" - building to a final climax) and *Crouching Tiger, Hidden Dragon* (classic multiple-protagonist quest featuring different versions of "The Warrior," standard character types like "The Traitor Within" and "The Outsider," and the group survival macro of "Will the good warrior be trounced by the evil one?").

12. Multiple protagonists and antagonists

The traditional three-act film structure typically follows one protagonist through an action line and a relationship line. Flashback narrative, tandem narrative and sequential narrative all fit a number of different stories (often with the same theme but different protagonists) into one film. However, there are certain kinds of films, particularly what are often known as *ensemble films*, which do not fit either the traditional three-act structure or any of the parallel story structures that we have looked at so far. Although they deal with one sequence of events and are set predominantly in one time frame, they do not have a single protagonist on a single journey. They tell the story of a group, each member of which has much the same importance, and is followed through their own journey as the group itself makes a journey.

Films like this are actually using a different form of parallel storytelling. This form employs a number of protagonists of more or less equal importance *who are all versions of the same character type*. In *The Big Chill*, for example, the multiple protagonists are all versions of "the radical student ten years on." *Tea with Mussolini* is a variant which uses only one protagonist – the boy telling the story – but has multiple charismatic antagonists (much like the charismatic antagonists of "mentor" films such as *Scent of a Woman*) who are all versions of "the ex-patriot English-speaking lady in Italy during World War II;" this even applies to the son who is forced to dress up as a girl. Another multiple antagonist film is *Saving Private Ryan* in which, even though the leader has most prominence, each of the soldiers on the mission is a charismatic antagonist. As in *Tea with Mussolini*, the protagonist is a person who appears only briefly and is caught in the process of remembering just how profoundly he was affected by actions of the group. *The Magnificent Seven* provides an interesting variant of the multiple antagonist film with a dominant antagonist (Chris, the character played by Yul Brynner). *The Magnificent Seven* actually has multiple protagonists as well as multiple antagonists, the protagonists being the Mexican villagers whose village needs to be saved.

All of these films fall into a structural category that can be thought of as *multiple protagonist/antagonist structure*. In films like these, multiple protagonists or antagonists take it in turns to fulfil the structural tasks carried out in the normal three-act structure by one character alone. This is why there is no sense of disjunction in films like *The Big Chill*, *Tea with Mussolini*, and *Saving Private Ryan* when suddenly a character whom we have been following as protagonist steps out of the limelight and another takes its place. We are not really following a different character; we are following a different version of the same character. Films employing multiple protagonists or charismatic antagonists have two aims: they explore versions of the same social role which display different approaches, concerns, and solutions; and they study the dynamics and story of the group itself.

Films with multiple protagonists or antagonists are usually either quests, reunions or sieges, whether real or metaphorical. Quests involve groups like soldiers, spies, or criminals whom circumstances force into a mission to survive and prevail. Reunions involve groups coming together either for a holiday, or for rituals of passage like weddings or funerals. Sieges involve a group in some way trapped together. Plots can range from literal siege situations, like the women prisoners of war in *Tea with Mussolini* and *Paradise Road* (1997), to a metaphorical siege, as in *American Beauty*, in which a group of alienated people are trapped together in Middle America. Mike Leigh's films are often metaphorical siege films in which multiple protagonists, trapped in social roles, are observed struggling or trying to escape.

Not all films set in sieges or siege situations such as prisons are group stories involving multiple protagonists or antagonists. Many are simply normal three-act structures featuring a single protagonist, as in *Cadillac Man* (1990) or, as in *The Shawshank Redemption* (1994), a protagonist and a charismatic antagonist. The same applies to disaster movies in which, while the story deals with a group under threat, it is really only the vehicle for one heroic figure to be seen triumphing against the odds. The test for a multiple protagonist/antagonist story of any kind is that it is always in some way about the survival of a group, a group under threat, and the group story answers the question of whether the group will survive.

Sometimes the group under threat reinvents itself and survives in a life-affirming way, as happens in *The Big Chill*, in which one member takes on the role of the dead man and two members of the group decide to have a baby. Sometimes the group is destroyed. This happens in *American Beauty*, in which the group is destroyed by murder and family breakup. Alternatively, the group can triumph even though its members suffer or even die, as exemplified by The *Magnificent Seven*, *Saving Private Ryan*, and *Tea with Mussolini*. Parallel protagonists and antagonists can also borrow from other multiple story structures, like flashback. For example, the story of the multiple antagonists in *Saving Private Ryan* and *Tea with Mussolini* is structured as one long flashback, with an opening and closing section in the present. The same thing happens in *American Beauty*. The multiple protagonist/antagonist form often features a dominant driven character whose actions threaten the safety or autonomy of the group.

How all the narratives fit together

Successful multiple protagonist/antagonist structures are well worth examining because so many ensemble scripts fail as a result of writers being unable to handle large numbers of characters in what are often inherently static forms like reunions and sieges. So is there a logic? If all of the characters are protagonists or antagonists, do they all have their own story? How do all these stories fit together? The key to understanding how to write in multiple protagonist/antagonist structures is that the form tracks the emotional journey of both a group and the separate individuals within it. You need to create an action line that will permit this journey, then create the emotional steps from its beginning to its end.

Group action line or survival macro

In practical terms, telling the story of the group and of its individuals requires several different sorts of story to be told in parallel. Firstly, the group itself has to have an action line, however skeletal, which brings the family of multiple protagonists/antagonists together in a crisis situation with a common problem. For example, the action line in *Tea with Mussolini* is what happens to a group of English and American ladies in Florence in the buildup to and duration of World War II. This idea of a common problem threatening the group is, of course, a macro. In its theme and its events it reveals in the most basic sense what the film is about.

But unlike the macro in tandem narrative, which can be about any theme that might affect a large number of people collectively – say, unemployment, or alien invasion – the macro in multiple protagonist/antagonist forms is always about the same thing: survival of the group. Another way of putting this is that the common problem is always a threat to the survival of the group and the macro plot is about why and how the group is threatened. We can call this the "survival macro."

In siege and mission forms, the survival macro is often a dynamic, ongoing narrative, with agents of the common problem actively causing trouble for the group, as do the fascists in *Tea with Mussolini*. In reunion forms, the survival macro may be less dynamic, but it still deals with the problem of whether or not the group will survive the ordeal it has to experience. Specifically, the survival issue is raised by the event that causes the reunion; for example, the suicide in *The Big Chill*. The action of the survival macro deals with the questions raised for the group and individuals in terms of solving unfinished business and establishing the future – in *The Big Chill* this means discussions about the group's past and about the motives of the dead man.

Siege films that deal with actual physical sieges have as their trigger (technically, their disturbance) the event that caused the siege; for example, a bank robbery causing people to be trapped in siege conditions in a bank. But siege films like *American Beauty* that deal with a community trapped in social roles need an internal trigger in the form of a decision by a member, or something happening to a member. This is because their normality is already a siege situation. In *American Beauty*, the trigger (disturbance) that causes a group threat, a common problem, is Lester, a middle-aged man who decides to break all the group rules.

Responses by individuals to the common problem (macro plot)

The film also has to show the different responses of each version of the protagonist to the events provided by the action line or macro; for example, in *Tea with Mussolini,* how each woman reacts to what is done to her by the siege and its agents.

Relationships between individuals

The film also has to show a range of interconnecting relationship lines that explain how the multiple protagonists/antagonists interact with each other and outsiders in terms of conflicts, shifting loyalties and, if the group has a past rather than being thrown together by circumstance, unfinished business.

In short, there are two main sorts of story in these films. There is what happened, is happening, and will happen to *the group*, and there is what happened, is happening, and will happen to *the individual*. This means there are at least five kinds of plotlines in multiple protagonist/antagonist films:

1. The action line or survival macro in the present: a common problem involving the survival of the group and demonstrated in the form of events or adventures happening to the group (for example, in *Tea with Mussolini* the war and imprisonment).
2. The action lines of each protagonist/antagonist: how each protagonist/antagonist is physically affected by outside events happening to the group (in *Tea with Mussolini*, how each woman comes to be imprisoned).
3. The action line in the past: the events that happened to the group in the past – in mission films this can be minimal, but in reunion films it is of great importance because reunion films are about unfinished business (in *Tea with Mussolini*, the group before the war).
4. The relationship lines in the past: how the past had an impact on each member and affected relationships and future aims – again, in mission films this can be minimal, but in reunion films it is of great importance (in *Tea with Mussolini*, specific antagonisms and conflicts between individuals in the past).
5. The relationship lines in the present: the stresses of the present crisis and, if the group has a past, interaction between group members based on unfinished business from the past (in *Tea with Mussolini*, how war and imprisonment affect relationships).

The group story (macro) provides meaning and closure

This content breakdown points to the enormous importance of the group's story or survival macro to the success of films like these. While multiple protagonist/antagonist films are usually thought of as being character-driven with plot a secondary matter, in fact the films of this sort that succeed all show high jeopardy and a strong, if skeletal, action line dealing with the future survival of the group. Less successful models ignore the group's story and the macro which has brought the group together until very late in the action, focusing almost exclusively on individual relationships within the group. This flaw – the lack of a common problem or macro set up at the beginning – can be seen in films like *Parallel Lives* (1994) (see Chapter 13) or *Peter's Friends* (1992), both of which deal with student reunions and both of which, despite fine acting and interesting characters, seem static and fail to engage, with audiences typically commenting that the films feel as if they are "not going anywhere." Successful group films like *The Magnificent Seven*, *The Big Chill*, *Saving Private Ryan*, *American Beauty* and *Tea with Mussolini* all present the group with a powerful threat to its survival. Significantly, in all cases this involves death. Death is also the common problem in both *Peter's Friends*, in which at the end Peter reveals that he is dying of AIDS, and *Parallel Lives*, in which almost at the end a member of the group is murdered, although in both of these cases it does not work as a proper macro because it is introduced too late to provide a useful means for exploring the individuals or the group as a whole. A strong group action line – a strong survival macro – permits powerful relationship lines. This should come as no surprise because it happens in all forms of the three-act structure: action lines permit relationship lines to happen. Unfortunately, writers often forget the need for a group story because they assume that assembling a group of interesting characters will automatically result in an interesting film.

In forms that use multiple antagonists as opposed to multiple protagonists, the macro will always revisit the protagonist at the end of the film, even if it is only momentarily. This is sensible storytelling because the protagonist is the person whose story is being told by the film, and there is no proper closure until this person's story is resolved. In *Saving Private Ryan*, after dealing with the past, the film returns to the protagonist standing in the military cemetery hoping his life has been worth his companions' sacrifices. In *Tea with Mussolini*, the film returns to the protagonist but only in a subtitle before the final credits. When a dominant character is involved (see below), the film will usually end with that person. This is seen clearly in *American Beauty*, which finishes with Lester's voice coming in over the visuals, even though he is dead. The return to a dominant character, like Lester, or a passive protagonist, like Ryan in *Saving Private Ryan*, is a means of achieving closure.

The dominant character

Lester in *American Beauty* is what can be called a *dominant character*. Many films built on a multiple protagonist/antagonist structure contain a dominant, driven group member whose decision, at the start of the film, to pursue a certain line of often extreme or obsessive behavior in some way threatens the safety or autonomy of the group. This is clearly visible in films like *Saving Private Ryan* and *American Beauty*, but it is also present in a film like *The Big Chill*, in which the dead man, once the group's leader and chief idealist, is the dominant character. His suicide and apparent disillusionment with the group's ideals call into question the values and identity of the group, not only in the past but in the present and for the future. His suicide changes everything. It forces the group to question its ideals and redefine itself. The group's action line or macro is actually a sort of murder mystery in which various pieces of information about the dead man's beliefs and behavior prior to suicide are revealed, each of which challenges the group's assumptions about him and creates more mysteries. The group's relationship line is its attempt to reinvent itself in the light of the suicide of its figurehead and the undermining of its old ideals. This is a classic symbiotic relationship between action line and relationship line. The action line permits the relationship line to happen – indeed, the relationship line could not happen without the action line.

A dominant, driven character is very useful. As *The Big Chill* so clearly shows, a character like this provides the others with a survival macro which is a genuine *group* problem, a *group* story *in the present*, to which they can react in their individual ways and thus fulfil the aim of the multiple protagonist/antagonist form, which is to show different reactions to the same dilemma, different versions of the same character. Reunion films very often have such a figure because, lacking an outside, *present* threat, they need one within the group. One of the reasons why *Peter's Friends* feels directionless is because there is no dominant character who decides at the start of the film that it will now engage in behavior that in some way threatens the group – so there is no survival macro. Had the film opened with Peter announcing he has called the group together because he has AIDS, he could have been the dominant character, in very much the same way as the dead man in *The Big Chill*.

While many siege films have clear external antagonists and a survival macro in the force or forces operating to oppose them, they need internal antagonisms as well, to maximize tensions within the group.

Structurally, a dominant character in siege and reunion films helps to solve the inbuilt problem of the action being static and confined. It permits psychological action within the "closed walls" of the physical action. It provides the group with internal problems which can cause conflict and shifting loyalties. In other words, it provides the basis for a relationship line. Without conflict and shifting loyalties in a siege situation, there can be no relationship line and all that remains is the action line, the macro or common problem, which is merely the force or forces threatening the group by keeping the group trapped together. To get some idea of how limiting this can be, imagine *American Beauty* without Lester's decision to break the rules of Middle America. The heart of the film is gone.

In quest movies, the dominant character is typically engaged in forcing the others to approach the quest in a way they think dangerous. This also serves to unite the other characters in a group survival problem. Here, the analogy is with journey movies. Unless there is conflict between the travellers, they can only react to outside forces, which means that when they are alone there is no conflict, hence no drama – nothing to quarrel about or discuss. To get some idea of how limiting this could be, imagine *Saving Private Ryan* without conflict between the soldiers about their leader.

The outsider

Another device which seems to help in films utilizing multiple protagonists or antagonists is *the outsider*. This is a character who exists alongside the group and questions it but is not part of it. In *Tea with Mussolini*, the outsider is the young protagonist, the boy who was adopted by the ladies. In *The Big Chill* it is the apparently fatuous young woman who was the dead man's lover. In *The Magnificent Seven* it is the young Mexican villager Chico, who wants to be a hired gun and is permitted to join the seven, but in the end leaves for love and a normal life in the village. In *American Beauty* the outsider is Ricky Fitts, the boy obsessed with beauty. The outsider helps to define the group. In *Tea with Mussolini*, the outsider even talks about the group in voiceover – and provides usefully energizing conflict within it. Technically, the outsider's great use is that it can ask questions about the group and challenge its beliefs. The outsider's identity and function are very much like the investigator figure's in flashback narrative: a voice from the present.

The traitor within

Another useful character is *the traitor within*. This is a group member who rebels against the dominant character, providing useful conflict and suspense. The traitor within disagrees with the dominant character's behavior and tries to get rid of this person. This is a very active way of trying to protect the group. In siege films dealing with people trapped in social roles, like *American Beauty*, the traitor within is often trying to restore the status quo – in fact, personifies it, even though this may only be a façade.

Creating a strong multiple protagonist/antagonist structure

Group action line (survival macro)

All parallel story forms have the potential to "lose the plot" and become slow, unfocused and either confused in meaning or devoid of meaning altogether. Losing the plot in multiple protagonist/antagonist structures means, in effect, losing the survival macro or group action line, because this is what holds the film together.

If you want to keep a strong hold on the film (that is, keep a strong hold on the survival macro) do not approach the form primarily as an excuse to get individuals together. This pushes the survival macro into the background. Films of this kind should be thought of as a way to explore the fate of a *group* as distinct from the individuals who form it. This is not to say that exploring the individual members is not important. It is vital, but for it to happen there must be a strong group action line in which a common element threatens the group's survival and pushes the characters into situations that make them reveal themselves. The macro permits interesting relationships to happen.

The group as a family

To focus on the macro it helps to think of the multiple protagonists/ antagonists in the film as a real or virtual *family*, to which group identity, in the present and future, are vital and must be told in tandem with the stories of the individual. Start the plotting process by thinking of the reunion not in terms of "a family of characters is forced together *and* …," but in terms of "a family of characters is forced together *because* …" Think of an action line which will throw the group together under threat and give opportunities for characters to deal with new problems or unfinished business. Do not assume that new problems and unfinished business will happen just by putting characters together.

The threat to the group

The "because" in the above equation is the core of the survival macro, that is, the event or series of events that is threatening to destroy the group. In reunion films, the death or impending death of a crucial group member is often used. *The Big Chill* is a clear example, but *Cat on a Hot Tin Roof* (1958), *The Four Seasons* (1981), and the Australian film *Radiance* (1998), about three half-sisters who meet up after their mother's death, also utilize it. In films involving the group on a mission or quest, the mission or quest is the macro, and it usually involves the chance of death for group members. This can be seen in *Saving Private Ryan* and *The Magnificent Seven*. In films about physical sieges, the core of the macro is the force (or its agents) that is causing the siege. In sieges where people are trapped by social roles, the core of the macro is usually a threat to the group in the form of a member who wants to change.

Steps in the action line

Once the survival threat is decided, the steps in the group's action line can be devised by thinking first what situations could credibly happen, then what each group member would do in response. Each individual needs a story in which they are seen to react in their individual way to the group threat. To create a good story to illustrate the individual's response to the group threat, first isolate aspects of the group threat that would impinge on the relevant character, then create a well-structured story to carry this, preferably using a three-act structure. A one-act structure will suffice as long as its turning point is strong. In films that have a dominant character who is instigating the threat to the group, this character will play the part of antagonist because it is this character who is causing all the trouble. This can be seen clearly in *American Beauty*, in which Lester causes such anger in each character that they all have a motive to kill him.

In films where the group is very large, for example in *Tea with Mussolini*, the action can only focus on part of the group. *Parallel Lives*, which tries to deal with twenty group members, gets completely bogged down. Six is probably about the maximum number that can be successfully handled in depth in multiple protagonist/antagonist form. For large casts, tandem narrative is better because it splits the actors into manageable groups. They are not all competing for the action in one narrative.

The disturbance and "Whose film is it?"

To make sure the audience knows as early as possible that the answer to the question "Whose film is this?" is "the group's film," make the disturbance of the macro happen early and with as much impact as possible, so the group and the macro are firmly established in the audience's mind. It is interesting that the disturbance in *The Big Chill*, the suicide – the event which answers the question "a family of characters is forced together *because* …?" – is set up during the opening credits, in under a minute. This minute is also used to show all the characters in their normal lives, before they go to the reunion. The same thing is done in reverse in *American Beauty*, but in a similarly short time frame. The voice of Lester, the dominant character, tells of his impending death. It then goes on to show his own normality followed by that of his wife and daughter, and the two Jims, all of whom are also protagonists. Neither *The Magnificent Seven* nor *Saving Private Ryan* shows the multiple antagonists quickly, but they do show the protagonists and set up the macro. In *The Magnificent Seven*, the macro (the threat to group survival) is about the bandit raids and the protagonists are the villagers. In *Saving Private Ryan*, the protagonist is Ryan, grown old, and the military graveyard easily sets up the wartime mission.

It is particularly important in multiple protagonist/antagonist films to establish early on that the story is the group's story, otherwise the audience will be trying to pick a sole protagonist out of the many. When the group's story is not established early on, the film can feel slow, as if it is "not going anywhere." This happens in *Parallel Lives* and *Peter's Friends*.

Normality

Since all multiple protagonist/antagonist films are about groups under threat and in crisis situations, it is necessary to establish what life is or was normally like for the group and its individuals. This is equivalent to the standard practice of establishing the protagonist's normality. It is easy to spend too much time establishing each individual's normality, but it can be done economically, as we have seen in *The Big Chill* and *American Beauty*. *Tea with Mussolini* cleverly establishes the pre-fascist dictatorship normality of the group by having it happen in the background to the setting up of the protagonist and his normality, thereby achieving two storytelling goals simultaneously. In contrast, *Parallel Lives* does not show its individuals in their normal lives, which means much time has to be taken to describe it via scenes at the reunion, where it often results in "talking heads."

Skeletal structure of the macro/action line

Because there are so many parallel stories to tell, the group's action line as seen in the macro plot often has to be skeletal. This is not to say that it has to be trite – quite the opposite – but it cannot contain too many twists and turns because there is simply not enough time. It needs to be carefully planned so that what steps there are can provide maximum potential for the development of the other stories. This is akin to making sure every stop in a journey movie is impelling the story forward.

Relationship lines

Multiple antagonist/protagonist movies are usually created with the intention of exploring the relationships within the chosen group. This means the relationship lines are of huge importance. There are usually many relationship lines within the group. Often, each character will have a number of complex relationship lines. In *American Beauty*, for example, Lester's wife, Carolyn, has a three-act story that involves the breakdown of her marriage with Lester, a three-act story involving meeting and having an affair with Buddy Kane, and a three-act story involving her relationship with her daughter.

It is very easy to create relationship line scenes that merely show characters bickering about the past. Unless this material pays off later, it is redundant. Careful planning is necessary to choose not only what information will be transmitted in each scene, but also to give the relationship line the best possible scenario. It needs a strong rising three-act or one-act structure to permit the required emotional movement.

Quest films

In quest films the quest is the film's survival macro. The basic steps of the quest are identical to the hero's journey model or other three-act restorative structures. The only real difference is that the adventure must happen to the group. The group of protagonists has to *do things* or, to put it another way, the group action line has to progress from a normality to a disturbance, a first-act turning point, complications, second-act turning point, third-act and, finally, a climax. The film will follow the classic pattern in which events take the group of protagonists on an adventure/journey well away from their regular life and into realms where major and often dangerous decisions have to be made. The action will force the group of protagonists to find new strengths and overcome new hurdles, and in the course of this adventure – indeed, as a direct result of it – the relationship lines happen.

Quest films that bring together individuals who have not previously existed as a group are obviously not concerned with a group past in the way that films dealing with long-established groups have to be. Because quest films often deal with heroic figures, that is, people who are enigmatic and charismatic and cannot be seen from the inside, they often feature multiple antagonists. The protagonists will typically be minor figures (as in *Saving Private Ryan*). This is useful to know if the group you are planning to write about is heroic. The chances are they will be charismatic mentor–antagonists, rather than protagonists. You might have to create a protagonist to be influenced by them.

Relationship lines

If the group in the quest film has a history, then the story will deal with unfinished business or changing loyalties. But in films where the group is formed purely for the sake of the quest, as in a war mission film or a robbery, relationship lines normally concern developing relationships within the mission. They may refer back to the individual's normality to show how the mission has changed that person. In *Saving Private Ryan* this presents as an obsession on the part of the soldiers to know each other's normal social role, particularly that of their leader.

Reunion films

In writing quest films it is almost impossible to forget that the film needs a good action line involving the survival and journey of the group; in other words, it is almost impossible to forget the need for a survival macro that will contain the other plots, give them meaning, and provide closure for the film. Unfortunately, this is not the case with reunion films. It is very easy to think of reunions just as a device to get characters together, forgetting that interesting character interaction depends on the creation of a strong emotional *journey under threat* macro for the group as a whole. There is a built-in problem here because reunions are physically static. Whereas a quest takes a character out of its normal environment and sends it on a physical adventure with other versions of itself and plenty of opportunity for character-revealing incidents, a reunion takes a character out of its normal life and traps it, with other versions of itself, in one location.

It is inherent immobility that makes it very easy to forget the need for an emotional journey with significant events. Writers can very easily feel they are providing a good group action line when all they are doing is inventing a series of scenes about eating, drinking, and entertainment. This happens in *Parallel Lives*, in which large sections are given over to social events like a ball, a dormitory raid and ball games which become boring because they are not taking the film anywhere. *Peter's Friends* suffers from similar scenes.

The same mistake can be made in relationship lines, whereby redundant chats or bickering take the place of scenes that deal with unfinished business from the past impacting on the present and future. Time is spent establishing the characters' foibles and describing their past and personal present (their normality) without linking these things to an ongoing personal dilemma. *Parallel Lives* has many examples of redundant conflict of this sort. In one scene Wynn and Nick quarrel intensely over the fact that Nick published an article about the time they slept together. This matter is never taken any further so, while out of context it might seem excellent character material, it is actually redundant and slows the film down. This redundant, unfocused conflict is a close cousin to the repeated normality seen in *Mr. Saturday Night*. It quickly becomes boring. Again, the moral is that good characterization and acting are not enough.

A macro that leads to closure

While reunions are bounded by a time factor which gives chronological closure, this is not sufficient of itself. Reunion films need a macro which will permit explanation of the group's past and suggestions about its future. In *The Big Chill*, the end of the reunion is marked not only by it being time to go home but by two life-affirming, group-reinforcing acts: the first being one of the group taking on the role of the dead man, and the second being the decision of two of the group to have a child. This answers the group survival question set up at the beginning by the suicide.

The group on the cusp of change

The clue to creating a good macro for a reunion film is to remember that good reunion stories are always about the group caught on the cusp of change, being forced to reinvent itself – if not end – as the result of a traumatic event, often the death of a key member.

Think of the reunion as an emotional journey. Decide where the journey starts and ends, then create a normal three-act structure: disturbance, first-act turning point, complications, second-act turning point, third act and climax. Choose events not because they are typical or odd things that could happen on a journey, but because each will advance the action line (the reinvention or death of the group) and fuel the relationship lines.

Siege films

Much of what applies generally to the writing of quest and reunion films applies to siege films. In terms of writing problems, siege is midway between quests and reunions. Siege films share with quest films an inbuilt survival macro and closure, because in most cases the siege is an exciting event which starts and ends, and stories can be structured around that. But, for the duration of the siege, the characters are trapped in one place, as they are in reunion films, and this means the film can become static. Siege films like *American Beauty*, which deal with people trapped in social roles, are more like reunion films because the siege has no real start or conclusion – indeed, the siege is the normality with which they are trying to cope, or from which they are trying to escape.

The siege in its literal form – people physically imprisoned – is a useful form for exploring character because it shows people thrown into a stressful and usually highly dangerous situation. Physical confinement creates anxiety which can fuel rising jeopardy. Like groups in reunions, the group in a siege is being forced to change against its will. Shifting loyalties, breakdown, unexpected courage and unexpected cowardice are natural subjects to explore in siege.

In planning siege films, remember that the onset of the siege itself is usually the first-act turning point because it is what the film is about. Work backwards to create the pre-siege normality and a suitable disturbance. Regard the second act as a place to examine changing relationships within the group as it copes with the siege (as usual, the second act is a good place for relationships to come into their own). Work out what emotional progression you want for individuals and the group and create a scenario that will permit it. Make the second-act turning point the lowest point for the group. Follow the traditional three-act structure by making the third act a battle (in this instance, to escape). Make the climax answer the first-act question of "Will the group escape the siege and survive?" Even the simplest action movies will show the group changed emotionally, often with some members dead. As you structure the various plotlines, remember that they will all need to climax in and around the conclusion of the siege. Sieges benefit from internal antagonists, dominant characters, traitors within, and outsiders. These add opportunities for conflict during the physically static part of the plot. Sieges can permit a third-act battle and triumph along traditional three-act structure lines.

Siege structure in *American Beauty*

In writing a film about people who feel their life is boring and stultifying, it is very easy to create a screenplay that is boring and stultifying in itself. One of *American Beauty*'s many achievements is that it presents trapped and frustrated people in a dynamic way. This is all the more remarkable because *American Beauty* is a siege film, therefore is inherently static and prone to repetition and consequent loss of suspense. Good structure is behind these achievements. It is what permits the film to transmit its extraordinary depth of character analysis, its wit, its tragedy, and its deeper meanings.

American Beauty is a siege film in which the group is trapped by social roles, in this case, the social mores of Middle America. It is recognizable as a multiple protagonist siege film because, while it does have a dominant character in Lester, there are several other characters who are highly prominent and well-developed stories. These are Lester's daughter, Jane; her friend Angela; his wife, Carolyn; the boy next door, Ricky Fitts; and the boy's father, Frank Fitts, a retired marine.

The macro plot is typical of the multiple protagonist/antagonist form in that it constitutes a threat to the group's survival. The macro is set up extremely well and extremely early – indeed, in the opening moments of the film. Significantly, it is actually set up in voiceover as the camera shows us the group story's normality: the streets of Middle America.

The macro is Lester's forewarned death and the events leading up to it in which Lester rebels against the role of respectable breadwinner, husband, and father. This will be the climax of the film. Since the climax of any film explains how the film's central problem is resolved, knowing what happens in the climax is an excellent way of knowing what film we are in. In other words, within moments of the film opening, we know what film we are in. This is good storytelling.

Like *Saving Private Ryan*, the body of the film occurs in one long flashback enclosed by events in the present. Lester's death is foretold both in voiceover and in a scene in which Jane talks to an unseen male about getting Lester murdered. Establishing Lester's death so early and so powerfully means the film starts with high jeopardy – in other words, it starts with an excellent hook. This is a good tip to remember in writing films about people with boring lives. The hook will keep the audience interested while the (necessarily) boring normality is being established. Also, forewarning of the death means not only that we know what the film is about, but that the film becomes a detective story – a whodunit – which adds continuing and building suspense. This is something badly needed in a form as static as a siege. Coincidentally, *American Beauty* shows how useful flashback can be in injecting jeopardy into siege form. It is flashback that permits the story to present itself as a detective story.

The film ends with Lester's death which, at the lowest level, concludes the detective story and, in terms of the film's higher meaning, provides closure to the macro, answering the problem of whether the group will survive (it will not). Returning to the present after the long flashback is also helpful in closure, and permits a startling end to the film in which the deceased Lester talks about the moment of death.

It is interesting that the flashback is set up and resolved in classic flashback as case history style. It starts at the triggering crisis: Lester's death. As usual, this is the climax of the story in the past and the start of the story in the present. Lester's death will also be the film's climax, as is standard in this sort of flashback narrative. The film even has the twist ending typical of flashback as case history, the twist being that Lester, dead, actually talks about the moment of his death, and the visions he describes are shown on screen.

The traitor and the outsider

The traitor within in *American Beauty* is Frank Fitts, who typically tries to maintain the status quo by shooting Lester. The outsider – who, in typical outsider style, questions the functioning and beliefs of the group and introduces conflicting and new views – is, of course, Ricky, with his drug dealing, his ever-present video camera, and his compulsion to capture and hold beauty.

The macro

The macro in any multiple protagonist/antagonist film is very important. In *American Beauty*, the macro is the story of Lester's fatal attempts to rebel against the status quo. It actually has a complete three-act action line (his career as breadwinner) and a complete three-act relationship line (his crush on Angela). In the opening moment of the film, Lester's normality in marriage and at work is established. The disturbance in his action line is being threatened with retrenchment, and in his relationship line it is encountering Angela. The first-act turning points in the action and relationship lines are the triggers for his rebellion. The first-act turning point in his action line is quitting his job and, in his relationship line, the moment when Angela suggests that he work out and he decides to pursue her sexually. As usual, the first-act turning point of these two storylines is what the film is about.

The second act covers Lester's rebellion. The second-act turning point in his action line is when he serves his wife and her lover at the fast food restaurant and declares that his role as husband and breadwinner is over. In his relationship line, it is when Angela tells him that she is a virgin, thereby aborting their attempt at sex. The climax of both stories is his death.

Stories of each multiple protagonist

While group members often have a number of stories dealing with various relationships they have across the group (parent to child, lover to lover, etc.), individuals are linked to the macro in three ways. The first way is by showing how each individual reacts to Lester, the embodiment of the group threat. The second is thematic, by making every story in the film a version of rebelling against the status quo. The third way is by making Lester the third person in relationship triangles.

1. Reactions to Lester, the dominant character

The first connection between group members and the macro (group problem) is that each protagonist in *American Beauty* has a well-structured three-act narrative that could be called "Lester causes trouble." This is a clever and dynamic way of demonstrating the effect of the macro on individuals, which all multiple protagonist/antagonist films need to do in order to tell the story of the group.

In all of these stories, Lester is the antagonist. Lester causes so much trouble that every version of "Lester causes trouble" tracks a developing motive for murder. Structurally, the climax of all of these stories is Lester's death. The film is deliberately structured so that each character's story seems to be moving towards a climax in which the protagonist will kill Lester. This is done so well that it is impossible to work out until the last moment who will be the murderer. Moments before Lester is shot by Frank, Carolyn sets out to shoot him herself. In effect this is providing a complex whodunit, and it provides very high levels of jeopardy.

2. Connections through theme

The second form of connection between the stories of individuals and the macro is thematic. All group members have stories that, like Lester's story, are versions of rebellion against accepted social roles. This even applies to Frank, the agent of status quo.

Carolyn rebels against the status quo by having an affair with Buddy Kane, by slapping Jane, and by planning to kill Lester. Jane rebels against the status quo by hating her parents (even fantasizing about getting Lester murdered), by the way she dresses, and by taking up with Ricky, the dreamy outsider and drug dealer who (jokingly, as it turns out) offers to murder Lester. Angela pretends to be a slut. Frank, who beats his son up and has him locked in a psychiatric institution, is a suppressed homosexual and a murderer. Ricky deceives his parents, makes a living by selling drugs, and entertains himself by videotaping anything that interests him, including corpses, with no regard for normal notions of privacy or propriety. He and Jane plan to run away and live on drug money.

While some of this antisocial behavior is not in the form of proper stories (the interaction between Jane and Carolyn, for example), frequently there are proper stories set up as genuine three-act structures, with a disturbance, act turning points and a climax. Carolyn's affair with Buddy is a good example.

3. Third person in the triangle

Interestingly, the personal stories all pull back towards Lester in the climax – indeed, they often involve Lester in some way as a third party, a third point in the triangle, causing problems and even triggering the story. Thus there is the Carolyn/Buddy/Lester triangle;

there is Jane/Angela/Lester; there is Ricky/Frank/Lester; there is Jane/Ricky/Lester and there is Jane/Carolyn/Lester.

The climax

While some siege films permit a third-act battle and a triumph, this does not happen as such in the macro of *American Beauty*. But it is interesting that just before Lester dies he seems to have found peace and happiness in himself, and particularly in the fact that Jane is in love. As he is shot, he is staring with a look of beatific peace and happiness at a family photo in which he, Carolyn, and Jane appear as the archetypal happy Middle American family. He seems to have transcended his lust for Angela. The look of peace and happiness is still on his face in death, something that Ricky clearly finds beautiful. Perhaps Lester's rebellion against convention and his search for beauty via sex has led him back full circle to a discovery of beauty and peace in Middle America.

In all of the "Lester causes trouble" stories, the climax was set up to be Lester's murder. This was what was going to reinstate the status quo or proper order of things – hence, Carolyn was going to shoot Lester so she could stop being a victim; Jane fantasized about getting Lester killed so that she would not have to put up with him drooling over her friend Angela – and so on. Only Frank's version of "Lester causes trouble" has a climax in which Frank actually kills Lester in a fruitless attempt to reinstate the old order. The other stories end with an avoidance of murder by the individual, but the destruction of the group as a whole. The climaxes to these different stories answer the question raised by the first-act turning points in Lester's two stories, which was "How is the group going to survive this antisocial behavior?" The answer is that the group will not survive, because the group will destroy itself from within.

Stopping the siege being static

To summarize, *American Beauty* uses a number of structural means to combat the inherent static quality of the siege form and create a dynamic film that permits the unfolding of its complex characterization and insights. Many of the techniques it employs are devices commonly used within multiple protagonist/antagonist structures, but it has some interesting and idiosyncratic methods of pumping up jeopardy and permitting maximum character exploration.

1. Interweaving the survival macro

The interweaving of individual stories with the survival macro through plot and theme is reminiscent of the crosswise interconnections in *City of Hope*. It tightens the story, permitting complex characterization, adding layers of meaning, and preparing for closure.

2. Setting up jeopardy early

Setting up Lester's death and the detective story element early establishes suspense and intrigue from the start. Flashback is used cleverly here.

3. Structuring suspense into individual stories

Creating an interesting murder motive for each character and structuring each "Lester makes trouble" story so that it appears to be heading towards murder in the climax is an excellent way to build tension.

13. Lost in the telling: films with structural flaws

W hy does a film become weak or boring? In general terms it is a lack of suspense, of jeopardy in the widest sense. Often this lack of suspense is because the idea is weak or clichéd. But how can we account for those films that fail to engage despite what seem to be so many of the ingredients for success – components like a good idea, top actors, fine performances and sensitive direction? Of course, whether or not a film works is ultimately subjective, but measuring by box-office performance there are quite definitely films which do not achieve as well as might reasonably be expected and it is interesting and useful to speculate why. In many cases the cause seems to be a structural flaw in the script, sometimes several flaws. In other words, the story has been lost in the telling.

What follow are analyses of a number of films which, although in many ways fine, were nevertheless lost in the telling as the result of specific structural weaknesses. Looking at films like this is a very helpful way to understand how structure works. In fact it is often easier to learn from films like these than from the copybook successes.

At the end of the chapter are some checklists for why a film feels slow, or boring, or fizzles. At the end of each film analysis you will find cross-references to information about the structural components that are causing problems.

Prelude to a Kiss
Problem

- Delayed first-act turning point.

Prelude to a Kiss stars Meg Ryan and Alec Baldwin in a love story about a man (protagonist) who falls in love with a beautiful and unconventional woman. They decide to get married. At the ceremony, a strange old man appears. The bride gives him a good luck kiss – and faints (surprise/obstacle or first-act turning point). After this, she starts behaving like a suburban housewife. Her husband is initially bewildered, becoming gradually hostile as he grows convinced that she is an impostor somehow located inside his wife's body. Eventually, the old man turns up at the husband's favorite bar. He reveals that his body now contains the soul and personality of the woman, and vice versa. The old man's body is dying, and unless the body swap can be reversed, the woman's soul and personality will die with him. This seems inevitable (second-act turning point). Finally, the reversal is achieved (climax).

The story of *Prelude to a Kiss* is a fascinating one and the film contains fine performances. Unfortunately, it soon becomes boring. The cause is a delayed first-act turning point (the kiss followed by the faint) that does not occur until a very long way into the film. Too much time is spent after the initial meeting and falling in love (the disturbance) on showing the lovers actually *in love* which, structurally, is really just a new "normality." There is a reason for this. The filmmakers feel they need to set up details that will later prove the woman to be an impostor. Unfortunately, the process takes much too long. The effect is of the plot "treading water" and the audience response is to ask, justifiably, "What is the point of all this?"

The film has lost so much momentum by the time the first-act turning point does occur that the moment does not have the impact it deserves. It is actually a good and striking first-act turning point – an exemplary model that raises the stakes and turns the film in an unexpected and interesting new direction. The rest of the film is also interesting. Unfortunately, many viewers simply do not persist long enough to see either.

For further information on the structural components that are causing problems, see:
Development Strategy 13: Finding the first-act turning point (surprise/obstacle)

Falling in Love
Problems
* No first-act turning point.
* Weak antagonists.
* Low jeopardy.

Falling in Love (1984) stars Robert de Niro and Meryl Streep in a love story about two married people who meet on a commuter train, fall in love, and eventually decide to leave their respective partners and stay together. Both actors give fine performances, the direction is sensitive, and the film is well shot. Unfortunately, for most audiences, the film does not engage.

Generally, the problem presents as low jeopardy. It is hard to see why the decision to leave their respective partners is so difficult. Neither of these partners is sympathetic and there is little left in either marriage (although some time but little weight is given to the problem of Robert de Niro's character leaving his two children). Neither of the lovers has a moral or religious problem with divorce. Right at the end of the film there is an issue over whether the Robert de Niro character will move away or not, but it comes at the point when the film has slowed too much for it to have a great deal of impact. The response of audiences, justifiably, is: 'what is their problem?'

In terms of the film's structure, this response hits the nail on the head. There is no problem. Specifically, there is no first-act turning point – no surprise/obstacle which complicates the protagonists' problem, turns the action in a new direction, and thereby lifts the jeopardy. A good first-act turning point – like the piano getting bogged in *The Piano* or, in *The Player*, the wrong person getting murdered – provides a whole range of complications that fuel the rest of the film. In fact, as the Development Strategies show, the first-act turning point is what the film is about (see Development Strategy 13).

Falling in Love would have been greatly energized had it been about "two people who fall in love and something major (moral or physical) comes in their path, forcing them to battle and agonize over their love" rather than "two people who fall in love'" Without a proper first-act turning point to put the lovers' relationship under genuine strain, *Falling in Love* does not have enough at stake to make an audience properly worry or empathize. The film would also have been helped by stronger antagonists in the form of the two jilted partners. Had they been more engaging or in some way more needy, the film would have had greater jeopardy.

For further information on the structural elements that are causing problems, see:
Development Strategy 13: Finding the first-act turning point
Development Strategy 11: Identifying the antagonist
Development Strategy 21: Checking that the relationship line is moving

Wedlock
Problems
- False start.
- Wrong protagonist?

Wedlock is an escape movie. One of a gang of thieves, the film's protagonist, is caught after a daring robbery. He is sent to a futuristic, mixed-sex prison where there are no walls or bars. Instead, each inmate is issued with a high-tech collar that will explode and kill its wearer unless a similar collar is within a certain distance. The thief, determined to find the other members of the gang, escapes with a beautiful woman and they eventually fall in love.

This is a clever idea for an escape movie, but the film does not fulfil its potential. It gets off to a bad start by opening with a lengthy section depicting the robbery and the protagonist's attempted escape from the police. There is no dramatic need for this section.

The action then switches to the protagonist's arrival at the prison, in the same bus as the woman with whom he will escape. The woman is a very weak character. It is obvious from the first scene on the prison bus that she will be the protagonist's love interest, and she has little to do in the escape but complain, follow, and sometimes render assistance. The escape generally is boring and predictable.

The film might have been greatly energized by making the woman the protagonist (representing the view of an ordinary person) and turning the thief into an enigmatic, charismatic antagonist whom she cannot fathom and of whom she is deeply afraid. This would immediately have provided extra interest and jeopardy. It would have provided the pair with room for a range of emotional interactions, everything from terror to manipulation, anger, and growing affection. Instead of being shown at the beginning of the film, the thief's background could have been slowly revealed, providing ongoing mystery combined with menace. This would have been cheaper than the expensive robbery and escape sequence, and dramatically much more interesting. All in all, the result would have been a much more complex, subtle, and interesting film.

For further information on the structural elements that are causing problems, see:

Action line
Development Strategy 7: Creating a simple story sentence
Development Strategy 20: Creating an advanced story sentence

Protagonist and antagonist
Development Strategy 10: Identifying the protagonist
Development Strategy 11: Identifying the antagonist

Jaws 3
Problems
- Not identifying the protagonist early enough.
- Not making the protagonist's problem clear enough (unfocused action line).
- Passive protagonist who is not central to the action (unfocused action line, poor understanding of genre).
- Weak hunt element (unfocused action line, poor understanding of genre).
- Lack of strong antagonists.
- Poor research.
- Poor research leading to incredible plot.

Jaws 3 is the second sequel to *Jaws*, a hugely successful film about a massive killer shark terrorizing a beach resort while the town's mayor and business community put profits before safety and deny there is a problem. In *Jaws 3*, a mother shark goes on a death rampage after her baby has become accidentally trapped in a lagoon that also accommodates a spectacular tourist attraction in the form of an underwater aquarium and dolphin pool. While, as in the original film, the owner of the resort denies there is a problem, many people are killed, the shark threatens the dolphins and, in a big climax, the underwater aquarium is smashed apart by the giant shark which is eventually blown up by the protagonist.

Whereas a successful film like *The Big Chill* starts identifying its multiple protagonists via the soundtrack even before the studio logo has gone from the screen and has established all of them in just over a minute, *Jaws 3* takes twelve minutes to properly identify its protagonist, Mikey. During these twelve minutes, the film gives a large number of characters screen prominence of a kind that suggests they might be the protagonist. This is trying for the audience, which becomes bored and irritated and rejects the film literally before the story has started. It would have been quite possible to start the film with the scene that properly identifies the protagonist and insert the other scenes (or the information that they contain) subsequently.

The problems *Jaws 3* has in establishing its protagonist and therefore in getting started reflect an unfocused action line and a weak protagonist generally. Far from driving the action, the protagonist has little to do until the climax when the shark is actually terrorizing people in the aquarium. It is only here that he is center of the action and properly takes on the role of protagonist as hunter and defender that is essential to successful monster films.

While protagonists in monster films often follow the typical hero's journey model – being initially reluctant to play hero – their reluctance is short-lived and normally they accept the quest very quickly. There is a good reason for this, namely, that monster stories only really start when the hunt starts. The whole point of monster movies is to create an exciting two-way hunt between the protagonist and vicious monster (or monsters) each bent on destroying the other. The hunt is the core of the monster movie, just as the core of a romance movie is the meeting, problems and final partnering of the lovers. Unfortunately, *Jaws 3* does not contain a proper hunt at all, and the protagonist is an essentially passive onlooker. Instead of a hunt there are many shark attacks, mostly on characters who have never appeared before and who therefore have little emotional pull on the audience.

There are three lessons to be learned from the treatment of the protagonist in *Jaws 3*. The first is that in any story, monster or otherwise, the protagonist must be established early, because until it is, the story cannot start and the audience gets bored. The second lesson is that in all stories the protagonist must be centrally involved in the action, otherwise the story is unfocused and cannot properly build. The third is that monster stories need to get the hunt started at an early stage.

Another weakness in *Jaws 3* is the lack of a strong antagonist with powerful allies who load the dice against the protagonist. In all films, monster or otherwise, the protagonist and the jeopardy is only as strong as the antagonist and its allies. The original *Jaws* gained enormous suspense from the fact that the mayor and business community of the town, acting as the shark's allies, would not listen to the protagonist and stop the monster's killing spree. There is the basis for this in *Jaws 3* – the owners are foolishly materialistic and will do anything to save the aquarium – but because the protagonist in *Jaw 3* is not a proper hunter engaged from the start with a proper mission, the antagonists cannot properly do their job of putting barriers in his way.

The problem of a weak action line with no proper role for the protagonist can be picked at an early stage by applying Development Strategies 7 and 20, which require the creation of a narrative sentence to describe the action of the story in terms of what the protagonist is *doing*. Development Strategies 10 and 11, which require identification of protagonist and antagonist, will help establish a strong antagonist and the antagonist's allies. Development Strategy 3, which involves pinpointing the genre to check audience expectations, will help identify the necessary plot components.

Another problem with the plot of *Jaws 3* was its inaccuracy. While the plot is based on the idea of a mother shark protecting her offspring, as Australian audiences were quick to point out sharks do not mother their young. They produce eggs and leave them to hatch. Also, while the plot of *Jaws 3* involved saving dolphins from sharks, in fact dolphins actually attack sharks and keep them at bay. Where dolphins are found, sharks are not found.

It is not worth losing audiences for the sake of an hour's research.

For further information on the structural elements that are causing problems, see:

Genre
Development Strategy 3: Pinpointing genre to check audience expectations

Action line
Development Strategy 7: Creating a simple story sentence
Development Strategy 20: Creating an advanced story sentence

Protagonist and antagonist
Development Strategy 10: Identifying the protagonist
Development Strategy 11: Identifying the antagonist

Jack and Sarah
Problems
- Poor combination of genre.
- Credibility.
- Weak climax.
- Too many barriers between lovers.

Jack and Sarah is set in London and opens with Jack's wife in late pregnancy. There are light, comic scenes about the difficulties of this predicament, and the film looks set to be a comedy about parenthood. But the mood changes drastically when Jack's wife dies in childbirth. Jack drops into deep depression and is uninterested in his child. He hires a young, self-confident American nanny. He and the nanny come into comic conflict. The climax is his realization that he loves her.

There are a number of problems with the film that make it an unsatisfactory experience. In the main they are associated with the use of death, grief and depression to trigger what is meant to be a "feel-good" screwball comedy (inter-class or inter-cultural love affair). Successful feel-good romantic comedies create jeopardy and strong audience involvement by stacking the odds against two lonely, worthy people who really deserve to come together. In *Jack and Sarah*, the presence of recent death seriously hampers the audience's enjoyment of the couple's coming together, and also raises the issue of credibility. Jack's depression over his dead wife was so profound and the film so successfully puts him and the nanny at odds for the rest of the film that, at the climax, it is hard to believe that Jack, only months after his wife's death, really does love Sarah, particularly since he does not realize he is in love until he is told so by others.

The first lesson to emerge from *Jack and Sarah* is that mixing tragedy with screwball romance is difficult, perhaps impossible. *Jack and Sarah* is really two films in sequence. The first is the incomplete tragedy of a man who loses his wife in childbirth and plunges into grief. The second is a romantic comedy about a man who falls for his child's wacky American nanny. Structurally, this means that the final climax (Jack discovering he loves Sarah) does not properly answer the problem raised by the film's first-act turning point – what happens to a man whose wife dies in childbirth and who plunges into terrible grief – which is part of the death story. That problem is never properly answered. What the film's climax does answer – or attempts to answer – is the standard screwball-comedy issue of whether two very different, mutually antagonistic people can come together as lovers. The fact that the climax, however well written, cannot really answer what the first-act turning point told the audience the film was about means that the ending of the film is probably bound to feel incomplete.

Perhaps connected with this disjunction is the matter of the barriers placed in the way of the lovers. There is so much conflict and so little in common between Jack and Sarah that their love is ultimately unbelievable. The lesson here is that barriers and conflicts put in the lovers' way must not be insurmountable. To be credible, love must be shown growing through a series of events, but here, as in *Guarding Tess*, it is not. This is probably because so much of the film's time and energy was taken up with the death of Jack's wife and his subsequent grief. There is simply not the time to properly develop the relationship, which is probably why the film gets itself into the dangerous territory of the protagonist being unaware that he is in love until told so by others. There was not the time for him to become self aware and explore all the complex emotions that such a turnaround from dislike to love usually merits in romantic comedy. Turnarounds like these usually provide some of the most delightful comic moments of the form, and should be exploited for all they are worth. But *Jack and Sarah* does not have time. The result is anticlimax. While anticlimax can be a valid artistic tool, in a romantic comedy it disappoints.

For further information on the structural elements that are causing problems, see:

Action line
Development Strategy 7: Creating a simple story sentence
Development Strategy 20: Creating an advanced story sentence

Turning points, climax, resolution
Development Strategy 13: Funding the first-act turning point (surprise/obstacle)
Development Strategy 16: Finding the climax
Development Strategy 17: Establishing the first-act turning point through the third-act climax
Development Strategy 18: Coming to a resolution and ending

Guarding Tess
Problems
- Delayed first-act turning point.
- Repeating the normality.
- Inappropriate action line.
- Unconvincing climax.

Guarding Tess is about a US government agent (Nicholas Cage) who has to guard Tess, a wilful but likeable ex-First Lady (Shirley MacLaine). Ultimately, Tess gets kidnapped and the agent has to find her. The agent is the protagonist, and Tess is the charismatic antagonist.

Guarding Tess has a very late first-act turning point (the kidnap). Prior to that, the film simply displays a range of different examples of the same normality, which is "Tess infuriates the agent by her wilfulness." While each example of this is interesting and humorous in itself, the repetition becomes boring – in the same way that the repetition in *Prelude to a Kiss* of scenarios of the "lovers in love" gets boring.

The repeated normality problem in *Guarding Tess* is probably caused by the poor choice of action line. Like many films, the main point of *Guarding Tess* is the exploration of a relationship, specifically, a mother–son relationship. Unfortunately, the action line chosen to carry and reveal the development of this mother–son relationship is inappropriate. A relationship film requires the two main players to be kept together so they can interact, but a plot where one of them is kidnapped necessarily separates them and so prevents this. In *Guarding Tess*, the temptation is to spend as much time as possible on the normality because once the plot starts, the couple will be separated.

The relationship line would have been much better served by the classic action line of relationship films, which is that events force the main players together in some joint enterprise, during which their relationship develops, moving from distance – even hostility – to closeness, often deep love. Almost every relationship film, comic or serious, displays this formula. Just a few examples are: *Driving Miss Daisy, Crocodile Dundee, Strictly Ballroom, The African Queen, Witness, Planes, Trains and Automobiles,* and *Romancing the Stone.*

It is very easy in films that are primarily concerned with relationships to forget the importance of the action line. It is important to remember that a relationship cannot change until events force it to change. Without an action line, the relationship is jammed in one spot. Structurally, the moments in a film that force a relationship to move out of its normality are the turning points and shifts in the action line plot: the disturbance, the first-act turning point, second-act complications, second-act turning point, and climax.

The kidnap movie can be a vehicle for a developing relationship, but the relationship will be between kidnapper and victim (*Ruthless People*, 1986) or kidnapper and ransom target (*Ransom*, 1996). It cannot be between the victim and the person who is trying to find them.

Another effect of this poor choice of action line is that the agent's profound emotion upon finally finding Tess is incredible because it has not been properly set up. An intense response like this has to be earned over the course of the film by a complex, developing relationship. This is what happens in *Driving Miss Daisy*. *Driving Miss Daisy* actually starts with an identical normality to *Guarding Tess* (wilful old lady infuriates those who have to look after her). The difference between the two films is that the central relationship in *Guarding Tess* is jammed at the normality stage. The inappropriate action line of the film has not permitted Tess to demonstrate any likeable, admirable, or lovable qualities that would provoke strong emotion of the kind her bodyguard ultimately displays.

For further information on the structural elements that are causing problems, see:

Action line
Development Strategy 5: Making sure the disturbance involves real change
Development Strategy 7: Creating a simple story sentence

Relationship line
Development Strategy 8: Differentiating the action line and the relationship line
Development strategy 9: Defining the steps of the relationship in the relationship line

Turning point and climax
Development Strategy 13: Finding the first-act turning point (surprise/obstacle)
Development Strategy 16: Finding the climax
Development Strategy 17: Establishing the first-act turning point through the
    third-act climax

Mr. Saturday Night
Problems
- Character study in place of plot.
- Repeating the normality.
- Weak action line.
- Redundant conflict.
- Life story in place of proper structure.
- Poor use of flashback narrative.
- Choosing the right action line.
- Whether to use flashback narrative.
- Wrong protagonist?

Mr. Saturday Night is the life story of a stand-up comedian (Billy Crystal) whose ego continually forces him to commit acts against his own professional and personal interests. We meet the comedian in old age, unable to get work because he has offended so many people. His life from adolescence onwards is depicted via flashbacks, while the story in the present follows his attempts to get work with the assistance of a young theatrical agent (Helen Hunt). Finally, he is given the chance of a comeback: a role in a film being made by an important director. Typically, he rejects the role as not good enough. There is a subplot about his difficult relationship with his daughter and his bullying treatment of his brother. At the end he is reconciled with both.

Billy Crystal wrote, directed, and starred in the film. Unfortunately, despite an acting *tour de force* from Crystal, fine performances from his supporting cast, and finely characterized individual sequences and scenes, the film does not engage the audience. The reason is structural. The film does not provide a story in which the protagonist is faced with a dilemma and moves through its ramifications to a climax. Instead it provides a range of different versions of the same normality, which is "good comedian bullies his brother and acts self-destructively." This is ultimately boring because each version of "good comedian bullies his brother and acts self-destructively" is providing essentially the same information. What is being shown is a character study, not a character driven to action by outside events.

Instead of being "good comedian bullies his brother and acts self-destructively" (which is a character in search of a plot, a character jammed in its normality), the film should have been "good comedian who acts self-destructively *is presented with a dilemma which will test him – and he is tested and resolves the problem successfully or unsuccessfully.*"

The difference can be pinpointed by asking what the film is about, as this question will usually provide the first-act turning point. It will describe a surprising event (a surprise which turns into an obstacle). If a description of what the film is about results in a character description rather than a surprising event, there is a major problem. It means that at best the plot lacks a first-act turning point. In the case of *Mr. Saturday Night*, the film does not have a useful action line at all.

Certainly people in real life do get stuck within the same normality. They do fail to change and they do repeat the same mistakes and the same jokes. But in a film, a little repetition goes a long way and the depiction of "real life" in storytelling generally can have a destructive, slowing effect, just as the use of "real life" dialogue can have a destructive, slowing effect within the individual scene (see Chapter 14 for differences between "real life" and "real time" dialogue). Films as a whole, like individual scenes, involve the selection of events to create a plot, plus a heightened reality. This even applies to films that appear to depict absolute reality, like the work of British filmmaker Mike Leigh. Each scene in a Mike Leigh film is carefully workshopped, after which Leigh selects the dialogue and events that are to appear.

If *Mr. Saturday Night* was intended to show a character who could not change, a better way might have been to give one or two examples of his repetitiveness within a plot in which special circumstances seem to give him no option but to change although, at the last moment, it turns out he can't. For example, a genuine dilemma would be if his marriage depended on him taking a role that he felt was beneath him and that, despite everything, he couldn't force himself to take. Putting a character in a dilemma engages the audience. They can empathize. A character not in dilemma is ultimately boring.

Actor–writers, whose training is so heavily biased towards character analysis, are particularly prone to mistake character study for plot, that is, they mistake scenes that depict character foibles for a scenario. The point to remember is that a plot places the protagonist in a dilemma which he or she has to resolve by action. If there is no dilemma, there is no story. Using a narrative sentence would have helped pinpoint the lack of an action line driven by the main character.

The need in a film for a heightened, selective reality and a specific dilemma is why a character's life story is not *of itself* suitable for a film. It is easy to assume that a character's life is a ready-made structure, but it is not, just as a journey is not automatically a ready-made structure (see Development Strategy 28: Writing journey films). To successfully depict a life (as in, for example, *Shine),* life-changing events have to be selected that will properly propel whatever interpretation of the life the writer wishes to depict. In *Shine,* each scene moved the story forward, and each flashback started and ended at a structural high point. The same thing happened in *The Remains of the Day* (see Chapter 10 for a structural analysis of both these films).

Unfortunately, *Mr. Saturday Night* assumes that major events from a life – as opposed to life-changing events from that life – provide a good structure, which results in plot sequences which are interesting of themselves but which, having no forward movement, slow the film and leave the audience without a story to follow. Again, identifying the film's narrative sentence would have pinpointed these weaknesses.

The film's relationship line in the past, which features the difficult relationship between the comedian and his brother, wife, and daughter, also suffers from repetition of the normality. They are all jammed in the same interaction. A proper, dynamic action line would have permitted the relationship line to move.

Mr. Saturday Night is also a useful example of redundant conflict. While the film is full of conflicts and quarrels, the conflict is redundant because the quarrels are all essentially the same quarrel, and nothing is changed by them.

With its failed protagonist in search of success, *Mr. Saturday Night* seems ideal for flashback as thwarted dream as used in *Shine* and *The Remains of the Day*. *Mr Saturday Night* does actually use flashbacks, but they are not successful, partly because of the film's lack of a strong action line in the past, meaning there are no strong turning points where flashbacks can start and end. Flashbacks in *Mr. Saturday Night* are also unsuccessful because the story in the present is not "a detective story of the heart" and because, in the present, the protagonist has not experienced a second act "death" from which he is re-born with a new agenda and the energy to restart the quest. These are all problems that cause low jeopardy.

The first question to answer in a situation like this where flashback appears to be an option is whether flashback narrative is indeed the right structure to use. The answer depends on what story is to be told. If the story is primarily about the present, then flashback narrative is probably not the answer. But if the intention is to tell of an at-tempt to achieve a thwarted dream, then flashback as thwarted dream would be suit-able. Similarly, if the story is about someone who persistently damaged himself, then possibly flashback as case history would be appropriate. (For content and structure of flashback narrative, see Chapters 8 and 9.) In both cases, the plot would have to be radically restructured in order to create proper turning points, in particular, a good triggering incident.

Another issue raised by an unsuccessful character-based film like *Mr. Saturday Night* is the question of whether the right protagonist has been chosen. While the obvi-ous assumption is that the comedian is the protagonist, the film structure might well work more successfully if the comedian – who is *par excellence* an unchanging, infuriat-ing but charismatic character – is the antagonist to a "normal" protagonist, like his daughter or the literary agent. The pattern then would be similar to *Scent of a Woman*.

The comedian as antagonist is compatible with either of the flashback narrative structures. In a version using flashback as thwarted dream, the comedian would be the protagonist in the past and an unknowable antagonist in the present, with his daughter or the young agent being the detective–protagonist. If flashback as case history is used, the comedian is charismatic antagonist in both past and present.

The lessons to be learned from *Mr. Saturday Night* are that flashbacks without a narrative structure become boring; that a life is not necessarily a ready-made structure; that an ongoing normality gets boring, and that even the most fascinating character becomes boring unless placed in a dilemma that creates a series of choices and builds to a climax; that conflict needs to be productive; that the most interesting character is often better handled as a charismatic antagonist rather than a protagonist.

For further information on the structural elements that are causing problems, see:

Action line
Development Strategy 6: Distinguishing an idea from a story
Development Strategy 7: Creating a simple story sentence
Development Strategy 20: Creating an advanced story sentence

Dramatic high points
Development Strategy 5: Making sure the disturbance involves real change
Development Strategy 13: Finding the first-act turning point (surprise/obstacle)
Development strategy 16: Finding the climax

Relationship line
Development Strategy 21: Checking that the relationship line is moving

Scene content
Development Strategy 22: Getting the right scenario for each scene
Development Strategy 23: Creating opening scenes

Protagonist and antagonist
Development Strategy 10: Identifying the protagonist
Development Strategy 11: Identifying the antagonist

Flashback narrative
Chapters 7–9

Conflict
Chapter 14: "Productive conflict and redundant conflict"

Parallel Lives
Problems
- No survival macro.
- Poor relationship lines.
- Too many characters.
- Ongoing normality.
- Delayed disturbance/first-act turning point.
- Redundant conflict.
- Poor climax.

Many writers are drawn to write film scripts about reunions of friends, family or colleagues for births, marriages, deaths, or holidays. The advantages are clear. Reunions provide the opportunity for a range of interesting, equally weighted characters, a particularly attractive option in days when ensembles of actors make good box-office sense. Also, because of the unfinished business built into any reunion, the story has ready-made conflict. But many reunion films fail, and many others are abandoned at early stages because they simply do not work. They become unfocused, slow and, in the worst cases, *actively boring*. These failings are structural problems related to a poor action line concerning the group. This is a major problem in *Parallel Lives*.

Parallel Lives is about a college reunion and is promoted on the basis that it is *The Big Chill* of the 1990s. It features twenty characters (ex-students of the college) who play a significant part in the action, and two others who appear at the end. After a lot of time has been spent introducing the characters and providing their backstory (characters are still being introduced twenty minutes into the film), the film shows the characters engaging in reunion activities like a dance, a raid on the women's dorm and a sports carnival. Then, close to the end, the much-disliked smooth-talking seducer, Peter, is found dead in his car in the river. Many people have a motive for his murder, and one woman, a senate candidate, was actually in the car. Her father, an elected senator, covers up. Everyone goes home, with many of the relationship subplots unresolved. Unfortunately, despite a stellar cast, fine acting, and interesting characters, the film is boring.

Parallel Lives assumes that a reunion is of itself a good structure, and therefore does not bother about a survival macro, that is, a unifying action line that threatens the group until well after an hour into the action, when it seizes on the cliché of a murder. In a proper structure, the murder would be the disturbance or the first-act turning point. It would be what the film is about in the way that *The Big Chill* is a mystery story about a group trying to find out why its charismatic leader committed suicide, and what that suicide means in terms of the future of the group and the identity of the individuals. In *Parallel Lives*, the murder story should provide the means through which the characters reveal themselves. As it is, it serves no useful purpose at all.

Instead of character being revealed through the pressure of events in an action line, character exploration in *Parallel Lives* is conducted through a vast number of scenes in which two characters discuss the past. Often the unfinished business between the characters is unconnected to their relationship at college, which means that that relationship dilemma is pulling away from the action line of the reunion. For example, one of the major relationship lines seems to be a love–hate relationship between two tough journalists, Wynn and Nick. They once slept together and Nick published a scathing article about the event, but since none of this happened at college it is not informing the premise of the film; rather, it is pulling the film elsewhere.

Similarly, the events that do happen to the group – the ball, the raid on the dorm and the sports carnival – are not used to take the characters anywhere either. They are used merely to show the characters behaving *in character*, in other words, repeating the same normality, as happened in *Mr. Saturday Night*. Like *Mr. Saturday Night*, *Parallel Lives* assumes that good characters with good conflict and interesting unfinished business will automatically make a good story – moreover, the more good characters, the better. In fact the vast number of characters makes the film very difficult to follow and the concentration on talking-heads relationship scenes to the detriment of an ongoing action line which involves all the characters makes the film slow and tedious. The film is very much a matter of characters in search of a plot.

That a film can be tedious despite good characters, good conflict, complex unfinished business, and good acting demonstrates that multiple protagonist films do not happen without planning and a good survival macro that will force the group and individuals on an emotional journey. *The Big Chill*, which *Parallel Lives* set out to emulate, is at all times vitally concerned with the group's past and its endangered future – indeed, its ideals and worth as a whole – and there are issues brought into prominence by the suicide of its most charismatic member. The individuals are dealt with in terms of their role in the group in the past, the present, and the future.

Parallel Lives would also be helped by useful multiple protagonist character types like "the traitor within," "the outsider" and the "dominant character."

For further information on the structural elements that are causing problems, see:

Chapter 12: 'Multiple protagonists and antagonists'
Chapter 14: 'Productive conflict and redundant conflict'

Common script problems
Why a script might feel 'slow'

By a "slow" script people usually mean one which takes uncomfortably long to start but eventually redeems itself by finding its story, even if that story is not properly developed. Of course, the issue of what is unacceptably slow is a matter of personal taste. Use the following lists in conjunction with the Development Strategies (given in full in Chapter 6). Slowness is usually caused by:

1. A poor set-up and wasted opening scenes. Key questions to ask are whether the writer knows the film's story sentence and has identified the protagonist.
2. The story starting too far ahead of the disturbance (for example, in *Out of Africa*, the disturbance consists of the protagonist going to Africa and meeting the Robert Redford character, but this event does not occur for some considerable time, so the film cannot properly move). Another way of understanding this problem of delayed disturbance is to say that too much of what is essentially backstory is being shown on screen.
3. Not enough twists and turns or else too much delay between twists and turns – really, poor second-act complications.
4. Insufficient conflict or dilemma facing the major characters (but note that conflict must be productive rather than redundant).

Why a script might feel boring

A script that is slow eventually finds its story. A script that is boring either never finds its story or its story is clichéd or unreal. Remedying a boring script means a complete rethink, and it is worth considering whether the script is really worth such an effort. A script is normally boring for a number or all of the following reasons:

1. It is not a good yarn, that is, it is clichéd or unbelievable.
2. Because it is clichéd, it is predictable.
3. The characters are static or underdeveloped.
4. It uses poor disturbance, turning points and second-act complications.
5. Backstory is handled badly, often with redundant flashbacks.
6. Plot information is transmitted poorly.

7. There is lack of conflict or redundant conflict.
8. The action is unfocused and doesn't move the story on.

Certain dramatic structures are prone to being boring and writers regularly have problems with them. Journey films and reunion films fit this category (see Development Strategy 28: Writing journey films, and Chapter 12, Multiple protagonists and antagonists.)

Why a script might "fizzle"

Scripts that fizzle at the end usually do so because their climax is not answering the question set up at the first-act turning point which is, effectively, "What is the film about?"

Anticlimactic endings are fixed either by changing the climax to answer the question set up at the first-act turning point, or by changing that question so that the climax, as it stands, *can* answer it. (See Development Strategy 13: Finding the first-act turning point (surprise/obstacles); Development Strategy 16: Finding the climax; and Development Strategy 17: Establishing the first-act turning point through the third-act climax.)

Part III
Getting it onto paper

14. Dialogue

I t is easy to think of dialogue as a single autonomous skill quite separate from structure. In fact there are a variety of dialogue skills that a working screenwriter may be called upon to use and, as we have seen in Development Strategies 22 (Getting the right scenario) and 23 (Creating opening scenes), good dialogue actually piggybacks on structure, particularly scenario. It is also inextricably linked to subtext. (For a brilliant analysis of how subtext drives story, hence dialogue, see Robert McKee, *Story*, "Scene Analysis.")

Different dialogue skills

Writing an original feature film permits lively and idiosyncratic dialogue like that of David Mamet or Harold Pinter. But much screenwriting, particularly television and film sequel writing, requires the writer to submerge personal style to produce dialogue and content in line with established styles and conventions. Characters in a television series must sound the same every week. The style and content of the program must be the same each week and, depending on time-slot, there will probably be limitations on subject matter, and often on bad language.

Dialogue and structure

Good dialogue ultimately depends upon a good scenario. It is very hard to make a clichéd or boring scene jump off the page. The chosen setting and action of a scene are vital. Another vital matter is whether a scene is actually useful – whether it is earning its keep. An example of a useless scene would be when a character announces in scene X that they are going to make a phone call, explaining what the call will be about, and then makes the call in scene Y exactly as already described, with no further information or characterization being added. Without more information, scene Y is redundant. An unnecessary scene slows down the film (as well as increasing the budget) because the film cannot move until some more information is transmitted. A series of unnecessary scenes can make a film dangerously slow.

Writing dialogue

Once you have planned the larger structure of the film and the content of the scene, you can start to think about action and dialogue. The process is very much an exchange between vertical and lateral thinking, with vertical thinking defining the structural and characterization requirements of the scene, and the lateral imagination exploring the emotions and intellect of the characters, to find dialogue that is realistic and true to character but will simultaneously carry the plot and character content required by lateral thinking.

Before rushing into writing dialogue, list on paper the content that must appear in the scene in terms of the action and relationship lines and characterization. Think about the emotional content and movement required in the scene. Think hard about the way you plan to establish backstory, date and setting.

Visuals and sound

Sound, silence, and visuals are partners to dialogue. Sound and visuals aid enormously in the transmission of information.

Real time

One of the most frequent problems new writers have with dialogue is writing it in "real time," as if they were recording what would really happen and be said if the scene were to occur in real life. In fact dialogue is not like real-life conversation at all. It is a very tightly and carefully structured illusion of conversation. Its point is to move the plot on while revealing character. Its intention is to manipulate the audience to feel and think as the writer intends. In *Writing the Screenplay*, Alan Armer defines the role of dialogue very well when he writes:

> Beneath a surface illusion of reality, effective dialog must meet these fundamental qualifications:
>
> 1. economy
> 2. simplicity
> 3. vernacular speech
> 4. invisibility
> 5. progression (p. 247).

Writing in real time most often happens when writers have not planned the structure of a scene or defined its content before they launch into dialogue. Without a sense of the importance (or relative unimportance) of the scene in terms of the whole script, it is impossible to gauge how much time the scene should be given or, indeed, what information should be transmitted. Writers tend to fall back on replicating reality, which has a slowing effect because the writing is not being directed to achieve a certain end.

Getting information across (exposition)

If you have compiled a list of information that needs to be included in the scene, don't assume that you have to insert it in the order of the list. Check that including this information at this point in the script is the right thing to do. It might be useful for suspense reasons to hold some information back. Recall, for example, how effective it is in *Thelma and Louise* that the audience is not told the details of Louise's rape until late in the film. Do not feel compelled to get too much information into each scene. Remember how possible it is to walk into a film late and pick up the plot within a few minutes. Mystery and suspense help drive the scene onwards.

Getting information across is called *exposition* and the problems of "how much" and "when" are perennial writing problems. Do not include in dialogue information that is obvious. Much can be deduced from actors' movements and the context. In general, keep dialogue lines short. One or two sentences is normal. Use long speeches only rarely.

Be careful that you are not making characters say the same thing in many different ways. For example, "The door is jammed" is the same thing as "I can't open the door." Make sure repetitions are moving the scene along.

Talking heads and poor exposition

Use characterizing action of some kind in as many scenes as possible. Give characters "business" to do as they speak. If budget demands impose a static scene on you, consciously seek ways to add psychological movement. Beware of clichéd "business" like pouring a drink. Try to combine character and plot points. Get over a plot point through a character point. In other words, make a character use their own idiosyncratic way to do what the plot requires – for example, James Bond will fight a villain in a very different way from Ace Ventura, Pet Detective.

Be lateral in the way you transmit information. Avoid talking-head scenes in which characters sit discussing matters – at tables in cafes, on couches, etc. It is boring to watch and, moreover, off-putting because it is so obviously exposition. Try putting the information into the first active scene as part of some action. For example, if the story demands that two police set out to catch a criminal, it is normally more interesting to open with them in the car on the way to catching the criminal than sitting in the cafeteria telling the audience the story so far.

Always write scenes with a view to budget limitations and act each scene as you write. Always read each scene for pace. If you need to get across theories or deeply held ideas, couch them, as you would any other exposition, in a character point. Try to split them up.

As a general rule, all exposition and backstory should be transmitted with subtlety. Never make characters volunteer information beyond credible limits. If you find yourself writing speeches that could be entitled "The story so far," or "What is going to happen," you have exposition problems. Here is an example of poor exposition.

For easier reading, the dialogue column in the following examples of scripts is wider than it would normally be in a real script.

> INT. KITCHEN.   DAY
>
> MARSHA and MUM are sitting at the kitchen table drinking coffee.
>
> MARSHA
>
> Isn't it annoying that Auntie Millie is coming to stay! Last time she came she upset everyone by drinking all the milk and breaking the crockery.
>
> MUM
>
> Nonsense, Marsha! Auntie Millie is a lovely woman and you should respect her because she's my oldest auntie. She drinks all the milk because she lives on a dairy farm (which we hope to inherit) and so is used to having lots of milk.

The main problem here is that too much exposition is being forced into too small a space. In action terms, the task of getting all the information across has distracted the writer from considering the movement of the scene, so that we are reduced to talking heads – seated characters spouting pure information, not character-loaded dialogue. In fact at times the dialogue starts to sound like extracts from the newspaper: "She drinks all the milk because she lives on a dairy farm (which we hope to inherit) and so is used to having lots of milk." Moreover, precious room is being taken up by words that state the obvious. For example, the statement "Isn't it annoying" could be deduced from the rest of the scene.

A better version of the scene could be produced if the writer considered, firstly, what information absolutely must appear in this scene, and secondly, ways of getting that information across through character points and possibly through credible conflict, however low-key.

A crucial issue here is the setting and scenario. The only point of creating this scene and here seems to be so that the two characters can have a conversation about Auntie Millie. It would have been better to get the conversation about Auntie Millie into another scene, a scene that had other functions in terms of the film as a whole.

An argument is a device often used to transmit information because the dynamics of an argument make it easy for characters to throw the past back at each other. In *Donnie Brasco* (1997), the time frame and nature of the protagonist's undercover work are first revealed in detail throughout an argument he has with his wife. This combines exposition with characterization and plot movement.

Keeping to the point

When writing the first draft of a scene it is normal for writers to take a few lines to find the essence or central dramatic dilemma of the scene. After all, every new scene is a new set of tasks and new set of problems to be solved. Check that the opening lines are actually moving the scene along, that is, that the scene gets right into the action it is supposed to transmit. Normally, particularly in the first days of writing the script where you are not really at home with the characters or the action, the first lines will need to be cut. If your scene is opening with redundant chat, like greetings, be ruthless. Ideally, the opening of the scene, like the opening of the film as a whole, should hook in the audience with an interesting idea or event. A good rule of thumb is that a scene should open at the last possible moment beyond which it becomes unintelligible.

The same ruthlessness needs to be applied to the end of the scene. You might find you need to cut the last lines of the scene because it is continuing beyond the vital piece of information that, for suspense purposes, you need as an exit line. This exit line is often a real or implied question that will keep the audience interested in watching further.

Pace

Keep reminding yourself of the context of the scene in order to best judge what pace and style your scene must have as well as what plot content and characterization. Variety of pace is important because too many scenes of the same length can be boring.

Character and emotions behind the words (subtext)

If good dialogue is dependent on good scenario, it is also dependent on good characterization. A character is defined by what it does not say as much as what it does say, and good dialogue is as much about what is not said as said. Subtext – when a character's words do not express their true feelings – is a supremely useful tool.

Just as inexperienced actors act only the words and ignore the possibilities of the pause, so inexperienced screenwriters forget both the power of the pause, and the usefulness of the actor's face and body language to transmit an idea. Get inside the pause and remember that the thoughts between the words determine the words. Understand and mentally script the thought progression that happens in pauses between speeches. Make the speeches sound as if they've appeared at the end of a thought progression.

Remember that in emotional situations, people do not describe their feelings in detail. They tend to skip stages of their mental progression. They often want to hide their vulnerabilities or conclude the conversation, particularly when they are in the wrong. Remember to look at matters from the point of view of all the characters in the scene.

Before writing, get into the characters' heads (see Development Strategy 12: Getting into character). Work out the range of reactions such characters would have. Practice writing in the voice of the character before starting to write scenes. To practice, do not use a scene that will appear in the script. Invent a new scene (for example, the character finding themselves locked out and getting help).

To get into character for the scene

1. Think what each character is – what has made them what they are and what is compelling them in the current situation.
2. Think what each character wants from the scene.
3. Think of how this particular character would suppress or cover up what they are thinking and how, despite themselves, their real feelings might come across in subtext.

Subtext, silence and meaningful looks are wonderful tools, but it can be dangerous to rely solely on visuals: the look of angst is also the look of indigestion!

Productive conflict and redundant conflict

Drama is about conflict. But conflict in individual scenes must move the story forward, either plot-wise or in terms of how the characters understand their situation. Productive conflict makes something change. Redundant conflict occurs when the characters are simply batting (usually the same) arguments or complaints back and forth: "You're a bad father!" "I'm a good father!" "No, you're a bad father!" … Nothing has changed at the end of the scene.

Productive conflict is: "You're a bad father!" "I'm a good father!" "No, you're a bad father because I overheard you/mother told me about/I found a letter…" whatever. Redundant conflict works to stop the plot in its tracks because the plot cannot move until the "yes, you did"/"no you didn't" static material is concluded. While redundant conflict is like a tennis game, with the issue being uselessly hit back and forth, productive conflict is like a game of football, where the participants have to move the "story ball" to the other end of the field while engaging in conflict all the way. The quarrels between Allnutt and Rose in *The African Queen* are a good example of productive conflict. The quarrels move the characters in a new direction. They show them changing. The quarrels in *Mr. Saturday Night* are redundant because they are all essentially the same row, and because nothing is changed by them.

As noted earlier in this chapter, quarrels are a useful way to get over backstory, exposition, or information generally.

Self-control

Screenwriters, like all dramatists, love to write dialogue. In fact it is usually a facility for dialogue that makes people become dramatists in the first place. But, it is easy to lose self-control when writing dialogue. So, do not fall in love with:

- your own dialogue skills (so that you write real dialogue in real time – for the sake of writing dialogue)
- your own deeply held ideas as articulated in stirring speeches
- your own jokes (if you are including a joke just for the sake of it, think hard. Such things slow a script down. Try to find a legitimate place for the joke – for example, where it will help with character or plot).

Acting and camera directions

Writing dialogue in scenes also means understanding the conventions governing the use of camera and acting directions and layout. The best way to do this is to read as many scripts as possible. Script layout guides with full glossaries of camera terms are available from organizations like the Writers' Guild and film-funding bodies. Television production companies sometimes vary a little in their in-house layout conventions. While it is important to understand the meaning of camera terms, in practice, writers use only a small range of camera directions, preferring to imply what the camera is doing through acting directions. Camera directions are always typed in capitals, to distinguish them. Figure 14.1 lists the most common camera terms.

ACROSS TO ...	Camera crosses to another person or thing.
ANGLE	The angle of the camera on what it is viewing.
BACK TO ...	Camera returns to a person or thing.
CU	Close up.
ESTABLISHING SHOT	Opening shot to a scene, establishing where it is set. Applied to a wide view.
EXT.	Exterior of a building, or outdoors.
FOOTAGE	Footage previously shot and stored, sometimes called STOCK SHOT.
HIGH ANGLE	An overhead, bird's eye view.
INT.	Interior of a building.
JUMP CUT	Dramatic cut to other action.
LONG SHOT (LS)	A view from a distance.
MED SHOT (MS)	View of a person or people from the waist up.
OFF CAMERA (OC)	When the person speaking is not visible on screen. See also VOICEOVER.
PAN	Camera, remaining in one spot, slowly sweeps a scene, describing an arc.
POINT OF VIEW (POV)	What a person is seeing.
PULL BACK	Camera pulls back to show a wider view of the action. Also known as WIDEN.
STOCK SHOT	Footage previously shot and stored (sometimes just called FOOTAGE).
TIGHT, or TIGHT SHOT	Something shot in a way that keeps everything else around out of frame.
TWO SHOT	Two people together.
VOICEOVER (VO)	When the person speaking is not visible on screen. See also OFF CAMERA.
WHIP PAN	A rapid sweep.
WIDE ANGLE	A very wide view.
WIDEN	Camera pulls back to show a wider view of the action. Also known as PULL BACK.
XCU	Extreme close up.
ZOOM	Camera zooms in on a detail.

Figure 14.1 Common camera terms

The general rule is to keep camera and acting directions (still often referred to as "stage directions") to a minimum. Partly this is so that the creative input of the director and the actors is not preempted, but it is also to keep the script readable. Unlike readers of fiction, people reading scripts are not merely reading for literary merit, they are trying to visualize the script and judge its pace and timing. Lengthy acting descriptions seriously distract from this. A good rule is to write acting and camera directions that will take the same time to read as they would to be seen on the screen. That way, the reader can maintain a genuine sense of the script as it will appear on film.

When describing an action or a place, make sure it is written in the order in which the camera will see it. For example, if a camera is supposed to be panning the ground floor of a house, do not describe the kitchen then, in the middle of the description of the living room, mention that there was a safe in the kitchen. The reason for avoiding this sort of jumping about is that the reader will have to reject the mental picture they have of the kitchen and start again, which is not only irritating but also interrupts their estimation of the timing of the film.

Never put in directions any information that is obvious from the action or dialogue.

For more material on how to write a description of what is happening on screen, see Chapter 16.

Writing well for the camera

Writing well for the camera means transmitting information about what is appearing on screen in an economical, vivid, but unobtrusive way. Here is an excellent example of good writing for the camera. It is an extract from a television drama scene written by well-known Australian screenwriter Cliff Green, who also wrote *Picnic at Hanging Rock,* and edited by Jo Martino, a highly respected Australian script editor. Notice the economy, wit, and minimal formal camera directions used to transmit a large amount of visual information, including detailed actions and characters' emotions.

INT. MERINDA/BEDROOM   DAY 1

DOUG, JULIA

We see, in BIG CU, a pair of tweezers pulling an individual hair from a large nose.

WIDEN to see DOUG sitting on a chair and JULIA plucking nasal hairs with as much loving compassion as the circumstances allow.

Suddenly one really hurts.

> DOUG

Ow!

He pulls back.

> JULIA

They'll be doing close-ups. They always do close-ups.

> DOUG

They can come as close as they like.

His face cupped in her hands. JULIA on guard for signs of any other facial debris.

Extract from "Getting to Know You," Episode 5 from the ABC TV series *Something in the Air* © 1999 Beyond Simpson Le Mesurier Productions and ABC TV.

15. Examples of flawed dialogue writing

L
ike the workings of good structure, the workings of good dialogue are sometimes easier to understand by looking at work that is flawed. What follow are variations on two different scenes – "Going on holiday" and "The breakup" – that each display a wide range of dialogue problems. Following each version of the scene is an analysis of its problems, with some suggestions for improvement. The faults have been exaggerated to make them easier to identify, but they are very common. For easier reading, the dialogue column in the following examples of scripts is wider than it would normally be in a real script.

"Going on holiday" (Version 1)

INT. LUCY'S BEDROOM [Unnecessary.] MORNING

PAN LUCY'S ROOM. [Unnecessary detail.]

MS LUCY IS <u>STANDING</u> BY HER BED.

Lucy is <u>standing by</u> her bed <u>wearing a short pink and white floral dress with a lace collar and belt matched with white, lace-up shoes and tan-colored pantyhose. She sighs, tips her head to one side, then, smiling warmly, picks up a grey stuffed elephant, hugs it, kisses it on its trunk, and puts it down again.</u>

[Redundant — has slowing effect.]

                         LUCY
                      (Happily)

[Repetition.]

[Clumsy exposition.] <u>I am</u> so <u>happy</u>! It is the first day of holidays and Auntie Jenny is arriving in five minutes to take us to her holiday cottage!

Lucy looks out of the window.

LUCY'S POV – THE STREET BELOW
WITH ITS TREES. A BLUE CAR PASSES.

> Time consuming –
> expensive and
> redundant.

BACK TO LUCY – SMILING.

ACROSS TO BELLA – <u>SITTING ON HER
BED WITH A HAPPY LOOK.</u>

> This is prose
> fiction writing.

BELLA is <u>sitting on her bed with a happy look.</u> She gets up, walks
to one corner and swings to face LUCY, a look of immense
excitement spreading across her freckled face.

BELLA
<u>(Excitedly, standing with her hands on her hips)</u>

> Redundant.

> Repetition – and
> unnecessary
> because dialogue
> should indicate
> mood.

The journey takes three hours but the cottage is
so beautiful! I am so excited! But I do hope Uncle
Bill has fixed the motor on the boat in case it
breaks down and the tide carries us out to the
island!

LUCY
(Bending to tie her shoelace)

> Clumsy
> exposition.

I must do up my shoes!

BELLA
(Bending to tie her shoelace)

> Redundant –
> 'real time'
> writing.

Me too.

> Redundant.

LUCY
<u>(Sighing with happiness, sinking onto the bed)</u>

> Repetition –
> needs
> tightening.

I really <u>love</u> holidays. I <u>love</u> to wake up in the
morning and think there is no school and hear
the waves in the distance and know that I can be
happy all day.

> Prose fiction

LUCY sighs to herself, remembering last year when she was at
the cottage and picked flowers every morning. She hopes the
grumpy neighbor will have moved.

> Redundant.

BELLA
<u>(Sighing, pulling a suitcase out from under the
bed, putting her books in it)</u>

> The action
> will show this.

<u>I think I will pack my books in this suitcase.</u> This
lock is always so stiff. There we are! Open! Now,

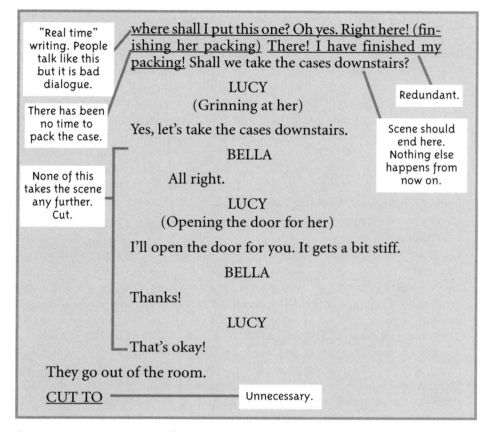

"Real time" writing. People talk like this but it is bad dialogue.

There has been no time to pack the case.

None of this takes the scene any further. Cut.

where shall I put this one? Oh yes. Right here! (finishing her packing) There! I have finished my packing! Shall we take the cases downstairs?

LUCY
(Grinning at her)

Yes, let's take the cases downstairs.

BELLA

All right.

LUCY
(Opening the door for her)

I'll open the door for you. It gets a bit stiff.

BELLA

Thanks!

LUCY

That's okay!

They go out of the room.

CUT TO

Redundant.

Scene should end here. Nothing else happens from now on.

Unnecessary.

Comments on "Going on holiday" (Version 1)

This scene contains too much "directing on paper" in terms both of camera directions and directions to the actors. These slow down the reader in the vital task of reading the script for its playing speed, credibility and emotional impact. Actors and director must be given the freedom to do their job. Note how repetitive the piece is, how like prose fiction narrative the directions often become. This is redundant. Stage directions are not literature, they are notes on a plan. The problems with this piece of screenwriting are:

- The instructions as to what is seen out of the window must be relevant to the plot or cut.
- The instruction CUT TO at the end is redundant because a cut is implied by the fact that this is the end of a scene.
- The dialogue frequently states what is self-evident: "I am excited." The dialogue does not use common spoken contractions like "can't" and "I'll."
- The exposition is very clumsy. When putting in exposition, try to get it across in fragments and avoid letting characters repeat the same piece of information unless it is a real springboard for delivering more information.
- The passages about doing up shoes and opening the door are repetitive and do not take the scene further. If either action is a set-up which will pay off later, they should be included but in a much more subtle way.

- Lucy thinking about picking flowers and the whereabouts of the grumpy neighbor are not transmittable to the audience. If it is important, it should be put into the dialogue.
- Nothing is happening while Bella packs her suitcase; moreover, there is no indication that the writer is imagining the action or thinking what is happening on screen while it is going on. The writer seems to have forgotten that packing a suitcase will take valuable screen time. If an action is specified in the script, enough time should be allowed for it to occur, and other action should occur as it is going on. If the action seems to be slowing the scene down, either get rid of it or imbue it with a point that will move along character. Seriously question its use in the film as a whole.
- Both characters have exactly the same speech mannerisms, and the speech mannerisms sound robotic rather than realistic. The dialogue is not credible as that of young people.
- The scene is giving us very little in terms of information about either plot or character.
- Often the dialogue and action are dropping into "real time" dialogue – that is, what people would say or do in the same situation in real life. This simply slows the scene down.
- The scene is repetitive and boring because there is no real characterization and no real plot movement after the first few speeches. It is not telling us anything about these girls after the first few speeches. It could be cut back massively.
- The task here is to get across as much about the personalities of the girls as possible. Characterization points that this scene could explore are:
    - whether the girls are related or just friends
    - whether they generally get on well
    - what class they are
    - where they live
    - how old they are
    - their possessions (which reveal character)
    - how tidy/untidy they are
    - whether they are timid, brave, poetical, etc.
- Plot points that could be revealed here are:
    - more about last year and what to expect
    - relevant detail about the uncle, aunt, and cottage
    - more about the geography of the area they are going to have their adventure in
    - details about their ability to cope with the adventure.

"Going on holiday" (Version 2)

This is the start of a better example of the scene.

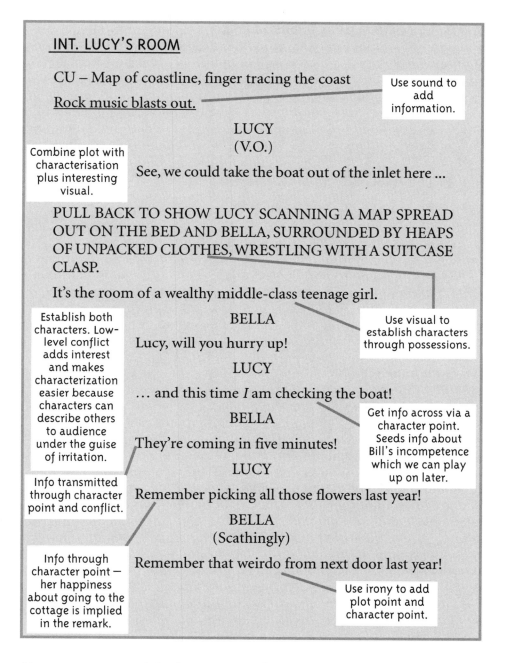

INT. LUCY'S ROOM

CU – Map of coastline, finger tracing the coast

Rock music blasts out.

Use sound to add information.

LUCY
(V.O.)

Combine plot with characterisation plus interesting visual.

See, we could take the boat out of the inlet here ...

PULL BACK TO SHOW LUCY SCANNING A MAP SPREAD OUT ON THE BED AND BELLA, SURROUNDED BY HEAPS OF UNPACKED CLOTHES, WRESTLING WITH A SUITCASE CLASP.

It's the room of a wealthy middle-class teenage girl.

Establish both characters. Low-level conflict adds interest and makes characterization easier because characters can describe others to audience under the guise of irritation.

BELLA

Lucy, will you hurry up!

Use visual to establish characters through possessions.

LUCY

... and this time *I* am checking the boat!

BELLA

They're coming in five minutes!

Get info across via a character point. Seeds info about Bill's incompetence which we can play up on later.

Info transmitted through character point and conflict.

LUCY

Remember picking all those flowers last year!

BELLA
(Scathingly)

Info through character point — her happiness about going to the cottage is implied in the remark.

Remember that weirdo from next door last year!

Use irony to add plot point and character point.

Comments on "Going on holiday" (Version 2)

Information is being transmitted via dialogue, visuals and sound, often simultaneously, and the lack of redundant dialogue means the pace is much faster. Notice how low-level conflict is used to transmit backstory, character and relationships. Note how Bill's incompetence is seeded so that it can be developed later on.

The "breakup" (Version 1)

The task here is to write a scene about Marie confronting her husband, Peter, in his office about his infidelity with a colleague, Stephanie. Peter confesses, but is torn between Marie and Stephanie. Marie leaves, saying that she and the children will be staying at a friend's. Left alone, Peter wonders how he will tell his beloved children.

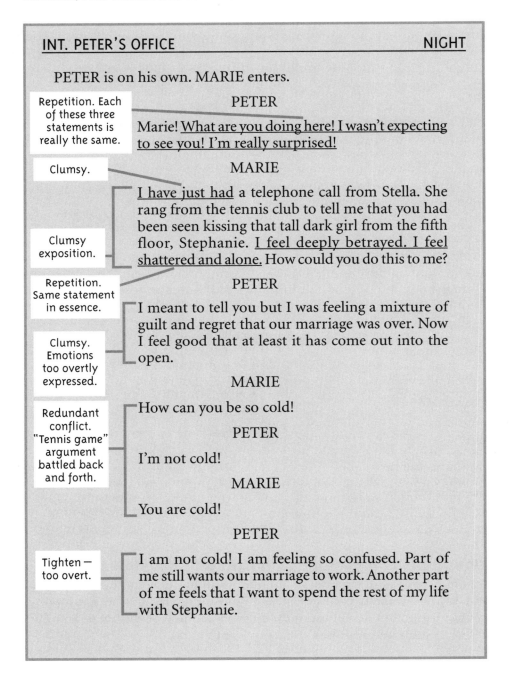

INT. PETER'S OFFICE   NIGHT

PETER is on his own. MARIE enters.

Repetition. Each of these three statements is really the same.

PETER

Marie! What are you doing here! I wasn't expecting to see you! I'm really surprised!

Clumsy.

MARIE

I have just had a telephone call from Stella. She rang from the tennis club to tell me that you had been seen kissing that tall dark girl from the fifth floor, Stephanie. I feel deeply betrayed. I feel shattered and alone. How could you do this to me?

Clumsy exposition.

Repetition. Same statement in essence.

PETER

I meant to tell you but I was feeling a mixture of guilt and regret that our marriage was over. Now I feel good that at least it has come out into the open.

Clumsy. Emotions too overtly expressed.

MARIE

How can you be so cold!

Redundant conflict. "Tennis game" argument battled back and forth.

PETER

I'm not cold!

MARIE

You are cold!

PETER

Tighten — too overt.

I am not cold! I am feeling so confused. Part of me still wants our marriage to work. Another part of me feels that I want to spend the rest of my life with Stephanie.

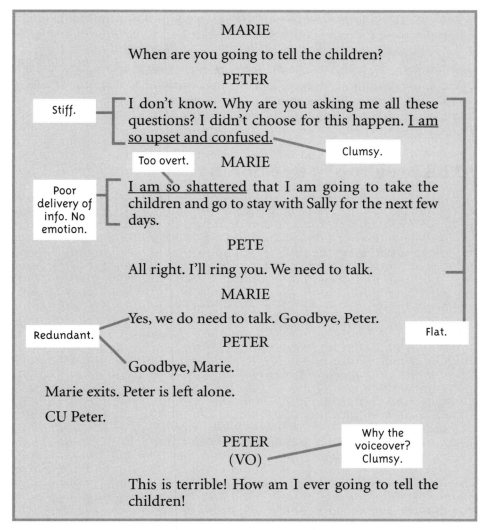

MARIE

When are you going to tell the children?

PETER

Stiff. — I don't know. Why are you asking me all these questions? I didn't choose for this happen. <u>I am so upset and confused.</u> **Clumsy.**

Too overt. MARIE

Poor delivery of info. No emotion. — <u>I am so shattered</u> that I am going to take the children and go to stay with Sally for the next few days.

PETE

All right. I'll ring you. We need to talk.

MARIE

Yes, we do need to talk. Goodbye, Peter.

Redundant. **Flat.**

PETER

Goodbye, Marie.

Marie exits. Peter is left alone.

CU Peter.

PETER
(VO)

Why the voiceover? Clumsy.

This is terrible! How am I ever going to tell the children!

Comments on "The breakup" (Version 1)

Generally, this version is poor because the characters are expressing too many of their feelings in words; moreover, they are saying things that are obvious (for example, "I am so upset and confused"). The "thoughts between the sentences" are not being considered at all. Specific problems are:

- The writer has missed the opportunity to characterize Peter when he is on his own.
- The writer has been so concerned to get across information that characterization has been forgotten.
- The tennis game of "You're cold," "No, I'm not," "Yes you are" is redundant, and thus reduces the scene's impact.
- The actor is not being given enough room to act. Sentiments like the following could almost be done through body language alone: "I am not cold! I am feeling so

confused. Part of me still wants our marriage to work. Another part of me feels that I want to spend the rest of my life with Stephanie."

- By setting the scene at night, the writer has missed the chance to have other people in the office who could raise the stress level by overhearing or interrupting. Even if the budget for this scene does not allow for other characters to appear, never miss the chance to imply they are there, if it helps the drama.
- The use of voiceover at the end is poor. Peter should either express himself through direct words or gestures.

"The breakup" (Version 2)

INT. PETER'S OFFICE   DAY

Peter is on his phone.

PETER

Yes … mmm … mmm … yes …

Marie throws opens the door.

PETER

Marie! (To phone) I'll call you back …

MARIE

[Melodramatic.] Oh, don't hang up on my account! I suppose that was her, was it? Little Miss Stephanie from the fifth floor?

PETER

[Cliché.] I … I … don't know what you mean.

MARIE

[Melodramatic.] Stella, Peter. She told me. She rang me up and told me that you were having an affair!

Peter gets up, walks about distractedly. **[Weak direction — leave actions to director and actor.]**

MARIE

[Melodramatic.] Well? Are you going to tell me it's not true?

PETER

Marie … I love you and the children …

MARIE

Cliché.
Melodramatic.

Ha!

PETER

Too
overt.

I do! I just ... I'm confused. Part of me wants the marriage to work. Another part wants to be with Stephanie for the rest of my life.

MARIE

You creep.

PETER

Don't call me that!

MARIE

Aren't you a creep?

PETER

Redundant
conflict.
Batting
argument
back and
forth.

No, I am not a creep. I'm a human being with needs and feelings! Something you seem to forget, Marie!

Marie slaps him around the face.

Melodrama.

Cliché.

PETER

Melodramatic,
implausible
response.

I didn't deserve that, Marie.

MARIE

When are you going to tell the children? Or should that be 'Are you going to tell the children?'

PETER

I'll tell them. I just need a little time.

Cliché.

MARIE

I'm taking them with me to Sally's. We'll stay there. You'll hear from my lawyers in the morning.

Peter steps forward to touch her.

PETER

Marie, I ...

Cliché.

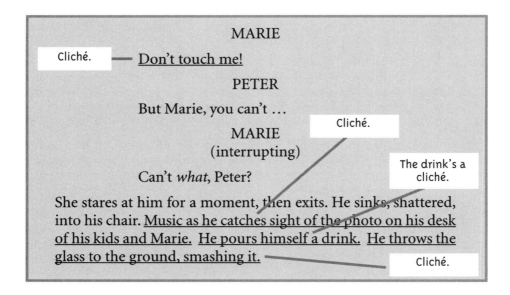

Comments on "The breakup" (Version 2)

This version incorporates all of the action clichés of melodrama: face slapping, pouring a drink, glass-breaking, photo-surveying (staring into a mirror is another cliché). The characters are very verbal and very sure of themselves, and tend to say what everybody wishes they could think of to say in such conversations. They talk in clichés and platitudes ("I … I … don't know what you mean." "I didn't deserve that, Marie." "You'll hear from my lawyers in the morning.") and there is little subtext or unscripted thought progression between the lines. While certain kinds of serial dramas operate on the overt and honest expression of emotions, this version of scene 2 is not acceptable even within such conventions. As well as wall-to-wall clichés, the scene shows a lot of redundant material. The opening phone conversation is redundant because it tells us nothing about the character or his state of mind. The tennis game of redundant conflict over the "creep" accusation is also poor.

"The breakup" (Version 3)

INT. PETER'S OFFICE   DAY

Peter is on the phone. He's looking through papers as he speaks. He's calm, in control.

PETER

No, I need delivery by the fifth or not at all … I …
(He sees Marie approaching) I'm sorry, what? I'll leave it with you. Bye.

He hangs up, gears himself to look normal. Marie enters.

                    PETER

        Hi!

She just stares at him. Peter gets up and closes the door. Marie realizes why, and gives a contemptuous snort. Peter comes back behind his desk. Tense pause.

                    MARIE

        I've just been driving around ... Stella rang this morning.

Pause.

                    PETER

        I was going to tell you.

Marie sighs – "the hell you were." Pause.

                    MARIE

        I'm taking the children to Sally's ...
                    PETER
            (Interrupting, stressed)

        Oh, don't do that!

The phone has started to ring.

                    MARIE
            (Cutting in)

Cut?

        When are you going to tell them? *Are* you going to tell them?

Beat.

                    PETER

        It's not as simple as that.

                    MARIE

        I think it's bloody simple!

PETER

Oh, shit. (Snatching up the phone) Masters? (He's watching her every movement, but it's his boss.) Oh, Mr Carter ... Yes ... (Marie waits a moment then gets up to go.) Look, I'm extremely sorry, sir, can I call you back? (The boss is clearly not pleased.) Thank you, sir.

He hangs up and grabs at Marie as she gets to the door.

PETER

Marie ...

MARIE

Go away!

PETER

No, we need to talk.

Cut? —

MARIE
(Fighting tears)

Go away!

PETER

Please ...

MARIE

Well talk! (BEAT) Talk then! Which of us do you want?

Cut?

She stares at him, anguished.

PETER

You always do this! You make everything black and white ...

He can't keep it up. He looks away. Her face flashes anguish then pride – and she's gone.

Left alone, Peter knows he's just lost the marriage and his kids.

Comments on "The breakup" (Version 3)

The scene is better because there is more characterization, subtext, and unspoken thought progression for the actors to utilize. Generally, the scene seems more rooted in reality.

Peter seems to be existing in a real office with its interruptions and gossip-minded colleagues. The phone call at the beginning has dialogue which tells us something about Peter's job and the way he does it. Moreover, it permits him to be seen reacting to Marie's arrival. There is also the opportunity, implied but not specified in the opening, that Marie's progression through the office towards Peter's room could be seen on screen.

The scene's drama and suspense levels (jeopardy) are raised because Marie is actually seen to interrupt Peter's work and Peter is shown being aware that they could be overheard. The mental jumps and matters left unsaid add suspense to the scene because we are not sure what is coming next. The interrupting phone call adds tension through putting Peter on the spot – his job and his marriage are both demanding his attention. The camera would be moving between both characters at this stage, monitoring their unspoken interaction.

At the end, Peter's inability to say anything is more dramatic than a weak line and gives Marie a chance to act her grief and hurt pride. His change of tack at the end is credible and characterizing. Marie's outburst at the end is a bit soapy but acceptable because she has been so restrained earlier.

The scene could be further cut back if required. Other possible versions might include an interruption from another office member, or other such tension-builders. Many writers would reduce the number of acting directions, feeling that they inhibit actors. Of course a real scene in a real film would present the writer with opportunities to seed later events or pay off material set up earlier. There would also be the possibility to develop character in a more precise and focused way. The bad language would have to be removed if this scene were to be screening as a family film.

For further information on writing specific scenes, see Development Strategy 22: Getting the right scenario for each scene; Development Strategy 23: Creating opening scenes; and Development Strategy 27: Writing short films.

16. Treatment writing and the script as instruction manual

As well as a piece of drama, a script in all its forms (including treatment and scene breakdown) is a technical instruction manual for everyone involved in the process of creating the film. This means it has to be written and laid out according to industry conventions. The scripts in the previous chapters have been laid out differently for ease of reading in a book format.

What is a treatment?

A "treatment" is a prose summary of a proposed film or other piece of screen drama. Essentially a selling document, its purpose is to provide potential investors of all kinds with a text that will let their mind's eye see the proposed film or telemovie as if they were sitting in a cinema watching it happen on screen. A treatment for a full-length feature film or telemovie is normally about 35 pages long. Shorter pieces require shorter treatments. Treatments are always written in the present tense and their closest affinity, stylistically and in function, is with stage directions.

Treatments are notoriously difficult to write because, at the same time as being meticulously precise and economical, they must be a good read – a piece of prose that jumps off the page. Treatments must depict, simply, vividly, and without any ambiguity, not only what the camera is seeing but also the order in which it sees it, so that no mental replays have to be done. In addition, the writer must be completely invisible because nothing, including an awareness of the narrator's sensibility, however unique or acute, must distract readers from the film or telemovie screening in their heads. Distractions mean the reader cannot maintain a proper sense of the planned film's pace. With every distraction, the film running in the reader's head risks losing its impact, suspense, and emotional build.

Of course, treatments, like all other pieces of scriptwriting, are a personal thing. They vary in tone from writer to writer. Some writers will include snippets of dialogue.

Others will open the treatment with a striking and detailed description of the script's first scenes, so as to excite and capture the reader. Others will be chatty, or in rare instances where the writer feels there may be mileage in it, openly idiosyncratic in description (although idiosyncracy of this sort is best avoided by new writers). Despite these differences, all treatments obey the same general rules about making sure readers can view the film in their heads undistracted.

What distracts readers from the film in their heads?

The most common distractions are:

1. repetition
2. redundant detail
3. out-of-sequence description
4. intrusive narrative voice.

Avoiding distraction while maintaining useful detail

Distractions can be minimized by working out in advance what information the reader has to be given to be able to visualize and understand the full import of a sequence. What is the scene about? What information is it vital that the reader receives?

What is the sequence about?
1. Action

What happens in this sequence?
The reader needs to know precisely and economically what is happening on the screen in the order it happens.

2. Emotional state of the characters

How are the characters feeling?
It may or may not be necessary to describe the characters' emotional state. This is something that must be treated with caution. If the sequence is showing something not emotionally charged, then there is usually no need to describe emotions. Again, if it is obvious what the characters are feeling from their actions or from what has just happened, there is usually no need.

3. New details that will be important later

Is this detail important for later?
If a detail that will be important later in the drama occurs in this scene, make sure it is neither submerged nor too heavily emphasized. Be aware that readers will assume details are significant.

4. Position

Where is the sequence in the film?

If the sequence is close to the end of the film, we will know the characters well and therefore not be in need of material descriptive of character. Conversely, if the sequence happens early in the film, character details (gender, age, response) might well need to be spelled out.

5. Mood

What mood is the sequence?

Capturing the mood of what is to be seen on the screen is vital. The treatment must do justice to the material. The reader must be engaged on an emotional level. If the sequence is an exciting chase, the description should be exciting to read. If the sequence shows a family after a death, the writing should capture the mood of grief. Similarly, comic scenes need to be described so as to show the reader how they will be funny.

Going to cards before writing the treatment

To make sure you fully understand the content and function of each sequence, it is a good idea to *go to cards* before you write the treatment. The first stage of going to cards means working out each plot point and writing it on a separate, numbered index card. The cards are then placed on a table, in order. This process permits the writer to visualize the whole piece of drama in its entirety. It is a great aid to objectivity and good structure. Once the cards are set out, plot points may then be rearranged, combined, and so on, for best effect.

Exercise in treatment technique

Here is a sequence that needs to be turned into part of a treatment.

What the sequence is about

1. Action

The sequence is about our protagonist, Joe, snatching up Old Harry's shotgun and running from his hotel through pouring rain to make sure that his girlfriend, Jenny, has not been attacked by a serial killer.

2. Emotional state of the character

Joe is distraught and feeling guilty that he didn't heed Jenny's warnings.

3. New details in the sequence that will be important later

None.

4. Position

This is a sequence late in the action, when we know Joe well. It is also just before the big climax, in which Joe and Jenny join forces against the serial killer.

5. Mood

Excitement, suspense.

Poor treatment writing

Here is the sequence poorly written.

Never mention the camera by name and try to make any vital shots part of the text. This direction is redundant, telling us nothing more than the obvious. If you want to specify exactly what we are seeing, you can say "stay with JOE" or, for close-ups, constructions like "JOE, panting and desperate, his face splattered with mud …" etc. Be sparing with this sort of writing. Do not "direct on paper."

Weak word, inadequate.

It is too late in the script for exposition. If the planting date of the trees is important it should have been set up earlier. If the trees and Harry are not of relevance here, cut, or risk distracting the reader and losing pace.

Out-of-sequence description. We already have a mental picture of him running out of the hotel — without a shotgun.

Redundant detail. We don't need to know about the leaves.

The camera shows JOE hurrying out of the hotel and being annoyed to find it raining. The rain is slashing down. It's pouring. JOE runs out of the hotel grounds, carrying Harry's shotgun, which he picked up in the hotel lobby. He dashes out along the street, which is carpeted with rain-sodden leaves in every color from yellow through red to dark brown, all fallen from the grove of plane trees planted by Old Harry sixty years ago to overhang the road. The gutters are running. Trees, dark sentinels of the night, are dripping. Cursing the rain, JOE jogs on down the black, glimmering road. Cars fly past, splashing him. His foot goes into a puddle and he turns his ankle. A car almost runs him over. He arrives at JENNY's house and runs through the rain up the drive and to the front door.

We know it's raining. Use only the most descriptive word, and use it once.

Repetition. We know he has just run out.

Intrusive narrative voice. This is distracting, adding nothing to what we are visualizing. Its only purpose is to draw attention to the way the writer sees the world.

While some of this detail might be powerful, too much could be distracting, becoming a red herring because the emphasis placed on it leads us to feel it must be important.

Better treatment writing – alternative versions

Here are some alternative versions that use much better treatment writing technique.

1. Very tight

> JOE snatches up OLD HARRY's shotgun. He runs frantically out into the slashing rain and up the road to JENNY's.

While extremely tight, this might be all that is needed if this is merely a link to the big climax and speed is of the essence. This version contains all the required elements. It maintains the mood of excitement and fear. It is colloquial rather than formal and literary. It is appropriate for its position in the script. It shows action in proper sequence. It shows the character's emotional state. It contains no distractions. Note that its shortness suggests a short sequence. Avoid depicting a short sequence at great length, because lengthy description will make the reader imagine a lengthy sequence.

2. Some detail

> JOE snatches up OLD HARRY's shotgun. He runs frantically out into the slashing rain and up the road towards JENNY's house. He's to blame for this, and he knows it. Cars fly past, hooting and splashing him. One narrowly misses him, and he slips, plunging down into a rut in the road. His ankle is twisted badly. He's in agony, but he struggles to his feet and forces himself on. He reaches JENNY's house.

This version addresses all the necessary points, but adds more detail on the specifics of the action and Joe's emotional state. Close-ups of Joe's face have been implied through saying that we see him in agony and that he feels guilty. This version gives both the director and actor more to work with without telling them how to do their job or cluttering up the page with distracting camera or acting directions. Notice that the actor and director are told Joe's emotional state without being given specific – and distracting – instructions as to how these emotions are to be shown, for example, "Joe's mouth quivers, his knees buckle, he sobs, raising his eyes heavenwards …"

Note also that this version suggests to the reader that the sequence takes longer than the first version, and that Joe's frantic run will be used in the film to raise suspense. But the sequence still feels like a link to the next main action point, namely, encountering the serial killer.

3. Very detailed, making the sequence very significant in Joe's emotional movement

> JOE snatches up OLD HARRY's shotgun. He runs frantically out into the slashing rain and up the road towards JENNY's house. He's to blame for this, and he knows it. Cars fly past,

hooting and splashing him. One narrowly misses him, and he slips, plunging down into a rut in the road. His ankle is twisted badly. He's in agony, but he struggles to his feet and forces himself on. The road seems endless. He's eaten up with despair. He's realizing how much JENNY means to him and how likely it is that he will be too late. He staggers on. JENNY's house comes into sight. He wills himself toward it. Near collapse, he staggers up the drive.

Here, the added detail about action and emotional state suggest a longer sequence and one which is crucial to Joe's emotional development. As it is now written, the run to Jenny's house shows Joe realizing, with pain, that he loves Jenny and that he might have lost her. The writing makes us imagine more close-ups because the film needs to display Joe's increasing distress. We can even imagine music.

Points to remember

The longer and more detailed the description of a sequence, the longer readers will expect it to play, and the more significance they will attribute to it. If the sequence is short, it should be described briefly. This can be tricky if the action, while brief in terms of time, takes a long while to describe on paper.

Do not accord all sequences the same amount of space. Go for variety based on the running time of the sequence. Try always to get the feel of the film. If the film is funny, keep the description funny but apposite. If the film is moving, keep the description moving but unsentimental and, as always, apposite. It is easy for treatments to become too dry. Remember, the treatment is a selling tool. It must be a good read. To summarize, think always of the film running in the reader's head. Avoid distractions in terms of redundant detail, intrusive narrative voice, repetition, and out-of-sequence description of action requiring a mental replay.

Scene breakdowns and stage directions

Treatments, scene breakdowns and stage directions all share the same aim, namely, to create a piece of prose which makes the drama screen vividly and without interruption in the reader's mind. Hence all rules about distractions (in the form of redundant detail, intrusive narrative voice, repetition, and out-of-sequence action requiring mental replays) are as equally applicable to scene breakdowns and stage directions as they are to treatments.

Like treatments, scene breakdowns and stage directions are also pieces of technical writing which must give all film personnel the information they need to do their job.

17. Writing under pressure

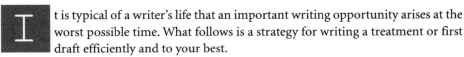

I t is typical of a writer's life that an important writing opportunity arises at the worst possible time. What follows is a strategy for writing a treatment or first draft efficiently and to your best.

Read this chapter in conjunction with Chapter 16: "Treatment writing and the script as an instruction manual," and cross-check with the Development Strategies. Chapter 6 contains the Development Strategies in detail. If you are writing in any of the parallel story structures, look for general guidance in Chapters 7–11. For flashback structures, see Chapter 9, Quick reference guide to using flashback narrative.

Strategy for writing under pressure

Here is a simple plan for writing when you are under pressure of time:

1. Work out how much time you can afford to devote to the writing, and create a plan with dates for completion of each stage of the work. Do not plan to do everything over the weekend or in a few consecutive days because the pressure on you will be too great. Instead, try to do a little a day. Remember that even a minute here and there can be used to brainstorm solutions to small problems. For example, a five minute coffee break devoted to brainstorming the demands of the genre in which you plan to write will give you a huge amount of information. Added together, these minutes will move the work on its way.

2. Consciously remind yourself that stress creates cliché. Look calmly at your strengths and weaknesses as a writer, and be aware that under stress you will make your normal mistakes. For example, if you have a weakness with structure, that weakness is liable to show itself under stress. This is not to be negative, it is to be focused. It is just a sensible approach to your weak spots, so you can attend to them and produce to your best. Write yourself reminders about problem areas in the script or with technique and stick them over your desk.

3. Throughout the writing, make use of the Development Strategies. Start by defining the task at hand, that is, refreshing your memory about the sort of material that is needed for the sort of script you have to write. Watch relevant films and read relevant scripts. Be aware of details.

4. Decide what the genre demands in terms of emotions and pattern.

5. If you are writing a short film, check that the story can be told in the length of screen time you have.

6. Check what specific limitations, if any, the piece of work might have, for example, no period pieces, no expensive effects, etc.

7. Brainstorm a range of ideas as shown in Chapters 2–4, exploring them as shown in Chapter 2. Do not jump at your first idea because it will probably be a cliché. Later ideas are likely to be more original. Choose an idea that fits with the above points and is original and unclichéd.

8. If your story is about a group reunion, siege or mission, see Chapter 12, Multiple protagonists and antagonists.

9. If your story has flashbacks, see Chapters 7–10.

10. If your film is running stories in parallel and/or looking at the same event from the points of view of different characters, with stories in sequence, see Chapter 11, Tandem and sequential narrative. Work out a Smiley/Thompson nine-point plan, and turn it into a chart (see Figure 5.6 on page 47).

11. Work out a simple story sentence which you keep developing. If you are writing a parallel story film, you will have a number of these.

12. Draw a "structure mountain," putting in the turning points (see Figure 5.1 on page 42). If you are writing a parallel narrative film, you will have a number of these.

13. Decide whether your story is an action line or a relationship line and create whichever you are missing. In parallel narrative, there might be a number of action lines and relationship lines.

14. For any relationship line, draw a "relationship road" with signposts indicating the developmental steps of the relationship. Make sure the relationship does develop (that is, that the signposts show development and cannot be interchanged).

15. If you are writing a tandem narrative or multiple protagonist/antagonist film, you will need to think of a macro and address the problems of unity, meaning and closure.

16. Check you have the right protagonist and antagonist, and that the antagonist is a worthy foil to your protagonist. Be aware that the protagonist in films that use a mentor–antagonist is often less colorful than the antagonist.

17. Be aware that you might have to invent a protagonist to match a charismatic mentor–antagonist.

18. Check that you have a good first-act turning point in your story or stories. Remember that it must be a physical surprise. Remember that your first-act turning point is what the story is about. If you know what your film is about, you will often have your first-act turning point without knowing it.

19. Make sure that the action does not slow down and meander after the first-act turning point.

20. Work out good second- and third-act complications. Remember that these

complications can be worked out logically by deciding what obstacles could be put in the way of the protagonist after the first-act turning point.

21. Check that your climax answers the problems raised by your disturbance and first-act turning point.

22. Make sure your climax is powerful and worth your audience's effort. In parallel narrative, you might have to think about how the macro pays off, and you will have to check you have sufficient unity, meaning and closure in the ending.

23. If your antagonist is pursuing your protagonist from a distance, consider inserting a companion for the antagonist, so they have someone to whom they can express their aims and thoughts. Insert some relationship conflict between these two people.

24. Keep checking that you are exploiting the intrinsic drama and essence of your story (for example, if your story is a thriller, is it really thrilling?). Ask what is "hot" (exciting, new, marketable) about your story, and make sure you are properly exploiting this. Try to leave enough time to edit your work. In your second draft, check that your story hasn't shifted so your climax no longer fits the first-act turning point.

25. In your second draft, run through the Development Strategies and other checklists again.

Filmography

The African Queen (1951)
American Beauty (1999)
Awakenings (1990)
Analyze This (1999)

Babe (1995)
Batman (1989)
The Battleship Potemkin (1925)
Being John Malkovich (1999)
The Big Chill (1983)
Blade Runner (1982)

Cadillac Man (1990)
Catch-22 (1970)
Cat on a Hot Tin Roof (1958)
Citizen Kane (1941)
City of Hope (1991)
Clockwise (1986)
Courage Under Fire (1996)
Crimes and Misdemeanors (1989)
Crocodile Dundee (1986)
The Crucible (1996)
The Crying Game (1992)

Dances with Wolves (1990)
Dead Poets' Society (1989)
Donnie Brasco (1997)
Driving Miss Daisy (1989)

The End of the Affair (1999)
The English Patient (1996)
The Entertainer (1960)

Falling in Love (1984)
Fatal Attraction (1987)
Field of Dreams (1989)
A Fish Called Wanda (1988)
Forrest Gump (1994)
The Four Seasons (1981)
The Fugitive (1993)

Go (1999)

Gods and Monsters (1998)
The Green Mile (1999)
Guarding Tess (1994)

Home Alone (1990)
Huozhe, aka To Live (1994)

Il Postino (1994)

Jack and Sarah (1995)
Jaws 3 (1983)
Jean de Florette (1986)
Julia (1977)
The Juror (1996)

The Killing Fields (1984)
Kiss of the Spider Woman (1985)

Lawrence of Arabia (1962)
Lethal Weapon (1987)
The Lion King (1994)

Magnolia (1999)
The Magnificent Seven (1960)
Man Without a Face (1993)
The Mighty Ducks (1992)
Monty Python and the Holy Grail (1975)
Mr. Saturday Night (1992)
Muriel's Wedding (1994)

Notting Hill (1999)
The Nutty Professor (1996)

Out of Africa (1985)

Parallel Lives (1994)
Paradise Road (1997)
The Piano (1993)
Planes, Trains and Automobiles (1987)
The Player (1992)
Prelude to a Kiss (1992)
Pretty Woman (1990)

Priscilla, Queen of the Desert (1994)
Psycho (1960)
Pulp Fiction (1994)

Ransom (1996)
Radiance (1998)
Rain Man (1988)
The Remains of the Day (1993)
Romancing the Stone (1984)
Romeo + Juliet (1996)

Saving Private Ryan (1998)
Scent of a Woman (1992)
The Shawshank Redemption (1994)
Shine (1996)
Short Cuts (1993)
Six Days Seven Nights (1998)
Sliding Doors (1998)
Sophie's Choice (1982)
The Stepford Wives (1975)

Strictly Ballroom (1992)
The Sweet Hereafter (1997)

Tea with Mussolini (1999)
Terminator II (1989)
Thelma and Louise (1991)
There's Something About Mary (1998)
Three Days of the Condor (1975)
Titanic (1997)
Tootsie (1982)
True Lies (1994)

The Usual Suspects (1995)

Wedlock (1991)
When Harry Met Sally (1989)
Withnail and I (1987)
Witness (1985)

You've Got Mail (1998)

Bibliography

HISTORY

STEMPEL, T, 1988, *Framework: a history of screenwriting in the American film.* Continuum, New York.

LAYOUT

TROTTIER, DR, 1992, *Correct format for screenplays and teleplays.* 3rd ed. Forbes Intitute, Anaheim, Ca.

SCRIPTWRITERS

BEAIRSTO, FG, 1998, *The tyranny of story: audience expectations and the short screenplay.* Vancouver Film School, Vancouver.

BRADY, J, 1981, *The craft of the screenwriter: interviews with six celebrated screenwriters.* Simon and Schuster, New York.

DUNN, I, 1999, *The writer's guide: a companion to writing for pleasure or publication.* Allen & Unwin, Sydney.

ENGEL, J, 1995, *Screenwriters on screenwriting.* Hyperion, New York.

FRANCKE, L, 1994, *Script girls: women screenwriters in Hollywood.* British Film Institute, London.

FROUG, W, 1972, *The screenwriter looks at the screenwriter.* Silman-James Press, Los Angeles.

FROUG, W, 1991, *The new screenwriter looks at the new screenwriter.* Silman-James Press, Los Angeles.

FROUG, W, 1996, *Zen and the art of screenwriting: insights and interviews.* 1st ed. Silman-James Press, Los Angeles.

GOLDMAN, W, 1983, *Adventures in the screen trade: a personal view.* Warner, New York.

McCREADIE, M, 1994, *The women who write the movies: from Francis Marion to Nora Ephron.* Carol Pub. Group, Secaucus, NJ.

McKEE, R, 1997, *Story: substance, structure, style and the principles of screenwriting.* Regan Books, New York.

POTTER, D, 1993, *Potter on Potter,* edited by Graham Fuller. Faber, London.

TECHNIQUE

ARMER, AA, 1988, *Writing the screenplay: TV and film.* Wadsworth, Belmont, Ca.

BALLON, RF, 1986, *Blueprint for writing: a workbook on structure and character development for screenplays and novels.* Write Word Press, Los Angeles, Ca.

BERGER, AA, 1990, *Scripts: writing for radio and television.* Sage Publications, Newbury Park, Ca.

BERMAN, RA, 1988, *Fade in: the screenwriting process.* Michael Wiese Film Productions, Westport, Ct.

BLACKER, IR, 1988, *The elements of screenwriting: a guide for film and television writers.* Collier Books, New York.

BRADY, B and LEE, L, 1988, *The understructure of writing for film and television.* University of Texas Press, Austin, Tx.

CHIARELLA, T, 1998, *Writing dialogue.* Story Press, Cincinnati, Ohio.

COOPER, D, 1997, *Writing great screenplays for film and TV.* 2nd rev. ed. Macmillan Publishing. New York.

COOPER, P & DANCYGER, K, 1994, *Writing the short film.* Focal Press, Boston.

CROMPTON, A, 1987, *The craft of copywriting.* Hutchinson Business, London.

DANCYGER, K & RUSH, J, 1995, *Alternative scriptwriting: Thinking Beyond the Rules.* 2nd ed. Focal Press, Boston.

DANCYGER, K, 1991, *Broadcast writing: dramas, comedies and documentaries.* Focal Press, Boston.

DAVIS, R, 1998, *Writing dialogue for scripts.* A. & C. Black, London.

DAWSON, J, 2000, *Screenwriting: a manual.* Oxford University Press, South Melbourne.

DI MAGGIO, M, 1990, *How to write for television.* Prentice-Hall, New York.

DMYTRYK, E, 1985, *On screen writing.* Focal Press, Boston.

DORR, A, 1986, *Television and children: a special medium for a special audience,* Sage Publications, Beverly Hills, Ca.

DROUYN, C, 1994, *Big screen, small screen: a practical guide to writing for film and for film and television in Australia.* Allen & Unwin, Sydney.

DUNN, I, 1999, *The Writer's guide: a companion to writing for pleasure or publication.* Allen & Unwin, Sydney.

EGRI, L, 1960, *The art of dramatic writing: its basis in the creative interpretation of human motives.* Simon & Schuster, New York.

Fallen Angels: six noir tales told for television, 1993. Grove Press, New York.

FARON, F, 1998, *Rip-Off a writer's guide to crimes of deception,* Writer's Digest Books, Cincinnati, Ohio.

FIELD, S, 1994, *Screenplay: the foundations of screenwriting.* Expanded [3rd] ed. Dell Publishing Co., New York.

FIELD, S, 1984, *The screenwriter's workbook*, Dell Pub. Co., New York.

FRIEDMANN, J & ROCA, P (eds), 1994, *Writing long-running television series: lectures from the first PILOTS workshop. Stiges, Catalonia, Spain, June/October, 1993*. Media Business School, Madrid.

FROUG, W, 1993, *Screenwriting tricks of the trade*. Silman-James Press, Los Angeles.

HAYWARD, S, 1977, *Scriptwriting for animation*. Focal Press, London.

HORTON, A, 1994, *Writing the character centred screenplay*. University of California, Berkeley, Ca.

HUNTER, L, 1993, *Lew Hunter's screenwriting 434*. Perigee Books, New York.

JOHNSON, MC, 1995, *The scriptwriter journal: an inner journey*. Focal Press, Boston.

KARETNIKOVA, I, 1990, *How scripts are made*. Southern Illinois University Press, Carbondale, Ill.

KEANE, C, 1998, *How to write a selling screenplay: a step-by-step approach to developing your story and writing your screenplay by one of today's most successful screenwriters and teacher*. 1st ed. Broadway Books, New York.

KING, V, 1988, *How to write a movie in 21 days: the inner movie method*. Perennial Library, New York.

LEFF, LJ, 1983, *Film plots: scene by scene narrative outlines*. Pieran Press, Ann Arbour, Mich.

LUCEY, P, 1996, *Story sense: writing story and script for feature films and television*. McGraw-Hill, New York.

McKEE, Robert, 1999, *Story: Substance, Structure, Style, and the Principles of Screenwriting*. Methuen, London.

McMAHAN, E, 1988, *The elements of writing about literature and film*. Macmillan, New York.

MEHRING, M, 1990, *The screenplay: a blend of film and content*. Focal Press, Boston.

MILLER, WC, 1980, *Screenwriting for narrative film and television*. Hastings House, New York.

MILLER, WC, 1998, *Screenwriting for film and television*. Allyn and Bacon, Boston.

POPE, T, 1998, *Good scripts, bad scripts: learning the craft of screenwriting through the 25 best and worst films in history*. 1st ed. Three Rivers Press, New York.

ROUVEROL, J, 1992, *Writing for daytime drama*. Focal Press, Boston.

SEGER, L, 1990, *Creating unforgettable characters*. H Holt, New York.

SEGER, L & WHETMORE, EJ, 1994, *From script to screen: the collaborative art of filmmaking*. H Holt, New York.

SEGER, L, 1994, *Making a good script great*. Samuel French, New York.

SEGER, L, 1999, *Making a good writer great: a creativity workbook for screenwriters*. Silman-James Press, Los Angeles.

SHAND, J & WELLINGTON, T, 1988, *Don't shoot the best boy! the film crew at work*. Currency Press, Sydney.

STEMPEL, T, 1982, *Screenwriting*. AS Barnes, San Diego, Ca.: Tantivy Press, London.

Style manual for authors, editors and printers. 1994. 5th ed. Australian Government Publishing Service, Canberra.

STRACZYNSKI, JM, 1996, *The complete book of script-writing*. Rev. ed. Writer's Digest Books, Cincinnati, Ohio.

SWAIN, DV, 1990, *Creating characters: how to build story people*. Writer's Digest Books, Cincinnati, Ohio.

SWAIN, DV & SWAIN, JR 1988, *Film scriptwriting : a practical manual*. 2nd ed., Focal Press, Boston.

SWAIN, DV and SWAIN, JR, 1991, *Scripting for the new AV technologies*. 2nd ed. Focal Press, Boston.

THOMPSON, K, 1999, *Storytelling in the new Hollywood: understanding classical narrative technique*. Harvard University Press, Cambridge, MA.

TROTTIER, D, 1998, *The screenwriter's bible*. 3rd ed. Silman-James Press, Los Angeles.

TRUBY, J, 1985, *Truby's story structure*. [United States] (16 sound cassettes ca. 60 min. each plus booklet)

VALE, E, 1982, *The technique of screen and television writing*. Prentice-Hall, Englewood Cliffs, NJ

VAN NOSTRAN, W, 1996, *The scriptwriter's handbook*. Focal Press, Boston.

VAN NOSTRAN, W, 1996, *The scriptwriter's workbook: a media writer's companion*. Focal Press, Boston.

VARCHOL, DJ, 1996, *The multimedia scriptwriting workshop*. Sybex, San Francisco.

VOGLER, C, 1992, *The writer's journey: mythic structure for screenwriters and storytellers*. M. Wiese Productions, Studio City, Ca.

Vorhaus, J, 2000, *Creativity rules! a writer's workbook*. Silman-James Press, Los Angeles.

WILSON, JM, 1998, *Inside Hollywood: a writer's guide to researching the world of movies and TV*. Writer's Digest Books, Cincinnati, Ohio.

WINGATE, A, 1992, *Scene of the crime: a writer's guide to crime-scene investigations.* Writer's Digest Books, Cincinnati, Ohio.

WOLFF, JM & COX, K, 1988, *Successful scriptwriting.* 1st ed. Writer's Digest Books, Cincinnati, Ohio.

SCREEN ADAPTATION

ARMER, AA, 1988, *Writing the screenplay: TV and film.* Wadsworth, Belmont, Ca.

BLACKER, IR, 1988, *The elements of screenwriting: a guide for film and television writers.* Collier Books, New York.

BLUM, RA, 1995, *Television and screen writing: from concept to contract.* 3rd ed. Focal Press, Boston.

BRENNER, A, 1980, *The TV scriptwriter's handbook.* Writer's Digest Books, Cincinnati, Ohio.

CARTMELL, D & others (eds) 1999, *Alien identities: exploring differences in film and fiction.* Pluto Press, Sterling, VA.

DMYTRYK, E, 1985, *On screen writing.* Focal Press, Boston.

McFARLANE, B, 1996, *Novel to film: an introduction to the theory of adaptation.* Oxford University Press, Clarendon Press, Oxford, New York.

MILLER, WC, 1980, *Screenwriting for narrative film and television.* Hastings House, New York.

PORTNOY, K, 1991, *Screen adaptation: a scriptwriting handbook.* Focal Press, Boston.

ROTHWELL, KS, 1999, *A History of Shakespeare on screen: a century of film and television.* Cambridge University Press, Cambridge.

SEGER, L, 1992, *The art of adaptation: turning fact and fiction into film.* H Holt and Co, New York.

SHANKS, B, 1986, *The primal screen: how to write, sell, and produce movies for television.* Norton, New York.

WHEELER, D, 1989, *No, but I saw the movie: the best short stories ever made into film.* Penguin Books, New York.

WILLIS, EE, 1981, *Writing scripts for television, radio, and film.* Holt, Rinehart and Winston, New York.

SCRIPT EDITING

ARMER, AA, 1988, *Writing the screenplay: TV and film.* Wadsworth, Belmont, Ca.

MILLER, W, 1980, *Screenwriting for narrative film and television.* Hastings House, New York.

SEGER, L, 1994, *Making a Good Script Great.* Samuel French, New York.

SERIES AND SERIALS

BRANDT, G (ed.), 1993, *British television drama in the 1980s.* Cambridge University Press, Cambridge.

CHALVON-DEMERSAY, S, 1999, *A Thousand screenplays: the French imagination in a time of crisis.* Translated by TL Fagan. University of Chicago Press, Chicago.

FRIEDMANN, J and ROCA, P (eds), 1994. *Writing long-running television series: lectures from the first PILOTS workshop. Stiges, Catalonia, Spain, June/October, 1993.* Media Business School, Madrid.

SITUATION COMEDY

BYRNE, J, 1999, *Writing comedy.* A & C Black, London.

NEALE, S, & KRUTNIK, F, 1990, *Popular film and television comedy.* Routledge, London.

PERRET, G, 1990, *Comedy writing step by step.* 1st Samuel French ed. Samuel French, Hollywood, Ca.

SCHWARZ, L, 1989, *The craft of writing TV comedy.* Allison and Busby, London.

VORHAUS, J, 1994, *The comic toolbox: how to be funny even if you're not.* Silman-James Press, Los Angeles.

WRITING DOCUMENTARIES

BERGER, AA, 1990, *Scripts: writing for radio and television.* Sage Publications, Newbury Park, Ca.

BEVERIDGE, JA, 1969, *Script writing for short films.* UNESCO, Paris.

CROTON, G, 1986, *From script to screen: documentaries.* BBC Television Training, Borehamwood, Hertfordshire.

DIMOND, P, 1980, *Writing documentary script and narration.* AFTS Open Program, North Ryde, NSW.

DIZAZZO, R, 1992, *Corporate scriptwriting: a professional's guide.* Focal Press, Boston.

EDMONDS, R, 1978, *Scriptwriting for the audio-visual media.* Teachers College Press, New York.

EUSTACE, G, 1990, *Writing for corporate video.* Focal Press, London.

FIELD, S, 1974, *Professional broadcast writer's handbook.* Tab Books, Blue Ridge Summit, Pa.

HESSE, J, 1987, *The radio documentary handbook: creating, producing and selling for broadcasting.* International Self-Counsel Press, Vancouver.

HILLIARD, RL, 1991, *Writing for television and radio.* 5th ed. Belmont, Ca. Wadsworth Publishing Company.

LOMASK, M, 1986, *The biographer's craft.* Harper and Row, New York.

McCARTHY, T, 1983, *Pictures and words: the use of words in film and television.* AFTS, North Ryde, NSW.

McGUIRE, J, 1978, *How to write, direct and produce effective business films and documentaries.* 1st ed. Tab Books, Blue Ridge Summit, Pa.

MATRAZZO, D, 1980, *The corporate scriptwriting book: a practical, step by step guide to guide to writing scripts for organizations.* Media Concepts Press, Philadelphia.

MILLER, W, 1980, *Screenwriting for narrative film and television.* Hastings House, New York.

ROSENTHAL, A, 1990, *Writing, directing, and producing documentary films.* Southern Illinois University Press, Carbondale, Ill.

ROSENTHAL, A, 1995, *Writing docudrama: dramatizing reality for film and TV.* Focal Press, Boston.

SEGER, L, 1992, *The art of adaptation: turning fact and fiction into film.* H Holt & Co., New York.

WILLIS, EE and D'ARIENZO, C, 1981, *Writing scripts for television, radio and film.* Holt, Rinehart and Winston, New York

PITCHING AND SELLING YOUR SCREENPLAY

CALLAN, K, 1993, *The script is finished, now what do I do?* Sweden Press, Studio City, Ca.

CRAM, A, 1985, *How to write and sell TV scripts in Australia and New Zealand.* William Heinemann Australia, Richmond, Vic.

DE ABREU, C & SMITH, HJ, 1995, *Opening the doors to Hollywood: how to sell your idea, story, book, screenplay.* Custos Morum, Beverly Hills, Ca.

DROUYN, C, 1994, *Big screen, small screen: a practical guide to writing for film and television in Australia.* Allen & Unwin, Sydney.

FIELD, S, 1989, *Selling a screenplay: the screenwriter's guide to Hollywood.* Delacorte Press, New York.

HAUGE, M, 1989, *Writing screenplays that sell.* Elm Tree, London.

McCARTHY, P & HATCHER, C 1996, *Speaking persuasively: making the most of your presentations.* Allen & Unwin, Sydney.

SAUTTER, C, 1988, *How to sell your screenplay: the real rules of film and television.* New Chapter Press, New York.

SILVER, D, 1991, *How to pitch and sell your TV script.* Writer's Digest Books, Cincinnati, Ohio.

STUART, L, 1993, *Getting your script through the Hollywood maze.* Acrobat Books, Los Angeles, Ca.

WHITCOMB, C, 1988, *Selling your screenplay.* Crown Publishers, New York.

INTERNET SCREENWRITING RESOURCES

The Australian Society of Authors at http://www.asauthors.org/

http://www.teleport.com/~cdeemer/scrwriter.html

Charles Deemer's site provides information about the craft of screenwriting, and has detailed information about writing, editing and selling scripts.

The Movie Script Gallery at http://www.screentalk.org/moviescripts.htm, has a comprehensive collection of movie scripts of various genres.

OTHER

BUNYAN, John, 1678, *The Pilgrim's Progress,* Penguin, London, 1970.

COLERIDGE, Samuel Taylor, quoted in Preface to *Lyrical Ballads,* 2nd ed., Penguin, London, 1999, first published 1800.

de BONO, Edward, 1970, *Lateral Thinking,* Penguin, London.

JOHNSON, Ben, 1999, *Ben Johnson: Five Plays,* OUP, Oxford.

MARLOWE, Christopher, 1633, *The Jew of Malta,* Manchester University Press, Manchester, 1997.

MOLIÈRE, 1959, *The Misanthrope and Other Plays,* Penguin, London.

SMILEY, S, 1971, *Playwriting: The Structure of Action.* Prentice Hall, NJ.

WORDSWORTH, William, 1999, quoted in Preface to *Lyrical Ballads,* 2nd ed., Penguin, London, first published 1800.

Index

About the Author

Linda Aronson is a highly respected, multi-award-winning
writer who has written widely for the screen in the U.K., Australia,
New Zealand and for U.S. television. While primarily a working writer, she is
also highly celebrated as a teacher for her unique and practical approach to
writing for the screen. Linda has a special expertise in working with new writers
and is regularly called upon as a script assessor and consultant.
She has also won awards for her novels – which have been
published in nine countries – and for her plays.